Health
Care

An American Crisis

D1454179

Health Care

An American Crisis

Edited by Lester A. Sobel

Contributing editors: Joseph Fickes, Russell Kahn

Indexer: Grace M. Ferrara

FACTS ON FILE, INC.   NEW YORK, N.Y.

Health
Care
An American Crisis

Library of Congress Catalog Card Number 75-20838
ISBN 9-87196-288-8

9 8 7 6 5 4 3 2 1
PRINTED IN
THE UNITED STATES OF AMERICA

Contents

19113621

Definition of a Crisis

MOST PEOPLE OF THE WORLD HAVE good reason to envy the health-care system of the United States. With one doctor for every 665 people, the United States has more physicians per inhabitant than any other country. (The runner-up is the Soviet Union with probably one doctor to about every 750 people.) The U.S. health-care system comprises some 325,000 doctors, 750,000 nurses, 7,000 hospitals, 3 million beds in hospitals or other inpatient facilities, 4.4 million workers in a variety of health-related occupations and an annual expenditure estimated at more than $105 billion, about 8% of the gross national product, or at least $500 for every American. This system's hospitals, health centers and doctors include some of the finest in the world. The U.S. health establishment's achievements in fighting disease, in research, in eradicating epidemics, in increasing life expectancy and in training medical personnel are justly admired.

Yet complaints about the U.S. health-care system are rife. Senator Edward M. Kennedy (D, Mass.) told the Senate Jan. 15, 1975 that "we are in the midst of a crisis in health care in America." In a foreword to an April 1973 statement by the Committee for Economic Development, Philip M. Klutznik and Marvin Bower asserted that: "American medical science has made great advances in curing disease, easing human distress and prolonging life. Yet unavailable to many people and even whole areas of the nation—the richest nation in the world—are the services required for adequate medical attention. Equally heartbreaking is the severe financial hardship that can and often does result from serious disease."

As Kennedy pointed out, the aspect of the health-care "crisis . . . known best by every American is the crisis in costs. Hospital costs have risen. Doctor bills have risen. And insurance premiums have risen to keep pace. Every American family feels the pressure of this inflation. The average wage earner works one month a year just to pay his health-care and health-insurance bills. And there is no limit in sight. There is nothing at present built into our health-care system that will assure an end to this inflation." "But the health-care crisis in America is not a matter of inflation and rising costs alone," Kennedy continued. "The crisis is also evident to the 5,000 American communities that have no doctor, and to patients who wait in city hospital emergency rooms six or eight hours for help because they have no doctor or because they cannot reach him after hours."

According to Kennedy: "The crisis is also evident to patients who spend hours waiting at the doctor's office only to be sent to a laboratory for tests, then waiting at a specialist's office perhaps only to be sent to yet another laboratory for more tests, then perhaps back to the first doctor or to a hospital or a drugstore. Each stop involves waiting, some involve traveling across town and back, and some involve making appointments way in advance. All in all, it can take days or weeks to complete the process; it can cost extra dollars for repeated tests and duplicate records, and worst of all, it can discourage the elderly, the infirm, or the poor from completing the course. And the whole process is geared more to responding to the patient for a specific disease, than to viewing the patient as a whole with the intention of preventing diseases and keeping him well. . . .

"The crisis is evident, too, to Americans who suffer needlessly because they can not get to the skilled services or facilities they need, or because they receive less than the best quality care. The fact is that the quality of health care varies greatly in America. There is too much unnecessary or ill-advised surgery performed. There are too many missed diagnoses. It is not necessarily due to greed, to incompetence, or to carelessness. It is simply that our nation is trying to offer sophisticated 20th century medical care through 19th century organizations.

"We have created scores of new and interrelated specialties but continue to think the physician can operate on his own with no close formal relations to other physicians of other specialties. Most physicians practice solo or in groups of the same specialty. The patient's medical records, like his physicians, are scattered all over town, and sometimes it is the patient who decides what specialist he needs for a given problem. It seems clear that, in this fragmented system, a patient is likely to be treated by the specialist he chooses from the perspective of that specialty. A surgeon, for example, is more likely to pursue a surgical solution to a problem than would an internist, if other approaches are possible—especially if consultation between the specialists is cumbersome and there is no real incentive to explore all possible solutions. The delay and clumsiness of referral and consultation can also lead to missed diagnoses—as can the absence of a complete medical record to the doctor who is making the diagnosis.

"Moreover, we have for the most part continued to license health professionals on a once and for all basis, while medical knowledge has literally exploded during recent decades. We have not required continuing education of physicians whose training was completed decades ago—and more importantly, we have made minimal efforts to establish continuing programs to meet these physicians' particular needs and problems. . . .

"But perhaps the crisis in health care is most obvious to Americans whose health insurance has run out, who cannot get insurance because of their medical history, or who simply cannot afford to buy good insurance. Many Americans of all incomes have been bankrupted by health-care costs which continue after their insurance runs out. They then join the ranks of Americans whose medical history makes it impossible to buy good insurance at all, and millions of other Americans of low income who are not eligible for group plans and cannot afford decent insurance. For these Americans who have no decent insurance every illness can turn into a financial disaster. Since every penny comes out of an already limited income, they weigh every decision as to whether or not to seek a doctor—and sometimes they wait too long and suffer needless pain.

"There is no way to tell how many children grow up in America with needlessly twisted limbs, dulled minds or other handicaps simply because fear of the cost kept his parents away from the doctor for too long. There is no way to tell how many Americans suffer needless pain and even early death simply because good health costs too much. It is clear, however, that these things can and do happen all too often for a country as advanced as America.

"The problem is our hopelessly fragmented health-insurance system which encourages insurance companies in the name of profit to exclude Americans who need care the most, or to limit their policies to the most profitable benefits that they can market. This crazy-quilt system also frustrates the providers of care. Doctors and hospitals are faced with providing expensive services to millions of Americans whose insurance may or may not pay—knowing frequently that if the insurance does not come through there is little hope of the patient being able to pay the bill.

"The provider deserves a fair fee for his services. The answer to our health-insurance dilemma is not to require the provider to offer free care—it is to create an insurance system that assures that every American is covered for basic health care. If we insist that health professionals should offer help to everyone who needs it, and Americans do insist on that, then we should make sure that every American is covered by an insurance policy that will pay the provider a fair fee for his service. Nor should insurance coverage influence the provider's method of treatment. Too often providers are encouraged to hospitalize a patient in order that insurance will cover the cost. Insurance should be comprehensive enough to cover whatever course of treatment the physician considers medically appropriate. . . .

"I believe that the private health-insurance industry has failed us. It fails to control costs. It fails to control quality. It provides partial benefits, not comprehensive benefits; acute care, not preventive care. It ignores the poor and the medically indigent. Despite the fact that private health insurance is a giant $20 billion industry, despite more than three decades of enormous growth, despite massive sales of health insurance by thousands of private companies competing with each other for the health dollar of millions of citizens, health insurance benefits today pay only 40% of the total cost of individuals covered by private health care, leaving 60% to be paid out of pocket by the patient at the time of illness or as a debt thereafter, at the very time when he can least afford it. . . .

"Too often, private carriers pay only the cost of hospital care. They force doctors and patients alike to resort to wasteful and inefficient use of hospital facilities, thereby giving further impetus to the already soaring cost of hospital care and unnecessary strains on health manpower. Valuable hospital beds are used for routine tests and examinations which, under any rational health care system, would be conducted on an outpatient basis. Unnecessary hospitalization and unnecessarily extended hospital care are encouraged for patients for whom any rational system would provide treatment in other, less elaborate facilities. . . ."

THE PURPOSE OF THIS BOOK IS TO RECORD the development of the U.S. health-care "crisis" as it grew during the period ending in the mid-1970s. This volume also details the efforts made to overcome the faults that were found with government programs such as Medicare and Medicaid as well as with the private health-insurance and fee-for-service medical systems. This narrative is preceded by an account of both the events that led to the adoption of the Medicare program and of the health-care developments of the period that followed. The material in this volume consists largely of the record compiled by FACTS ON FILE in its weekly coverage of world events. As in all FACTS ON FILE works, a conscientious effort was made to keep this book free of bias and to make it a balanced and accurate reference tool.

LESTER A. SOBEL

New York, N.Y.
January, 1976

The Road to Medicare

The Truman Health Program

DESPITE SEVERAL EARLIER ATTEMPTS to revise the American medical system, the struggle for a national health-insurance program is generally regarded as having begun Nov. 19, 1945 when President Harry S. Truman proposed, in a special message to Congress, a "comprehensive health program." A key element of the program was Truman's plan for health insurance under "our compulsory social insurance system." Truman said in his 1945 message:

"In my message to the Congress of Sept. 6, 1945, there were enumerated in a proposed Economic Bill of Rights certain rights which ought to be assured to every American citizen. One of them was: 'The right to adequate medical care and the opportunity to achieve and enjoy good health.' Another was the 'right to adequate protection from the economic fears of . . . sickness. . . .'

"Millions of our citizens do not now have a full measure of opportunity to achieve and enjoy good health. Millions do not now have protection or security against the economic effects of sickness. The time has arrived for action to help them attain that opportunity and that protection.

"The people of the United States received a shock when the medical examinations conducted by the Selective Service System revealed the widespread physical and mental incapacity among the young people of our nation. . . . The number of those rejected for military service was about 30% of all those examined. . . . In addition, after actual induction, about a million and a half men had to be discharged from the Army and Navy for physical or mental disability, exclusive of wounds; and an equal number had to be treated in the Armed Forces for diseases or defects which existed before induction. Among the young women who applied for admission to the Women's Army Corps there was similar disability. Over one-third of those examined were rejected for physical or mental reasons. . . .

"It is not so important to search the past in order to fix the blame for these conditions. It is more important to resolve now that no American child shall come to adult life with diseases or defects which can be prevented or corrected at an early age.

"Medicine has made great strides in this generation. . . . In spite of great scientific progress, however, each year we lose many more persons from preventable and premature deaths than we lost in battle or from war injuries during the entire war.

"We are proud of past reductions in our death rates. But these reductions have come principally from public health and other community services. We have been less effective in making available to all of our people the benefits of medical progress in the care and treatment of individuals. . . .

"People with low or moderate incomes do not get the same medical attention as those with high incomes. The poor have more sickness, but they get less medical care. People who live in rural areas do not get the same amount or quality of medical attention as those who live in our cities. Our new Economic Bill of Rights should mean health security for all, regardless of residence, station, or race—everywhere in the United States. . . .

"There are five basic problems which we must attack vigorously if we would reach the health objectives of our Economic Bill of Rights.

"(1) The first has to do with the number and distribution of doctors and hospitals. One of the most important requirements for adequate health service is professional personnel—doctors, dentists, public health and hospital administrators, nurses and other experts. The United States has been fortunate with respect to physicians. In proportion to population it has more than any large country in the world. . . . It is not enough, however, that we have them in sufficient numbers. They should be located where their services are needed. In this respect we are not so fortunate. The distribution of physicians in the United States has been grossly uneven and unsatisfactory. Some communities have had enough or even too many; others have had too few. Year by year the number in our rural areas has been diminishing. Indeed, in 1940, there were 31 counties in the United States, each with more than a thousand inhabitants, in which there was not a single practicing physician. The situation with respect to dentists was even worse. . . .

"Inequalities in the distribution of medical personnel are matched by inequalities in hospitals, clinics and health centers to take proper care of the people of the United States. About 1,200 counties, 40% of the total in the country, with some 15 million people, have either no local hospital, or none that meets even the minimum standards of national professional associations. . . .

"(2) The second basic problem is the need for development of public health services and maternal and child care. The Congress can be justifiably proud of its share in making recent accomplishments possible. Public health and maternal and child health programs already have made important contributions to national health. But large needs remain. Great areas of our country are still without these services. . . . Although local public health departments are now maintained by some 18,000 counties and other local units, many of these have only skeleton organizations, and approximately 40 million citizens of the United States still live in communities lacking fulltime local public health service. . . .

"If we agree that the national health must be improved, our cities, towns and farming communities must be made healthful places in which to live through provision of safe water systems, sewage disposal plants and sanitary facilities. Our streams and rivers must be safeguarded against pollution. In addition to building a sanitary environment for ourselves and for our children, we must provide those services which prevent disease and promote health.

"Services for expectant mothers and for infants, care of crippled or otherwise physically handicapped children and inoculation for the prevention of communicable diseases are accepted public health functions. So too are many kinds of personal services such as the diagnosis and treatment of widespread infections like tuberculosis and venereal disease. A large part of the population today lacks many or all of these services.

"Our success in the traditional public health sphere is made plain by the conquest over many communicable diseases. Typhoid fever, smallpox, and diphtheria—diseases for which there are effective controls—have become comparatively rare. We must make the same gains in reducing our maternal and infant mortality, in controlling tuberculosis, venereal disease, malaria, and other major threats to life and health. . . .

"(3) The third basic problem concerns medical research and professional education. . . . Research—well directed and continu-

ously supported—can do much to develop ways to reduce those diseases of body and mind which now cause most sickness, disability,
and premature death—diseases of the heart, kidneys and arteries,
rheumatism, cancer, diseases of childbirth, infancy and childhood,
respiratory diseases and tuberculosis. And research can do much toward teaching us how to keep well and how to prolong healthy
human life.

"Cancer is among the leading causes of death . . . and should
receive special attention. Though we already have the National
Cancer Institute of the Public Health Service, we need still more
coordinated research on the cause, prevention and cure of this disease. We need more financial support for research and to establish
special clinics and hospitals for diagnosis and treatment of the disease especially in its early stages. We need to train more physicians
for the highly specialized services so essential for effective control
of cancer.

"There is also special need for research on mental diseases and
abnormalities. We have done pitifully little about mental illness.
. . . Mental cases occupy more than one-half of the hospital beds,
at a cost of about $500 million per year—practically all of it coming
out of taxpayers' money. . . . We need more mental-disease hospitals, more out-patient clinics. We need more services for early diagnosis, and especially we need much more research to learn how to
prevent mental breakdown. Also, we must have many more trained
and qualified doctors in this field. . . .

"(4) The fourth problem has to do with the high cost of individual medical care. The principal reason why people do not receive
the care they need is that they cannot afford to pay for it on an individual basis at the time they need it. This is true not only for
needy persons. It is also true for a large proportion of normally
self-supporting persons.

"In the aggregate, all health services . . . absorb only about
4% of the national income. . . . But 4% is only an average. . . . Individual families pay their individual costs, and not average costs. They may be hit by sickness that calls for many times
the average cost—in extreme cases for more than their annual income. When this happens they may come face to face with
economic disaster. Many families, fearful of expense, delay calling
the doctor long beyond the time when medical care would do the
most good.

"For some persons with very low income or no income at all
we now use taxpayers' money in the form of free services, free

clinics, and public hospitals. Tax-supported, free medical care for needy persons, however, is insufficient in most of our cities and in nearly all of our rural areas. This deficiency cannot be met by private charity or the kindness of individual physicians. . . .

"(5) The fifth problem has to do with loss of earnings when sickness strikes. Sickness not only brings doctor bills; it also cuts off income. On an average day, there are about seven million persons so disabled by sickness or injury that they cannot go about their usual tasks. Of these, about 3¼ millions are persons who, if they were not disabled, would be working or seeking employment. More than one-half of these disabled workers have already been disabled for six months; many of them will continue to be disabled for years, and some for the remainder of their lives. Every year, four or five hundred million working days are lost from productive employment because of illness and accident among those working or looking for work—about forty times the number of days lost because of strikes on the average during the ten years before the war. . . .

"These then are the five important problems which must be solved, if we hope to attain our objective of adequate medical care, good health, and protection from the economic fears of sickness and disability. To meet these problems, I recommend that the Congress adopt a comprehensive and modern health program for the nation, consisting of five major parts. . . .

"First: Construction of Hospitals & Related Facilities—The federal government should provide financial and other assistance for the construction of needed hospitals, health centers and other medical, health and rehabilitation facilities. With the help of federal funds, it should be possible to meet deficiencies in hospital and health facilities so that modern services—for both prevention and cure—can be accessible to all the people, federal financial aid should be available not only to build new facilities where needed, but also to enlarge or modernize those we have now.

"In carrying out this program, there should be a clear division of responsibilities between the states and the federal government. The states, localities and the federal government should share in the financial responsibilities. The federal government should not construct or operate these hospitals. It should, however, lay down minimum national standards for construction and operation, and should make sure that federal funds are allocated to those areas and projects where federal aid is needed most. . . .

"Adequate emphasis should be given to facilities that are particularly useful for prevention of diseases—mental as well as physical—and to the coordination of various kinds of facilities. It should be possible to go a long way toward knitting together facilities for prevention with facilities for cure, the large hospitals of medical centers with the smaller institutions of surrounding areas, the facilities for the civilian population with the facilities for veterans. . . .

"*Second: Expansion of Public Health, Maternal & Child Health Services*—Our programs for public health and related services should be enlarged and strengthened. The present federal-state cooperative health programs deal with general public health work, tuberculosis and venereal disease control, maternal and child health services, and services for crippled children. These programs were especially developed in the ten years before the war, and have been extended in some areas during the war. They have already made important contributions to national health, but they have not yet reached a large proportion of our rural areas, and, in many cities, they are only partially developed.

"No area in the nation should continue to be without the services of a full-time health officer and other essential personnel. No area should be without essential public health services or sanitation facilities. No area should be without community health services such as maternal and child health care. Hospitals, clinics and health centers must be built to meet the needs of the total population, and must make adequate provision for the safe birth of every baby, and for the health protection of infants and children.

"Present laws relating to general public health, and to maternal and child health, have built a solid foundation of federal cooperation with the states in administering community health services. . . . The federal government should cooperate by more generous grants to the states than are provided under present laws for public health services and for maternal and child health care. The program should continue to be partly financed by the states themselves, and should be administered by the states. Federal grants should be in proportion to state and local expenditures, and should also vary in accordance with the financial ability of the respective states. The health of American children, like their education, should be recognized as a definite public responsibility.

"In the conquest of many diseases prevention is even more important then cure. A well-rounded national health program should, therefore, include systematic and wide-spread health and physical education and examinations, beginning with the youngest children and extending into community organizations. Medical and dental examinations of school children are now inadequate. A preventive health program, to be successful, must discover defects as early as possible. We should, therefore, see to it that our health programs are pushed most vigorously with the youngest section of the population.

"Of course, federal aid for community health services . . . should complement and not duplicate prepaid medical services for individuals, proposed by the fourth recommendation of this message.

"*Third: Medical Education & Research*—The federal government should undertake a broad program to strengthen professional education in medical and related fields and to encourage and support medical research. Professional education should be strengthened where necessary through federal grants-in-aid to public and to non-private institutions. Medical research, also, should be encouraged and supported in the federal agencies and by grants-in-aid to public and non-profit private agencies. . . .

"*Fourth: Prepayment of Medical Costs*—Everyone should have ready access to all necessary medical, hospital and related services. I recommend solving the basic problem by distributing the costs through expansion of our existing compulsory social insurance system. This is not socialized medicine. . . . If instead of the costs of sickness being paid only by those who get sick; all the people—sick and well—were required to pay premiums into an insurance fund, the pool of funds thus created would enable all who do fall sick to be adequately served without overburdening anyone. . . .

"During the past 15 years, hospital insurance plans have taught many Americans this magic of averages. Voluntary health insurance plans have been expanding during recent years; but their rate of growth does not justify the belief that they will meet more than a fraction of our people's needs. Only about 3% or 4% of our population now have insurance providing comprehensive medical care.

"A system of required prepayment would not only spread the costs of medical care, it would also prevent much serious disease. Since medical bills would be paid by the insurance fund, doctors would more often be consulted when the first signs of disease occur instead of when the disease has become serious. Modern hospital, specialist and laboratory services, as needed, would also become available to all, and would improve the quality and adequacy of care. Prepayment of medical care would go a long way toward furnishing insurance against disease itself, as well as against medical bills.

"Such a system of prepayment should cover medical, hospital, nursing and laboratory services. It should also cover dental care—as fully and for as many of the population as the available professional personnel and the financial resources of the system permit.

"The ability of our people to pay for adequate medical care will be increased if, while they are well, they pay regularly into a common health fund, instead of paying sporadically and unevenly when they are sick. This health fund should be built up nationally, in order to establish the broadest and most stable basis for spreading the costs of illness, and assure adequate financial support for doctors and hospitals everywhere. . . .

"Medical services are personal. Therefore the nationwide system must be highly decentralized in administration. The local administrative unit must be the keystone of the system so as to provide for local services and adaptation to local needs and conditions. Locally as well as nationally, policy and administration should be guided by advisory committees in which the public and the medical professions are represented.

"Subject to national standards, methods and rates of paying doctors and hospitals should be adjusted locally. All such rates for doctors should be adequate and should be appropriately adjusted upward for those who are qualified specialists.

"People should remain free to choose their own physicians and hospitals. The removal of financial barriers between patient and doctor would enlarge the present freedom of choice. The legal requirement on the population to contribute involves no compulsion over the doctor's freedom to decide what services his patients needs. People will remain free to obtain and pay for medical service outside of the health insurance system if they desire, even though they are members of the system. . . .

"Likewise physicians should remain free to accept or reject patients. They must be allowed to decide for themselves whether they wish to participate in the health insurance system full time, part time, or not at all. A physician may have some patients who are in the system and some who are not. Physicians must be permitted to be represented through organizations of their own choosing, and to decide whether to carry on in individual practice or to join with other doctors in group practice in hospitals or in clinics.

"Our voluntary hospitals and our city, county and state general hospitals, in the same way, must be free to participate in the system to whatever extent they wish. In any case they must continue to retain their administrative independence.

"Voluntary organizations which provide health services that meet reasonable standards of quality should be entitled to furnish services under the insurance system and to be reimbursed for them. Voluntary cooperative organizations concerned with paying doctors, hospitals or others for health services, but not providing services directly, should be entitled to participate if they can contribute to the efficiency and economy of the system. . . .

"I repeat—what I am recommending is *not* socialized medicine. Socialized medicine means that all doctors work as employees of government. The American people want no such system. No such system is here proposed.

"Under the plan I suggest, our people would continue to get medical and hospital services just as they do now—on the basis of their own voluntary decisions and choices. Our doctors and hospitals would continue to deal with disease with the same professional freedom as now. There would, however, be this all-important difference: whether or not patients get the services they need would not depend on how much they can afford to pay at the time.

". . . I believe that all persons who work for a living and their dependents should be covered under such an insurance plan. This would include wage and salary earners, those in business for themselves, professional persons, farmers, agricultural labor, domestic employees, government employees and employees of non-profit institutions and their families. In addition, needy persons and other groups should be covered through appropriate premiums paid for them by public agencies. . . .

"The plan which I have suggested would be sufficient to pay most doctors more than the best they have received in peacetime years. The payments of the doctors' bills would be guaranteed, and the doctors would be spared the annoyance and uncertainty of collecting fees from individual patients. The same assurance would apply to hospitals, dentists and nurses for the services they render. . . .

"*Fifth: Protection Against Loss of Wages from Sickness & Disability*—. . . Sickness brings with it loss of wages. Therefore, as a fifth element of a comprehensive health program, the workers of the nation and their families should be protected against loss of earnings because of illness. A comprehensive health program must include the payment of benefits to replace at least part of the earnings that are lost during the period of sickness and longterm disability. This protection can be readily and conveniently provided through expansion of our present social insurance system, with appropriate adjustment of premiums. . . ."

The National-Health-Insurance Approach

For more than half a century Americans have been arguing over whether some form of national health insurance can solve the growing problem of health costs. A proposal for tax-financed, national health insurance had been made by the American Medical Association during World War I days—before AMA leaders soured on the idea as an entering wedge for "socialized medicine." National health insurance plans were brought up again during the Roosevelt and Truman Administrations but were defeated, largely as a result of growing AMA opposition. Legislation for a compulsory national health insurance program had actually been introduced in 1943—the height of World War II—by Senators Robert F. Wagner (D, N.Y.) and James E. Murray (D, Mont.) and Rep. John D. Dingell (D, Mich.), but President Franklin D. Roosevelt apparently considered the time inappropriate for a political fight on the issue. A new Wagner-Murray-Dingell health-insurance bill was introduced Nov. 19, 1945, the day Truman issued his landmark health message.

Within a year of the passage of the Social Security Act in 1935, efforts had been started to broaden this government-run pension program by creating a parallel or associated national health insurance program. Initially, opposition to the idea was strong. But as Rep. Claude Pepper (D, Fla.) pointed out recently, when World War II came along, "the nation was shocked by the fact that over 40% of . . . [U.S.] selectees were found physically unfit for military duty." "At least a sixth of these had defects which were remediable," he continued, and "many more had preventable defects." A Senate Subcommittee on Health & Education was set up in 1943 under Pepper, who was then a Senator. After investigating the nation's health care needs, the subcommittee reported in March 1946:

". . . . More than 23 million people in the country have some chronic disease or physical impairment. On any one day, at least seven million people in the United States are incapacitated by sickness or other disability, half of them for six months or more. Illness and accidents cause the average industrial worker to lose about 12 days from production a year, a loss of about 600 million man-days annually. Sickness and accidents cost the nation at least $8 billion a year, half of this amount in wage loss and half in medical costs.

. . . Even before modern medicine had reached its present peak of complexity and specialization, the fee-for-service, individual practice method of providing medical care did not meet the nation's health needs. Now it is a complete anachronism. It results in barriers to good health care which keep not only low-income people, but most middle-income families, from the fruits of modern medical science. It inhibits the full use of modern preventive medicine since it forces most people to wait until they are seriously ill before going to a doctor. And it leaves any family the prey of unexpected crippling costs from medical bills and wage loss. On top of the natural tragedy of illness may be heaped economic catastrophe. . . . The need for health insurance has become clear. The well-tried American way of meeting the hazards of life by spreading risks and by prepaying costs is applicable to health services.''

By May 1946, a Gallup Poll indicated that 55% of the public supported the idea of a federally sponsored, comprehensive health insurance program for all Americans.

President Truman urged Congress again April 22, 1949 to enact a nationwide system of compulstory health insurance to meet this two-fold objective: "To make available enough medical services to go around, and to see that everybody has a chance to obtain these services." Since current voluntary insurance plans "are not adjusted to income, those who need protection most cannot afford to join," he declared. Although 50 million Americans had "some form of health insurance," only 3½ million "have insurance which provides anything approaching adequate health protection." Furthermore, the poorest areas, where doctors were needed most, had the fewest of them. With payment of doctors' fees assured under the President's proposal, however, "doctors will be able to practice where they are needed most, without sacrificing incomes."

Rejecting objections that compulsory health insurance means medical "regimentation" and "socialization," Truman said that his plan would not make doctors government employes, would leave patients "free to choose their own doctors" and permit patients, doctors and hospitals "to make their own arrangements for care outside the insurance system if they so choose." Deriding rumors of the system's high cost, he said: "The truth is that it will save a great deal more than it costs. We are already paying about 4% of our national income for health care. More and better care can be obtained for this same amount of money under the program I am recommending." Truman Administration plans called for a 3% payroll tax—1½% on employers and 1½% on employes' earnings up to $4,800 a year. The government would put up ½ of 1% of payrolls the first year, 1% thereafter. Everyone under the Social Security System would be covered. The Administration had estimated that complete medical, surgical, dental and hospital care would cost $6.5 billion a year; the American Medical Association (AMA) said it would be as high as $18 billion. The nation then spent about $8 billion. Under the plan, the government would pay doctor bills at prevailing rates, with adjustments to encourage doctors to practice where they were most needed.

A Republican bill to provide federal aid to state health programs had been introduced April 14 by Sens. Robert A. Taft (Ohio), H. Alexander Smith (N.J.) and Forrest C. Donnell (Mo.). Intended as a rival to the President's program, the measure would authorize $1¼ billion in grants over a period of five years. The states would bear part of the cost of their health plans themselves but would get federal assistance on a sliding scale ranging from 33⅓% to 75% according to need. The Committee for the Nation's Health, which supported the President's plan, denounced the Republican proposal as "a subterfuge" and a "charity system." The committee met with Truman April 15 and told him that the American Medical Association had influenced legislation in 22 states to restrict private health insurance systems.

Neither the Truman plan for the Republican proposal won Congressional approval. (The AMA House of Delegates voted unanimously Dec. 8, 1949 to impose $25 annual dues on each of the 145,000 AMA members to fight Truman's plan. Penalty for failure to pay: expulsion. The 102-year-old association had never charged dues before, being financed entirely by its *Journal*. In 1948, $25-a-member assessments to fight the health plan had brought $2,330,000 from 80% of the members.)

The national-health-insurance dispute was a major issue debated during the 1952 Presidential election. Dwight D. Eisenhower, the Republican candidate, said in a prepared statement Sept. 14 that he opposed "a federally operated and controlled system of medical care, which is what the [Truman] Administration's compulsory health insurance scheme is." Eisenhower rejected "compulsory methods" and warned that they would mean "less and poorer medical care for more" money. Truman retorted in a speech at the American Hospital Association convention Sept. 16 that Eisenhower's health views would bring back "the horse and buggy days," and he called again for national health insurance.

In 1952 the Republican National Convention adopted a platform that included this plank: "The health of our people as well as their proper medical care cannot be maintained if subject to federal bureaucratic dictation." "We are opposed to federal compulsory health insurance" but "shall support [government] health activities . . . which stimulate the development of adequate hospital services without federal interference."

The health plank of the 1952 Democratic platform said: "We also advocate a resolute attack on the heavy financial hazards of serious illness. . . . Costs of medical care have grown to be prohibitive for many millions of people. We commend President Truman for establishing the . . . Commission on Health Needs . . . to seek an acceptable solution. . . ."

The commission for which the Democratic platform lauded Truman was a 15-member President's Commission on the Health Needs of the Nation. Truman had created it Dec. 29, 1951 with Dr. Paul B. Magnuson as chairman. Truman directed the commission to study the U.S.' "total health requirements" and to make "recommendations for safeguarding and improving the health of the nation." Dr. Gunnar Gundersen, La Crosse, Wis. physician whom Truman had named to the commission, resigned Dec. 30. Gundersen, an American Medical Association trustee, denounced the commission as "an instrument of practical politics [created] to relieve President Truman from an embarrassing position as an unsuccessful advocate of compulsory health insurance." Magnuson, however, also opposed Truman's compulsory health insurance plan and had proposed locally-sponsored clinics.

The commission Dec. 18, 1952 presented to Truman a report containing proposals for giving complete health services to all Americans. The report said that "access to the means for the attainment and preservation of health is a basic human right." But it noted that the "fee-at-the-time-of-service" method of paying for medical service was breaking down and that many Americans did not get needed medical care simply because they did not have the money to pay for it. A majority of the commission's members urged: (1) acceptance of "the principle of prepaid medical insurance . . . as the most feasible method of financing the costs of medical care"; (2) expansion of "present prepayment plans . . . to provide as much health service to as many people as they can"; (3) "a cooperative federal-state program . . . to assist in the financing of personal health services" and establishment of "a single health authority . . . in each participating state." Members Albert J. Hayes, Elizabeth S. Magee and Walter P. Reuther objected that leaving participation to the option of each state "could not possibly accomplish the objective of giving 'all persons in the country' ready access to high quality comprehensive personal health services" because many people in non-participating states would not be covered. Clarence Poe urged that those who could fully or partly pay their own way should do so with "government and philanthropy providing the remainder" of needed funds. Dr. Joseph C. Hinsey insisted that health plans should "maintain free choice of health personnel, freedom of type of practice, and a system of remuneration" mutually satisfactory to the health professions and patients.

A majority of the members also backed a proposal for the establishment of a Cabinet-rank Health & Security Department. Hinsey, dissenting, urged more study. Evarts A. Graham and Russel V. Lee, dissenting, favored a Health Department but opposed combining it with security. The report urged Congress to create a permanent 18-member Federal Health Commission to keep the nation's health status under continuous scrutiny and to make annual reports to the President and Congress.

Truman lauded the report and said it would be unfortunate if its "proper evaluation" were hindered by "the same emotionalism which has prevented open-minded study of major health proposals advanced during the past few years." Dr. Louis H. Bauer, AMA president, denounced the report and charged that a proposal to use old-age and survivors' insurance for prepayment of personal health service benefits was "national compulsory health insurance."

Increased voluntary health insurance with financial support by the federal, state and local governments was recommended by the commission Feb. 22, 1953 in an additional section of its report. Statistics included in the report: (1) Consumers spent about 4% of their total disposable incomes for medical care; (2) their total spendings on such service rose from about $2 billion in 1933 to nearly $9 billion in 1951; (3) about 28% of such spendings went to doctors, 25% to hospitals, 17.6% for drugs during 1951; (4) about 20% of U.S. families owed an average of $105 each (median debt: $50) to doctors, dentists and hospitals at the beginning of 1952; (5) medical expense was the most frequent reason for borrowing during 1951 from the U.S.' three largest small-loan companies (they handled more than 46% of the nation's small-loan business); such loans accounted for more than 20% of the three companies' $1.1 billion loan total in 1951; (6) disability cost the U.S. economy an estimated $34 billion to $40 billion in 1951, when national income totaled $278 billion.

(After the Eisenhower Administration had been in office for nearly two years, Vice President Richard M. Nixon charged in Los Angeles Oct. 13, 1954 that when the Eisenhower took power, "we found in the files a blueprint for socializing America . . . for adding $40 billion to the national debt by 1956." He said "it called for socialized medicine, socialized housing, socialized agriculture, socialized water and power" and socialized atomic energy.)

Eisenhower Health Proposals

Eisenhower proposed March 12, 1953 that the Federal Security Agency (FSA) be transformed into a Cabinet-rank Department of Health, Education & Welfare, and he won the AMA House of Delegates' qualified approval of the plan by assuring the doctors March 14 that he opposed national health insurance. "I don't like the word 'compulsory'; I am against the word 'socialized'," he said. He asserted his "faith" that "the medical profession will provide the kind of services our country needs better, with the cooperation and the friendship of the Administration, rather than its direction or any attempt on its part to be the big "Pooh-Bah' in this particular field." The AMA House, which had been holding a special meeting in Washington to consider the FSA plan, then voted that the Eisenhower proposal was "a step in the right direction." With Congress' approval, the change was made April 1.

But in 1954, Eisenhower also proposed a health insurance plan—and Congress refused to approve it.

Eisenhower asked Congress Jan. 18, 1954 to provide government reinsurance for private health insurance plans. In a special health message that rejected "socialization of medicine," Eisenhower reported that good medical care was unavailable to many Americans. Where available, "its costs are often a serious burden," he said. "Major, longterm illness can become a financial catastrophe" for a normal family. The President listed two "national health goals": (1) "The means for achieving good health should be accessible to all"; (2) "the results of our vast scientific research . . . should be broadly applied for the benefit of every citizen." He discussed these proposals "to bring us closer to these goals":

"I recommend . . . a limited federal reinsurance service to encourage private and nonprofit health insurance organizations to offer broader health protection to more families [by reinsuring] the special additional risks involved in such broader protection. It can be launched with a capital fund of $25 million provided by the government, to be retired from reinsurance fees." "The government need not and should not go into the insurance business to furnish the protection which private and nonprofit organizations do not now provide." The Public Health Service should continue technical assistance to states, industrial hygiene work and other field projects through which it helps control "health hazards on the farm, in industry and in the home." It should strengthen its research activities, including those of its National Institutes of Health, its new sanitary engineering laboratory in Cincinnati and its research grants to states, localities and to private institutions. "Continued support" should go to Children's Bureau programs for maternal and child health and crippling diseases. A new "simplified" formula of federal grants-in-aid would be "based on three general criteria": (1) aid in inverse proportion to states' financial capacity and related to "degree of need"; (2) aid, in proportion to population, to extend and improve health and welfare services provided by the programs; (3) a set-aside of part of the aid to support "unique projects of regional or national significance which give promise of new and better ways of serving the human needs of our citizens."

Eisenhower made these further recommendations to improve two of the grant-in-aid programs: Grants should provide, "under state auspices": (a) "specialized training for the professional personnel" needed in an "expanded program" for rehabilitating the disabled and to foster research into "ways of overcoming handicapping conditions"; (b) "clinical facilities for rehabilitative services in hospitals" and elsewhere. "We should encourage state and local initiative in [developing] community rehabilitation centers and special workshops for the disabled." "A program of matching state and local tax funds and private funds [for building] nonprofit hospitals where these are most needed is . . . essential." For illnesses that need not be treated in costly and "elaborate" general hospitals, facilities could be provided by amending the Hospital Survey & Construction Act to authorize added aid in building: (a) hospitals for chronic cases, (b) "medically supervised nursing and convalescent homes" (c) "rehabilitation facilities for the disabled," (d) "diagnostic or treatment centers for ambulatory patients." The President recommended that the federal government help states pay for surveys of their needs.

Eisenhower warned that "much remains to be done" to improve American health despite such advances as: (a) in the past half-decade the average U.S. life span rose from 49 years to 68 and deaths from infectious disease dropped from 676 per 100,000 to 66; (b) maternal deaths per 100,000 live births since 1916 dropped from 622 to 83 and the number of babies who died in their first year declined from 10% to less than 3%. He cited these problems of 1954: Cancer killed 224,000 Americans in 1953, would kill "25 million of our 160 million people unless the present cancer mortality rate is lowered." Diseases of the heart and blood vessels took over 817,000 lives annually. Over seven million Americans suffered from arthritis and rheumatic diseases. Twenty-two thousand Americans lost their sight, 100,000 became diabetics, each year. Two million disabled Americans "could be, but are not, rehabilitated"; rehabilitation programs at that time returned only 60,000 each year "to full and productive lives" whereas 250,000 more were disabled annually. Ten million Americans "will at some time in their lives be hospitalized with mental illness." The Northeast had 150 doctors for every 100,000 persons, the West 126, North Central area 116, South 92. Hospital beds per 1,000 persons ranged from 10 to 11 in some states to four or five in others. Ten percent of American families spent more than $500 a year for medical care. About 6% of Americans reporting incomes under $3,000 spent almost 1/5 of their gross income for medical and dental care. The nation's hospital bill exceeded $9 billion a year—"an average of nearly $200 a family"—and "is rising."

The House of Representatives July 13, 1954 rejected Eisenhower's $25 million health reinsurance plan by voting, 238-134 (162 D., 75 R. and one independent vs. 120 R. and 14 D.), to return it to the Commerce Committee. The measure was opposed by the American Medical Association, by conservative Democrats and Republicans who considered it a start toward "socialized medicine" and by New Deal-Fair Deal Democrats who thought it did not go far enough. But Eisenhower had emphasized his support of the program by introducing Health, Education & Welfare Secretary Oveta Culp Hobby when she made a telecast from the White House July 9 in support of it. Eisenhower, obviously angered at th bill's defeat, declared at his press conference July 14 that those who voted against the bill "just don't understand what are the facts of American life." It was the first time since taking office that he assailed members of Congress. "I don't consider that anyone lost yesterday except the American people," he said. He pledged to fight for health reinsurance as long as he remained President. (Eisenhower July 12 had signed into law a bill authorizing $60 million a year, to be matched by state funds, for construction of hospitals for chronic ills, nursing homes, rehabilitation clinics and treatment centers. It was the first item of his four-point health program to be enacted.)

Eisenhower, in New York Oct. 21 at the annual Alfred E. Smith Memorial Foundation dinner, defended his health reinsurance program. He reiterated his opposition to "socialized medicine" and denied that his plan would be "the entering wedge" to such a scheme. He warned his audience not to "confuse social progress with socialism."

⹁ The Commission on Financing of Hospital Care had recommended in an unpublished report disclosed Jan. 16, 1954 that hospitalization be linked with Social Security and unemployment insurance so that it could be provided for all who needed it regardless of ability to pay. The commission, sponsored by the American Hospital Association, was headed by Gordon Gray, president of the University of North Carolina. (Its study took two years and cost $556,000.)

In his 1955 State-of-the-Union message, delivered in person before the Democratic-controlled 84th Congress Jan. 6, Eisenhower called for a coordinated health program that would reject "socialized medicine," provide "a federal health reinsurance service to encourage the development of more and better [private] voluntary health insurance" and improve medical care for those receiving public assistance. The program would: "facilitate construction of needed health facilities"; "help reduce shortages of trained health personnel"; "combat the misery and national loss involved in mental illness"; improve services for crippled children and for maternal and child health; provide "better consumer protection under our existing pure food and drug laws"; strengthen "programs to combat the increasingly serious pollution of our rivers and streams and the growing problem of air pollution."

Eisenhower submitted to Congress Jan. 31, 1955 a national health program similar in most respects to measures that Congress had rejected in 1954. A key feature was the President's plan for a "Federal Health Reinsurance Service to encourage private health insurance organizations in offering broader benefits to insured individuals and families and coverage to more people." "A reasonable capital fund" would be used as necessary in reinsuring health insurance plans that: (1) provided "protection against the high costs of severe or prolonged illness"; (2) provided "coverage for individuals and families in predominantly rural areas," and (3) were "designed primarily for coverage of individuals and families of average or lower income against medical care costs in the home and physician's offices as well as in the hospital.'' The program "involves no government subsidy and no government competition with private insurance carriers,'' Eisenhower declared.

In his message, Eisenhower requested federal funds to match "state and local expenditures for the medical care needed by public assistance recipients"—the needy aged, blind, permanently disabled and dependent children. The message recommended "tested" government-insured loan procedures to stimulate construction and repair of "hospitals, clinics, nursing homes and other modern technical facilities required for the protection of the people's health.'' It urged that insurance be limited "to less than the face amount of the loan" and that a loan, to qualify for insurance, be "for less than the full value of the property.'' The President also proposed: (a) "a five-year program of grants to state vocational education agencies for training practical nurses,'' (b) "expansion of Public Health Service operations to establish traineeships for graduate nurses in specialties such as nursing service administration, teaching and research,'' (c) "traineeships in all public health specialties, including mental health.''

The message recommended funds and authority for: (a) improvements in the Public Health Service, Children's Bureau and Food & Drug Administration, (b) improvement of grant-in-aid programs aiding mothers, crippled children and children needing special services, (c) "greater flexibility" in state use of federal grants for public health, (d) increased research on air pollution, (e) greater aid to states for water pollution control. The message called for: (1) "strengthening of present aid to state and community programs for the early detection, control and alleviation of mental and emotional derangements"; (2) more financial aid for training mental health personnel; (3) "a new program of mental health project grants" to improve "the quality of care in mental institutions and the administration of the institutions" and to "search out ways of reducing the length of stay and the necessity for institutional care.''

In a Feb. 12 press release, the AMA expressed "complete accord" with the stated purpose of Eisenhower legislation designed to promote voluntarily health insurance, but it said that the AMA "still believes" the President's medical reinsurance proposal "will not achieve the desired results.'' Mrs. Hobby again assured the House Commerce Committee March 2 that the program would not be an "entering wedge" for socialized medicine. But the legislation again failed to win Congress' approval.

In 1956, submitting his budget proposals for fiscal 1957,

Eisenhower recommended "renewed consideration" of his federal
health reinsurance proposal if the Health, Education & Welfare
Secretary failed in plans for private insurance organizations to pool
risks to cover abnormal losses possible under broader health plans.
He urged Congress to adopt his 1955 recommendations "to provide
mortgage insurance for the construction of health facilities, to train
health personnel, to expand mental health programs, to abate water
pollution and to strengthen state and local public health services."
He urged authorization of $40 million in federal aid to build medical
and dental research and training facilities.

Eisenhower Jan. 26, 1956 sent to Congress a special message
proposing a five-point national health program in which the federal
government would assume a "partnership" role and "provide assistance without interference in personal, local or state responsibilities." In the message Eisenhower said:

● "More than 100,000 persons are now enrolled in prepayment
health insurance plans of some type." But this protection "remains
inadequate" in important respects and "is still not available to many
who need it." "There are now indications that the organizations
writing [voluntary] health prepayment plans might progress more
rapidly by joining together—sharing or pooling their risks—to offer
broader benefits and expanded coverage on reasonable terms. . . . If
practical and useful methods cannot be developed along these lines,
then I will again urge enactment of the proposal made last year" for
federal reinsurance. "I again recommend . . . a separate program
through which the federal government would match [state and local]
funds . . . for medical care of the indigent aged, the blind, the permanently and totally disabled and dependent children. . . ." (Congress in 1956 again took up but did not approve the health reinsurance plan.)

● $250 million was recommended "for a five-year program to as-
sist in construction of research and teaching facilities for schools of
medicine, osteopathy, public health and dentistry and other research
institutions. These institutions would . . . supply at least equal
amounts in matching funds."

● The program "will permit a major increase in trainees and research fellows," expansion of "student capacity" and "training of
more physicians, scientists, dentists and other health workers."
Legislation was requested to implement the 1955 proposals for "(A)
a five-year program of grants for training practical nurses, (B)
traineeships for graduate nurses and (C) . . . traineeships in other
public health specialties." (Modified legislation for this part of the

program was passed by Congress and was signed by Eisenhower Aug. 2.)

● Congress was urged "to authorize the Public Health Service to secure periodically needed information on the incidence, duration and effects of illness and disability in the nation." A two-year extension was proposed for the federal-state program of aiding the "construction of chronic disease hospitals, nursing homes, diagnostic and treatment centers and rehabilitation facilities." The budget provided a $19 million increase in funds for this. (Legislation covering the hospital-construction program was passed by Congress in 1956 and was signed by Eisenhower Aug. 2.) Eisenhower renewed his request for federal insurance of mortgage loans for the construction of hospitals, clinics and other private medical care facilities. He renewed his request for "a new program of mental health project grants . . . to seek ways of improving the quality of care [and administration] in mental institutions" and "of reducing the length of stay." He recommended that authority granted under the Water Pollution Control Act, scheduled to expire June 30, be strengthened and made permanent. He urged strengthening of the Food & Drug Administration, more research on public health aspects of civil defense, continued expansion of the federal-state program "of restoring handicapped men and women to more productive lives."

● The fiscal 1957 budget of $126,525,000 for the National Institutes of Health—a 28% increase over fiscal 1956 appropriations—would include these research funds: cancer $32,437,000, heart disease $22,106,000, mental illness $21,749,000, arthritis and metabolic diseases $13,345,000, neurology and blindness $12,196,000, infectious and parasitic diseases $9,799,000, dental disorders $2,971,000, general research $11,922,000. "By far the major share of the increased funds would be for research grants to medical schools, hospitals and private laboratories," which would receive 47% more than in fiscal 1956. The National Science Foundation's $7 million increase in research grants "would provide for additional research in the biological and medical sciences." (In 1956 Congress approved a three-year, $90 million program of government grants to help build public and non-profit health research facilities. Eisenhower, signing the authorization bill July 30, complained that it failed to provide an adequate amount or give needed assistance to new facilities for training medical scientists.

Adlai E. Stevenson, preparing in 1956 for a second Presidential election campaign against Eisenhower, discussed the health-care problem at the Los Angeles Press Club May 9. Stevenson said: The most promising approach to "the crisis of medical care" seemed "to be the development of voluntary, private, prepayment health insurance programs providing comprehensive service at low rates. . . . To stimulate growth of these plans there is urgent need . . . [for] long-term, low-interest government loans to help new prepayment groups to come into existence, and government grants to meet part of the cost of comprehensive care" for people with limited financial means. Federal action was needed to support medical school construction and medical research and inclusion of disability insurance in the Social Security System.

Stevenson in Chicago Oct. 8 proposed a national health program whose key feature would "make comprehensive private health insurance available on a voluntary basis to all Americans, so that no American will be denied good medical care for financial reasons." "Some form of federal aid will be required to achieve this goal," Stevenson said. Acceptable federal aid, he indicated, would include (a) "long-term interest-bearing loans" to help groups start cooperative health insurance plans, (b) "matching grants to the states to pay part of the costs of voluntary health insurance for low-income families and individuals." Stevenson repeated his opposition to "socialized medicine" and insisted that there should be no compulsion to join health insurance plans and no restriction on an individual's freedom to choose his own doctor. The program's administration, Stevenson said, "should rest with the states," but the federal government should not make grants until assured that federally aided health insurance policies "meet certain standards . . . [and provide] true comprehensive protection." "The federal government should do, toward promoting health in America, only what cannot be done—or as a practical matter will not be done—privately or through any other agency," Stevenson declared. His statement also urged federal aid for medical research, for medical education and for construction of hospitals and other medical facilities.

After being reelected President in 1956, Eisenhower continued to recommend enactment of his health proposals, although his health program appeared to receive a lower order of priority both from him and from Congress. Submitting his fiscal 1958 budget Jan. 16, 1957, Eisenhower told Congress it was time to enact his program "for expansion and improvement of voluntary health insurance plans under which smaller insurance companies and non-profit associations could pool their resources and experience." Congress, however, took no action on his suggestion. Neither did it act on legislation, introduced Jan. 25 by Sen. James E. Murray (D, Mont.) and

Rep. John D. Dingell (D, Mich.), to establish a national health insurance system similar to old-age, survivors and unemployment insurance with employed persons contributing 1½% of their earnings
(maximum annual contribution $90) and employers matching the
payments.

A Presidential Commission on National Goals for the 1960s
made public Nov. 27, 1960 a report that included a detailed section
on health. It said: "The demand for medical care has enormously
increased. To meet it we must have more doctors, nurses, and other
medical personnel. There should be more hospitals, clinics and nursing homes. Greater effectiveness in the use of such institutions will
reduce over-all requirements. . . . Federal grants for the construction of hospitals should be continued and extended to other medical
facilities. Increased private, state and federal support is necessary
for training doctors. Further efforts are needed to reduce the burden
of the cost of medical care. Extension of medical insurance is
necessary, through both public and private agencies. . . . To meet
our medical needs, we must not only increase the number of places
in medical school by about one-half in this decade; we must also
make it much more practicable for young men and women of talent
and modest means to enter the profession. Scholarships during medical school and internship training are necessary. The study of environmental health measures should be increased. We need to
mobilize our resources better to understand such problems as air and
water pollution, radiation hazards, and food additives. . . . Some 17
million persons suffer from mental illness in this country; it costs
state governments over $1 billion per year. A maximum research ef-
fort, a substantial increase in the number of mental health clinics,
and further progress in improving state mental hospitals are all part
of the necessary effort to cope with it."

Medical Care for the Aged

By 1959, Congress was beginning to give serious consideration
to proposals to provide medical care for the aged under the Social
Security System. A bill to enact such a plan was introduced Feb.
18, 1959 by Rep. Aime J. Forand (R, R.I.). During hearings of the
House Ways & Means Committee on the Forand bill, Secretary of
Health, Education & Welfare Arthur S. Flemming opposed the measure July 13 as likely to halt the broadening of health-insurance
plans for the elderly. U.S. Chamber of Commerce spokesman A. D.
Marshall, vice president of General Dynamics, opposed it July 14 as

so costly "as to jeopardize public acceptance of Social Security." Nelson Cruikshank, director of the AFL-CIO's Social Security Department, backed the plan July 14 on grounds that "adequate alternatives to federal action have not been developed" and that rising costs were sweeping away the "whole underpining of retirement." The plan was opposed July 15 by representatives of the American Medical Association and American Dental Association but backed by spokesmen for the American Nurses Association and the American Public Welfare Association. United Auto Workers President Walter P. Reuther indorsed the bill July 16 as providing a "basic minimum standard" of health insurance on which voluntary plans could build. Dr. Donald Stubbs, spokesman for the Blue Shield Surgical Insurance Plans, opposed the bill July 17 as being made unnecessary by rapid advances in voluntary plans. Dr. Caldwell B. Esselstyn, speaking for the Group Health Association of America, said Sept. 17 that the plan would help hospitals by giving them full fees instead of making them continue to depend on welfare rates or less.

The Forand bill was finally rejected by the House Ways & Means Committee by 17-8 vote (10 R. and 7. D. vs. 8 D.) June 3, 1960.

Earlier in 1960, a proposal that medical care be added to Social Security had been made Feb. 8 by the Democratic majority of a Senate Labor subcommittee headed by Sen. Pat McNamara (Mich.). They charged that "at least half of the aged—approximately eight million people—cannot afford decent housing, proper nutrition, adequate medical care." They proposed that minimum Social Security benefits be raised from $33 monthly to at least $50 and that an "Office of the Aging" be set up for problems caused by a "population explosion" among aging Americans.

Flemming had presented at a closed House Ways & Means Committee session May 4, an Eisenhower Administration proposal that the states set up federally subsidized "Medicare" systems to provide health insurance for persons over 65. This "Medicare Program for the Aged" was offered as an alternative to the Democratic proposals that Social Security provide medical care. Flemming said Medicare would cost the federal and state governments about $1.2 billion a year and enable 12½ million of the U.S.' 16 million persons over 65 "to cope with the heavy economic burden of long-term or other expensive illnesses." Those eligible would be single elderly persons with adjusted gross incomes of up to $2,500 a year and married couples with incomes of up to $3,800 a year. The 3½ million persons over 65 with incomes above these figures would be excluded. The state Medicare systems, operating under statutory federal standards, would collect fees of $24 a year each from covered persons who could afford the payments. Aged persons on relief would get free coverage. Medicare benefits in any year would start for single persons after they already had paid $250 that year for medical and hospital expenses and for married couples who had paid $400. Medicare funds would defray 80% of the year's expense beyond these sums, and the beneficiaries would have to pay the remaining 20%. Coverage would include up to 180 days of hospital care in a year, up to a full year of care at home or in nursing homes, up to $350 a year for prescribed drugs and up to $200 a year for laboratory and X-ray fees. Full payment would be made for the indigent. Eligible persons who decided against entering the Medicare program could buy private major-medical insurance, and the program would provide joint federal-state payment of 50% of the cost (up to $60 annually). The federal share of the total subsidy would be about 50%, but federal grants to individual states would range from two-thirds of the cost in the poorest states to one-third in the wealthiest.

Flemming told the committee that the Administration was willing to consider modifications that conformed with Eisenhower's requirements that a health-care plan for the aged be voluntary and that its costs be shared by the states and by beneficiaries financially able to contribute.

Most Democrats indicated opposition to the plan on grounds that it would be too costly and that some states would not cooperate. Republican reaction was mixed. New York Gov. Nelson A. Rockefeller told reporters May 4 that it would cause a "very serious fiscal situation." He urged that Social Security include health care and that beneficiaries contribute. The Medicare plan was denounced May 5 by the American Medical Association and the AFL-CIO Executive Council.

An advance announcement that the Administration would propose the plan had been made by Vice President Nixon in a Chicago TV interview May 1. Nixon said Republicans who opposed health legislation were "irresponsible and wrong." Nixon had participated in an Apr. 5 White House session with the President, Flemming and Republican Congressional leaders at which Administration guidelines were formulated for a program of medical care for the aged. Senate GOP leader Everett M. Dirksen (Ill.) said the guidelines specified that the program be voluntary, not "excessive," geared to the private insurance system and "limited in scope" and that it cause no increase in Social Security taxes. Eisenhower and the Republican Congressional leaders, at an earlier White House legislative conference Mar. 22, had rejected several proposals by Flemming for federally-subsidized voluntary health insurance for the aged. Flemming had prepared the proposals at Nixon's suggestion. Eisenhower and the GOP leaders insisted that the Administration should wait for more study of the issue before deciding on whether to submit legislation to Congress. After the Republican leaders had finally agreed to the submission of legislation for health aid to the aged, Nixon took the lead in calling for the rejection of the Forand proposal. He warned in a May 7 statement that the Forand plan "would open the door for socialized medicine." He said it "would set up a great state program which inevitably would head in the direction of herding the ill and elderly into institutions, whether they desired this or not." It "would threaten the high standards of American medicine," he said.

Eisenhower had said at his press conference March 30 that he opposed compulsory federal medical-care insurance for the aged. "I have been against any compulsory insurance as a very definite step in socialized medicine," he declared. "I don't believe in it, and I want none of it myself." He said he was seeking a voluntary program in which state and local governments would help finance medical and surgical care for those over 65 years old. Answering criticism that he did not understand the problem because he had always received free medical care as an Army officer and as President, Eisenhower said: "There are lots of governments, and the thing I object to is putting everything on the federal government."

Although the House Ways & Means Committee had rejected the Forand bill, it found the Administration's Medicare proposal also unacceptable. The committee June 3, just hours after voting down the Forand plan, approved a limited $325 million-a-year program of federal subsidies to help pay the medical bills of about 1½ million needy persons 65 and older who were not poor enough to qualify for public assistance. The bill would authorize annual federal grants of $185 million to the states, which would have to pay $140 million, or 35% to 50% of the cost of the program in each state.

The Senate Aug. 23 rejected (a) a proposal to provide medical care benefits through Social Security for all Social Security eligibles over 68, and (b) a liberalized version of the Eisenhower Administration's contributary Medicare plan for the aged. The Senate Aug. 23 then passed by 91-2 vote its Finance Committee's bill for federal contributions to state medical aid to the needy poor. Only Sens. Barry Goldwater (R., Ariz.) and Strom Thurmond (D., S.C.) voted "no." The two defeated plans had been offered as amendments to this bill. The Social Security approach, calling for higher Social Security taxes to finance its benefits, was co-sponsored by Sens. John F. Kennedy (D, Mass.) and Clinton P. Anderson (D, N.M.) and was voted down by 51-44 (32 R. and 19 D. vs. 43 D. and 1 R.). The liberalized Medicare version was introduced by Sen. Jacob K. Javits (R, N.Y.) with the indorsement of Nixon and assurances that Eisenhower backed it. The Javits plan was a voluntary scheme allowing beneficiaries to chose from three optional forms of coverage, requiring contributions of at least 10% (more if financially able) on the part of the beneficiaries, setting income limits for beneficiaries and providing for annual federal contributions of $320 million to $460 million and state contributions of up to $520 million. It was defeated by 67-28 vote.

A compromise bill for medical care for the needy aged was finally passed by 368-17 House vote (9 Southern Democrats and 8 Republicans opposed) Aug. 26 and 74-11 Senate vote Aug. 29. Eisenhower signed the measure Sept. 13. In the Senate 10 Southern Democrats and Sen. Barry M. Goldwater (R., Ariz.) voted "no." This Kerr-Mills bill (a version produced by Sen. Robert S. Kerr, D, Okla., and Rep. Wilbur D. Mills, D, Ark.) provided for federal contributions starting Oct. 1 to existing state medical-care programs for needy persons 65 and over (at the rate of $12 monthly for each recipient). It authorized federal grants on a matching basis to help states start new programs for "medically needy" persons over 65 who otherwise were self-supporting. About 12,400,000 persons were potentially eligible for both programs but would have to pass "means tests" to get the aid. The grants, to come from general revenues, were to be pro-rated to the states on the basis of each state's per-capita income. Payments under the two programs would go to the health-care vendors, not to the beneficiaries. It was estimated that it would cost the federal government $202 million and the states $61 million the first year and that the cost would rise after 5 years to $340 million a year for the federal government and $180 million for the states.

Kennedy & the Health-Care Problem

In 1960 Sen. John F. Kennedy (D, Mass.) was elected President in a race against Vice President Richard M. Nixon. Kennedy ran under a Democratic platform, adopted July 12, that listed in the Democratic-promised "economic bill of rights": " 'The right to adequate medical care and the opportunity to achieve and enjoy good health.' " The platform promised that a new Democratic administration would "provide medical care benefits for the aged as part of the time-tested Social Security insurance system. We reject any proposal which would require such citizens to submit to the indignity of a means test—a 'pauper's oath.' "

The Republican platform pledged "support of federal-state grant programs to improve health, welfare and rehabilitation services for the handicapped older persons and to improve standards of nursing home care and care and treatment facilities for the chronically and mentally ill. . . . Development of a health program that will provide the aged needing it, on a sound fiscal basis and through a contributory system, protection against burdensome costs of health care. Such a program should: provide the beneficiaries with the option of purchasing private health insurance . . . ; protect the personal relationship of patient and physician; include state participation. . . . Continued federal support for a sound research program . . . and intensified efforts to secure prompt and effective application of the results of research. This will include emphasis on mental illness. . . . Federal help in new programs to build schools of medicine, dentistry, public health and nursing and to provide financial aid to students in those fields. . . . Additional resources for research and training in the field of radiological medicine."

Shortly after becoming President, Kennedy sent Congress Feb. 9, 1961 a special health message proposing steps "to strengthen the indispensable elements in a sound health program—people, knowledge, services, facilities and the means to pay for them." The message said more than $25 billion a year, or over 6% of the U.S. national income, was being spent from public and private funds for health services, "yet there are major deficiencies" in these services.

The message recommended enactment of a health-insurance program under the Social Security System for all persons aged 65 and over who were eligible for Social Security or railroad retirement benefits. The message asserted that this was "not a program of socialized medicine" but "a program of prepayment of health costs with absolute freedom of choice guaranteed. Every person will choose his own doctor and hospital." The message said: "We must meet the needs of those millions" of aged persons who were "staggered by the drain on their savings . . . caused by an extended hospital stay"; "the high cost of ill-health in old age" denied "to

all but those with the highest incomes a full measure of security'';
the ''annual medical bill [of aged persons] is twice that of persons
under 65—but their annual income is only half as high.''

The health-insurance program was to be financed entirely (a)
by an increase in Social Security contributions of ¼% each on employers and employes, effective Jan. 1, 1963 (yielding $1.1 billion);
(b) by an increase in the maximum taxable earnings base from
$4,800 a year to $5,000 a year, effective Jan. 1, 1962 (yielding
$400 million). This program for the aged would provide: (a) in-
patient hospital services of up to 90 days for a single illness, including payment of all costs over $20, payment of all costs over $10 per
day for the first 9 days and payment of full costs for the remaining
time; (b) skilled nursing home services of up to 180 days immediately after hospital discharge, and, as an incentive to use these
facilities, 2 days of nursing care in place of one day of hospital
care; (c) hospital out-patient clinic diagnostic services for all costs in
excess of $20; (d) community visiting nurse and related home health
services for up to 240 days a year. 191.3621

The message called for legislation: (1) to double the current
$10 million authorization in matching grants for the construction of
more skilled nursing homes; (2) to provide an initial annual $10 mil-
lion appropriation for stimulatory grants to the states, and through
them to the communities, to improve health services; (3) to create a
Bureau of Community Health to provide states and communities
with leadership and assistance; (4) to eliminate an ''arbitrary ceiling
for research'' by allowing Congress to determine each year the
amount necessary for hospital research and development and by allowing the Surgeon General to make project grants for the construction of experimental or demonstration hospitals and other medical
facilities.

The message warned that health personnel ''shortages are growing. . . . We . . . fall short of our goal'' to export doctors ''to provide a nucleus for a world health program. . . .'' To maintain in the
next 10 years the current ratio of doctors and dentists to population,
the U.S. would need 20 new medical and 20 new dental schools
(the U.S. already had 92 medical and 47 dental schools). The message said that the U.S. should begin: (1) an immediate program of
planning grants and a 10-year program of matching grants ($25 mil-
lion the first year and $75 million annually thereafter) for construc-
tion and expansion of medical and dental school capacities; (2) a
program for medical and dental students of federal scholarships
equal to $1,500 for one-quarter of the newly entering students of

each institution, awarded in individual four-year scholarships by the institution in proportion to the student's need. The schools would receive a cost-of-education grant of $1,000 for each federal scholarship.

According to the message, the U.S. had fallen from 6th to 11th place among the advanced nations in saving of infant lives. It said Congress should establish a National Institute of Child Health and Human Development (to include a center for research in child health) and privide more appropriations for existing maternal and child health, crippled children and child welfare programs of the Children's Bureau. The Secretary of Health, Education & Welfare was designated as chairman of the President's Council on Youth Fitness. (Kennedy Feb. 6 had ordered that a center for research in child health be established within the National Institutes of Health of the Public Health Service. The President said more work should be done to find the causes of mental retardation.)

Congress took no action during 1961 on the proposal for health insurance under Social Security. But it adopted compromise legislation to provide increased federal aid for expanding community health services. The measure, as signed by Kennedy Oct. 5, (a) raised from $30 million to $50 million the limit on annual expenditures for the five-year program of grants in aid to states for public health services; (b) authorized $50 million annually for a five-year program of grants to states, communities and nonprofit organizations for research for improved health facilities outside hospitals; (c) increased from $10 million to $20 million the limit on annual expenditures for a three-year program of grants in aid to states for construction of nursing homes.

Kennedy urged the U.S. Oct. 11, 1961 to undertake "a comprehensive and coordinated attack on the problem of mental retardation." He also announced his intention to appoint a special panel to explore the possibilities for prevention and cure of mental retardation and to appraise existing programs. (He appointed the panel Oct. 16.) Kennedy said in his Oct. 11 statement: (1) The number of mentally retarded persons in the U.S. was expected to rise from approximately five million currently to six million by 1970; (2) one out of every four beds in state institutions was assigned to a mentally retarded person, but 96% of the retarded lived in private homes and put a "staggering financial burden on the families"; (3) it was "just as important to integrate the mentally retarded within our modern society . . . as it is to make a special effort to do this for the physically handicapped." (The Children's Bureau of the Health, Education & Welfare Departmentment began a mass screening program July 1, 1962 to detect phyenylketonuria, a congenital metabolic disorder leading to mental retardation, in newborn infants. The new test was devised by Dr. Robert Guthrie of the University of Buffalo and required a few drops of blood from an infant's heel. The test represented an advance over previous tests, which detected the disease in older infants, when the damage could still be arrested but not reversed.)

In his State-of-the-Union message Jan. 11, 1962, Kennedy asserted that "in matters of health, no piece of unfinished business is more important or more urgent thatn the enactment under the Social Security System of health insurance for the aged." He added that Congress also should approve legislation for: (1) aid for "medical and dental colleges and scholarships and to establish new national institutes of health"; (2) a mass immunization program against poliomyelitis, diphtheria, whooping cough and tetanus; (3) strengthening of the food and drug laws.

The American Hospital Association and the Blue Cross Association Jan. 4 had proposed a plan to provide medical care for the aged under a voluntary program to be administered by Blue Cross and partailly financed by the government. The AHA said the latter financing could be through Social Security, but the Blue Cross deleted the specific reference. The program, indorsed by both groups at a joint meeting held in Chicago Jan. 3-4, would be available to persons over 65. It would cover many hospital costs but not doctor or surgery costs and would scale premium costs to a person's income. The government would finance premiums for persons whose income was below a certain level. (The AHA opposed the Kennedy Administration's King-Anderson bill, which would finance hospitalization and nursing home costs through increased Social Security taxes but not cover doctors' fees.)

A voluntary insurance program to provide surgical and medical care benefits to cover doctors' services for aged persons was announced Jan. 17 by the National Association of Blue Shield Plans and the American Medical Association. The plan, to be submitted to Blue Shield affiliates for approval, was offered as a counter-measure to efforts to "socialize" medicine. It would have a uniform premium of "about $3 a month per person." It would cover the full cost of medical and surgical services for single persons whose annual income was $2,500 or less and for couples whose income was $4,000 or less. Doctors would be allowed to make additional charges to patients with higher incomes. Blue Shield payments to doctors would vary from area to area to conform with local patterns. Health, Education & Welfare Secretary Abraham A. Ribicoff criticized the Blue Shield plan Jan. 20 as capable of doing "nothing whatever to meet the staggering problem of high cost of hospital care in a serious illness which faces all the aged." He said Jan. 29 that if the doctors "would come along with provision for hospital care, I'd go along with the AMA-Blue Shield plan." He offered the AMA a "deal": "I'll go for your program if you will go for mine."

Kennedy, sending his second special health message to Congress Feb. 27, 1962, repeated his requests for enactment of a health insurance program for the aged financed through Social Security and of other pending Administration health proposals. He also proposed several new health programs. The federal role in health care, Kennedy said, was to share the responsibility "by providing leadership, guidance and support in areas of national concern." In addition to the controversial program for the aged, the message reiterated requests for a 10-year program of grants for planning and building medical schools, a medical-scholarship program, increased fiscal 1963 funds for the National Institutes of Health, establishment of an Institute for Child Health & Human Development, increased research on maternal and child health and crippled children's services, a further extension of the matching grants program for construction of health research facilities, training of additional mental health personnel.

The new programs requested (the cost to the U.S. was estimated at $850 million in the next five years): (1) a $35 million grant program to pay the entire cost of vaccines and help state and local governments pay operational costs of a program to immunize all children under 5 against poliomyelitis, diphtheria, whooping cough and tetanus; (2) a $31 million program of grants and technical aid to state and local agencies for air-pollution control; (3) establishment of a National Environmental Health Center to coordinate the fight against air and water pollution and radiation hazards; (4) a loan program for construction and equipment of group-practice medical and dental facilities, especially clinics in small communities; (5) a program (estimated federal cost—$3 billion a year) to aid states in providing medical services and facilities for migrant agricultural workers.

Dr. Leonard W. Larson, president of the AMA issued in Chicago Feb. 28 a statement saying: The Administration's proposed program to provide medical care for the aged "is not a program of health insurance; it is political medicine. The medical profession is for the Kerr-Mills Law to help the aged who need help. We are for voluntary enterprise, including health insurance and prepayment plans, for the non-needy aged."

The Social Security Administration reported Feb. 27 that 25 states and territories had programs of medical aid for the elderly under the Kerr-Mills Act, which took effect in October 1960; 18 states reported paying under the program in December 1961 a total of $13,919,818 in federal, state and local funds for the aid of 72,159 elderly persons. Gov. John B. Swainson of Michigan, the first state to enter the Kerr-Mills plan, told Kennedy in a letter Feb. 27 that "the Kerr-Mills program has not worked in Michigan." Despite a "vigorous" effort to provide aid under the legislation, Swainson said, only 11,800, or 1.85% of the state's over-65 population, were receiving aid under it after one year's operation. HEW Secretary Ribicoff, releasing his department's report on the first year's operation of the Kerr-Mills Law, said March 27 that the Kerr-Mills medical care program for the aged was inadequate. As of January, Ribicoff reported, it had aided only 64,700 persons, and only 22 states and territories participated in it. (Six more had joined since January.) Chairman Patrick V. McNamara (D, Mich.) of the Special Senate Committee on Aging released June 19 a committee staff report also indicating that the Kerr-Mills program failed to provide adequate health care for the aged. According to the report: About 90% of all federal funds disbursed under the program went to only four states—California, New York, Massachusetts and Michigan; only 88,264 medically indigent elderly persons (about .5% of the total population 65 and over)—were aided by the Kerr-Mills program in March 1962; benefit standards varied, and the program resulted in such inequities as rules under which many elderly persons had to put up their homes as security in order to qualify.

About 10,000 elderly persons March 26 attended a New York rally addressed by Mayor Robert F. Wagner, who called for support of the Administration's proposals as embodied in the King-Anderson bill. A voluntary committee—the Physicians Committee for Health Care for the Aged Through Social Security—was formed in Washington March 28 by 27 doctors to rally support from other doctors for the Administration's aged care plan. The group, led by Dr. Caldwell B. Esselstyn of Hudson, N.Y., president of the Group Health Association of America, had met with Kennedy Mar. 27 to pledge their support.

Two hundred New Jersey doctors were reported May 3, 1962 to have signed a resolution to treat aged patients under the King-

Anderson bill. The resolution was originated by Dr. J. Bruce Henriksen, 54, of Point Pleasant, who said that if the patients "can't pay their bills out of their own pocket or through insurance, then we'll treat them free." He described the King-Anderson bill as "a step toward creeping socialism." The doctors' action was condemned by Gov. Richard J. Hughes May 5 and by the New Jersey Assembly in a resolution passed by voice vote May 7. Hughes held that "the source of a person's income or the manner in which his hospital bill is paid, should have no bearing in whether a doctor will treat a . . . patient." Ribicoff May 5 called the doctors' plan "blackmail." He said May 8 that "these doctors apparently believe it is all right for the federal government to help build hospitals in which they practice but that an insurance plan that would help their patients pay their hospital bills would not be good." (In a speech at the 43d convention of the American Nurses Association in Detroit May 14, Ribicoff praised the group because "you, unlike most of your sisters—or brother organizations in medicine," had supported the Administration's aged-care plan.) The New Jersey doctors' boycott plan was indorsed by the Louisiana State Medical Society at its annual meeting in Monroe, La. May 9. The Louisiana society resolved not to "participate in the implementation" of the King-Anderson bill if it became law. The American Urological Association, holding scientific meetings in Philadelphia, announced May 14 its unanimous opposition to the King-Anderson bill. Sen. John G. Tower (R, Tex.) attacked the Administration's bill during a speaking engagement before the Texas Hospital Association and Texas Medical Association. The Texas Blue Cross and Blue Shield nonprofit health insurance groups conceded May 14 that they had paid Tower's expenses for the week-end engagement, but they denied that the money was used for lobbying. Tower called such payment common practice.

A committee to support the King-Anderson bill was formed in New York by 500 Columbia University faculty members, including 140 physicians associated with the Columbia-Presbyterian Medical Center. Its formation was announced May 12 by Dr. Frank Van Dyke. Dr. James Howard Means, professor emeritus of clinical medicine at Harvard University, attacked the AMA's opposition to the bill and described the AMA May 14 as a "medieval guild." He made the comparison in a speech at the annual institute of the Group Health Association of America, a non-profit group administering prepaid medical programs for community or labor groups.

Support for a program of medical care for the elderly financed through Social Security was reaffirmed by the American Nurses' Association at its convention in Detroit May 18.

Kennedy May 20 addressed a New York rally in support of his Administration's pending program of medical care for the elderly. The rally was sponsored by the National Council of Senior Citizens of Washington and the Golden Ring Council of Senior Citizens of New York. The President's speech was nationally televised and also televised to 32 other similar rallies across the country. Main speakers at some of the other rallies were Vice President Lyndon B. Johnson in St. Louis, Sen. Clinton P. Anderson (D, N.M.), co-sponsor of the King-Anderson bill, in Houston, Interior Secretary Stewart L. Udall in Kansas City and Commerce Secretary Luther H. Hodges in Boston. Similar rallies in 12 other cities were also held May 19 and 21.

Speaking extemporaneously, Kennedy said that doctors should write to him or to others in the Administration for explanation of the King-Anderson bill because "they do not comprehend what we're trying to do." Charging that the AMA and other opponents of the bill had "misinformed" the public, the President said: "This is not a campaign against doctors, because doctors have joined with us." It was, he said a campaign to help the elderly pay hospital bills so they could meet their other financial responsibilities. He said the bill would not (a) cover doctors' bills, (b) "affect the freedom of choice" of patients to choose their own doctors, (c) "sap the individual self-reliance of Americans," (d) "solve our problems in this area . . ., but it will do part of it." His appeal for support, he said, was made "as a citizen" asking other citizens to exert their power "to petition" government. "The business of government is the business of the people, and the people are right here," he said.

The AMA paid for and put on an hour-long, nationally televised program from New York May 21 to rebut the aged-care rally addressed by Kennedy May 20. The AMA program, estimated to have cost $100,000, was broadcast by NBC and by 190 NBC affiliates and 15 other stations covering every major U.S. metropolitan area except Boston, where the AMA could not get a station to carry it. The program was broadcast from the deserted Madison Square Garden to dramatize AMA President Larson's charge May 19 that the Administration was pressing its program with "the biggest lobbying campaign this nation has ever seen." (Larson had said May 2 that AMA requests for equal TV time to rebut the May 20 Kennedy rally had been refused on the ground the President would not make a political speech.) An announcer opened the AMA program with the statement that "the AMA and its member doctors strongly favor other forms of medical care for the aged," including the Kerr-Mills Law. Larson then spoke, making a plea for continuance of the "system of private medicine," which had "added an average of 10 years to the life of every American" and in which patients were treated "individually and intimately" and not "as numbers." The program's main attack against the King-Anderson bill was delivered by Dr. Edward R. Annis, 49, a Miami surgeon. He denounced the King-Anderson bill as "a cruel hoax and a delusion." He said the bill would "wastefully" cover "millions who do not need it" and "heartlessly" ignore "millions who do need coverage," "create an enormous and unpredictable burden on every working taxpayer," offer "sharply limited benefits," "undercut and destroy the wholesome growth of private, voluntary insurance and pre-payment health programs for the aged," "lower the quality and availability of hospital services," "stand between the patient and his doctor," "serve as the forerunner of a different system of medicine for all Americans," "put the government smack into your hospitals" and impose "a federally administered financial budget on our houses of mercy and healing." The program ended with an appeal for viewers to ask their physicians for information on the King-Anderson bill and to write their views to Congress.

A compromise version of Kennedy's medical-care-for-the-aged program was killed for the 1962 session of Congress July 17 when the Senate voted, 52-48 (31 R. and 21 D. vs. 43 D. and 5R.), to table the measure. Every one of the 100 Senators was present and voted. The program, calling for financing of health care through Social Security, had been brought up as an amendment to a bill to expand federal participation in state public assistance and child welfare programs. Kennedy made an unusual TV appearance an hour after the vote to term the bill's rejection "a most serious defeat for every American family." He said: Americans would "have to decide . . . in November, in the Congressional elections, whether we want to stand still or whether we want to support this kind of legislation. . . . I hope that we will return in November a Congress that will support a program like medical care for the aged, a program which has been fought by the American Medical Association and successfully defeated. This bill will be introduced in January 1963. . . . With your support in November, this will pass in 1963."

The compromise program had been introduced June 29 by a bipartisan group of 21 Democratic Senators led by Clinton P. Anderson (N.M.) and five Republican Senators led by Jacob K. Javits

(N.Y.). It was generally referred to as the Anderson-Javits bill. In the showdown vote July 17, the five co-sponsoring Repbulicans were the only GOP Senators to back the measure. The compromise would have provided health insurance coverage through Social Security for all persons 65 or over regardless of whether or not they were eligible for Social Security or other federal retirement benefits. It also would have (a) authorized at the option of those covered, that benefits be administered through Blue Cross or other private health insurance plans, (b) put the money for the medical care program into a special trust fund and not kept it with the rest of Social Security money, (c) provided for American Hospital Association and American Medical Association accrediting of hospitals participating in the program. Anderson said on opening debate on the compromise July 3 that the program would not lead to "socialized medicine" and that "the AMA should stop worrying."

Kennedy, asked at his press conference July 5 why the program did not cover doctors' bills as well as hospital, medicine and similar costs, replied: ". . . Doctors are very strong against being included. They feel that this would involve the government in the doctor-patient relationship. . . . It is because we have not included doctors that I have found it very difficult to understand why the American Medical Association has found this legislation so unsatisfactory. It involves the payment of hospital bills, and in view of the fact that the federal government participates in the construction of hospitals through the Hill-Burton Act, I have found the AMA's extreme hostility to the bill somewhat incomprehensible."

Three GOP substitutes for the measure had been rejected by the Senate before the compromise plan was killed: The Senate, by voice vote July 6, had turned down a proposal of Sen. Thruston B. Morton (R, Ky.) to provide federal payments totaling more than $1.2 billion a year in the form of subsidies of up to $125 each to persons 64 years or older for private health insurance. By 50-34 vote July 12, the Senate rejected a proposal of Sen. Leverett Saltonstall (R, Mass.) and six Republican co-sponsors for about $500 million a year in federal matching grants to the states for health insurance for the aged. The Senate, by 75-5 vote July 13, defeated a proposal of Sen. Prescott Bush (R, Conn.) to increase Social Security taxes as recommended in the Administration bill but to use the funds as supplementary payments of up to $9 a month to Social Security beneficiaries to reimburse them when they bought private health insurance.

Kennedy Aug. 16 appointed a 12-member Health Resources

Advisory Committee, headed by Dr. William R. Willard, vice president of the University of Kentucky's Medical Center, to help formulate emergency plans for allocating national health resources.

A special message on health was presented to Congress by Kennedy Feb. 7, 1963. In it, Kennedy said his medical-care program for the aged financed through Social Security "must be enacted this year." The message proposed several new programs and renewed pleas for health programs he had proposed in 1962 and for the attack on mental illness he had proposed Feb. 5. His new proposals included: (a) federal aid to help finance expansion of nurse training facilities and assist nursing students; (b) air-pollution-control legislation authorizing government intervention whenever such problems involved two or more states; (c) tightened control over food, drugs and cosmetics, including a requirement that cosmetics be tested and proven safe for use before being marketed; (d) a five-year extension of Hill-Burton Act aid to build hospitals. The financing requested for the programs, all provided for in the budget, included: (a) $69,300,000 in fiscal 1964 (expenditures of $14 million) for aid to relieve manpower shortages and to improve health facilities; (b) $34,300,000 in the first year of operation and $813 million over 10 years for increasing the number of professional health personnel by aiding school and facility construction and providing student loans to doctors, dentists and osteopaths; (c) increasing Hill-Burton funds from $180 million to $215 million in fiscal 1964 ($50 million for nursing homes); (d) increasing national Institutes of Health expenditures by $113 million and its authorization by $50 million (to $980 million); (e) $13,200,000 in supplemental appropriations for community vaccination and migrant health programs; (f) $5 million to start an international program to wipe out yellow fever mosquitoes. Kennedy also requested: (1) a five-year program of insuring mortgages and providing loans for building and equipping group-practice facilities for health specialists; (2) creation of a Bureau of Environmental Health; (3) pay raises for government medical officials; (4) more funds for rehabilitation of handicapped children (to raise such rehabilitation by 25%).

Kennedy sent to Congress Feb. 21, 1963 a fresh proposal to provide hospital insurance for the aged through Social Security. The plan was the main feature of the first Presidential message to Congress devoted entirely to problems of the aged. "It is not enough for a great nation merely to have added new years to life," Kennedy said in his message. "Our objective must also be to add new life to those years." He said the U.S. had 17½ million persons aged 65 or older and that there would be nearly 25 million by 1980. The President asserted that the health insurance he proposed should be available to all aged persons covered by Social Security or Railroad Retirement. It would be financed by increasing both the employer's and employe's Social Security taxes from 3⅝% to 3⅞% and the annual wage base on which it was paid from $4,800 to $5,200. A covered person would be offered his choice of alternative plans: (1) 90 days' hospital care at a maximum cost to him of $90; (2) 44 days' hospital care at no cost to him; (3) 180 days' hospital care at a maximum cost to him of 2½ times the average cost of one day's hospital care (about $92.50, currently). For elderly persons not covered by Social Security (about 10% of those currently reaching 62), the Administration proposed to provide hospital insurance paid from the Treasury (estimated cost: $360 million a year). Kennedy also recommended a tightening of the laws governing sale of "quack" medicines. The President, at his news conference Feb. 21, said: "Social Security has shown for 28 years that it is a logical first line of defense in this field. The revised bill would give every individual the option of selecting the kind of hospital insurance protection that will be most consistent with his budget and health outlook, to be administered without any interference with medical practices, much as Blue Cross is administered today."

(The Special Senate Committee on Aging had held additional hearings in Washington Jan. 15-17 on quacks and cheats. Sen. Pat McNamara [D, Mich.], committee chairman, said as the hearings ended that $2 billion a year was a "conservative" estimate of the money going to those who prey on the elderly; the Food & Drug Administration had estimated that $1 billion was wasted on quack medicine, vitamins and nutritional compounds. The committee Feb. 13 issued a 200-page report on its two-year investigation. On some issues, the committee was divided. The majority, headed by McNamara, criticized the Kerr-Mills Act [which provided aid to states to help the "medically indigent"] as "too little, too late to too few"; it strongly indorsed the Administration's plan for medical care under Social Security. The minority, led by Senate GOP leader Everett M. Dirksen [Ill.], denounced the Administration plan's Social Security approach, its "compulsory" aspect, and its coverage of many wealthy employers and exclusion of many poor employes.)

A comprehensive program against mental illness and mental retardation had been proposed to Congress by Kennedy Feb. 5, 1963 in the first special Presidential message on the subject. The program, designed to stimulate state, local and private action by limited-term federal aid, would establish health centers and provide for child care, retardation research and vocational rehabilitation. The program was aimed at halving the number of patients in mental hospitals and the number of retarded children born each year. The overall cost of the program was estimated at more than $400 million over four to five years, about $85 million the first year. The direct cost to the taxpayer of caring for the 800,000 persons institutionalized for mental reasons—600,000 ill, 200,000 retarded—was more than $2.4 billion a year. A new approach to mental illness based on new treatment and new drugs, he said, his program would initiate a shift of the problem from the "cold mercy of custodial isolation" of state institutions to the community health centers. By the proposed new methods, he said, two of three schizophrenics "can be treated and released within six months, whereas under the current prevailing system the average stay was 11 years. Kennedy specifically proposed: (a) grants to the states, beginning in fiscal 1965, to establish comprehensive mental health centers in communities (the federal share would be 45% to 75% of the project cost; each center would cost an estimated $1 million to $2 million and serve about 100,000 persons); short-term grants for operating costs during the first four years; (b) a five-year program of project grants to local and state health departments to plan and develop maternity and child health care programs; (c) grants to states for planning state and local action on retardation (the federal funds would cover up to 75% of construction costs for mental retardation research centers); (d) amendment of the vocational rehabilitation act to permit increased federal aid for the mentally retarded.

An Administration bill amending the Social Security Act to provide additional funds to combat mental retardation was passed by the Senate Oct. 2, 1963 and House Oct. 15 and was signed by Kennedy Oct. 24. The bill increased the federal share of federal-state matching grants for both maternal and child health services and crippled children's services from $25 million annually to $30 million each for fiscal 1964, to $35 million each for 1965, to $40 million each for 1966 and 1967, to $45 million each for 1968 and 1969 and to $50 million each for 1970 and subsequent years. Three new programs were authorized by the bill: (1) a five-year, $110 million grant program to public health agencies for prenatal care of low-income, expectant mothers with special health problems; (2) an $8 million annual grant program for research relating to maternal child health and crippled children's services; (3) a $2,200,000 grant for planning projects to increase public awareness of mental retardation programs.

A companion bill embodying a large part of Kennedy's proposed program for the construction of facilities to combat mental retardation was passed Oct. 21 by 298-13 House vote and Senate voice vote and was signed by the President Oct. 31. The bill authorized a four-year program costing $329 million, $91 million more than originally approved by the House Sept. 10 but $519½ million less than approved by the Senate May 27. The House had amended the Senate bill to delete $427 million requested by the Administration for an eight-year program to help pay staffing costs in community mental health centers. The conferees upheld the deletion. The final bill authorized (four-year programs unless otherwise noted): (a) $26 million for grants to public and private non-profit institutions to build research centers; (b) $32½ million in construction grants for university-affiliated clinical centers; (c) $67½ million in construction grants for public and private non-profit facilities for treatment and training (federal share of costs: 33⅓% to 66⅔%); (d) $150 million in three years for grants to help pay construction costs of community mental health centers (federal share: 33⅓% to 66⅔%); (e) $45½ million in three years for expansion of programs to train teachers of mentally retarded and deaf children.

A key Kennedy Administration bill authorizing a three-year $236,400,000 program to provide medical facilities and loans to students of medicine, dentistry and osteopathy had been passed by 63-18 Senate vote Sept. 12. Kennedy signed it Sept. 24. The bill authorized $175 million in matching grants for construction ($105 million for new medical training facilities, $35 million for dental training facilities, $35 million to replace or rehabilitate existing training facilities) and $30,700,000 in student loans plus another $30,700,000 to phase out the loan plan. A proposal to kill the loan program, on the ground that the American Medical Association had a student loan program, was offered by Sen. Barry M. Goldwater (R, Ariz.) and defeated by 63-18 vote. Sen. John O. Pastore (D, R.I.), opposing Goldwater's proposal, said the AMA loans were offered at a 6½% interest charge. The Senate also defeated, by 43-39, a proposal by Sen. Norris Cotton (R, N.H.), to cancel half a student's indebtedness if he practiced in an area having a shortage in his field. (During House debate on the plan April 24, Rep. Albert H. Quie's [R, Minn.] proposal to eliminate the student loans had been defeated by 239-171 vote. Quie's proposal was backed by

House Republican leaders and the AMA.)

Johnson & the Enactment of Medicare

Lyndon B. Johnson became President of the United States Nov. 22, 1963 following the assassination of John F. Kennedy. It was during the Johnson Administration, with its programs for a "Great Society," that Congress finally enacted Medicare, under which the Social Security System was broadened to finance medical care for the elderly.

Johnson, as President, had made a strong appeal for such a program as early as Jan. 8, 1964 when he delivered his first message on the State of the Union. In his message, he called on Congress to provide hospital insurance for the elderly "financed by every worker and his employer under Social Security contributing no more than $1 a month." He repeated this proposal Jan. 21 in his first budget message.

A new appeal for the enactment of a program to finance hospital and nursing-home care for the aged through Social Security was made by Johnson in a special health message to Congress Feb. 10, 1964. Johnson urged all states to adopt "adequate programs" of medical aid under the Kerr-Mills Act and indicated that there was a need for supplementary private insurance for the elderly. He said he was creating a commission to recommend ways of reducing the incidence of heart disease, cancer and strokes. Referring to his entire health program, Johnson said "there is no need and no room for second-class health services." He called for a "vigorous and many-sided attack on our most serious health problems." Among his proposals: (a) a grant program for construction of nursing schools; (b) a scholarship program for nurses; (c) a five-year program of federal mortgage insurance and loans for building and equipping group-practice medical and dental facilities; (d) a five-year extension of the Hill-Burton Hospital Construction Act with emphasis on renovation of older facilities in big cities. A similar appeal for passage of a health-care bill for the elderly and for state adoption of Kerr-Mills programs had been made by Johnson in Texas Feb. 8 after he received an 87-page report from his Council on Aging, headed by Health, Education & Welfare Secretary Anthony J. Celebrezze. Johnson told Democratic Congressional leaders at their weekly White House breakfast with him April 28 that he wanted the medical care for the aged program enacted during the 1964 session of Congress. He also appealed for the aged-care program in a talk at the 1964 Campaign Conference for Democratic Women April 30.

The Senate, in considering Social Security amendments legislation, accepted by 49-44 vote Sept. 2 an amendment, sponsored by Sen. Albert Gore (D, Tenn.), to provide medical care for the aged financed through Social Security. The Gore proposal was similar to the King-Anderson bill, and its passage marked the first time either chamber had approved the program. The entire Social Security amendments bill was approved by 60-28 Senate vote Sept. 3. But the measure died in Senate-House conference when the Senate conferees refused to accept a bill without a health plan whereas the House conferees, led by Rep. Wilbur D. Mills (D, Ark.), refused to accept the health plan. (The 49-44 Sept. 2 vote to add the Medicare amendment to the bill: 44 D. and 5 R. vs. 28 R. and 16 D.)

Johnson was reelected President in 1964 by a landslide victory over Sen. Barry M. Goldwater (R, Ariz.). Johnson campaigned under a Democratic platform that made these health assertions:

. . . The needless suffering of people who cannot afford adequate medical care is intolerable: We will continue to fight until we have succeeded in including hospital care for older Americans in the Social Security program. . . . We will further expand our health facilities, especially medical schools, hospitals and research laboratories. . . .

. . . In 1960, we proposed to: "Provide medical care benefits for the aged as part of the time-tested Social Security system. Step up medical research on the major killers and crippling diseases. Expand and improve the Hill-Burton hospital construction program. Federal aid for construction, expanding and modernizing schools of medicine, dentistry, nursing and public health. Greatly increased federal support for psychiatric research and training and community mental health programs."

More health legislation has been enacted during the past 3½ years than during any other period in American history. The Community Health Services and Facilities Act of 1961 has made possible 149 projects for testing and demonstrating new or improved services in nursing homes, home care services, central information and referral centers; and providing additional personnel to serve the chronically ill and aged. . . . The Hill-Burton Amendments of 1964 extend the program of federal grants for construction of hospitals, public health centers, long-term facilities, rehabilitation facilities and diagnostic or treatment centers for five additional years. For the first time provision is made for the modernization and renovation of hospitals and health facilities. . . . . The Mental Retardation Facilities & Community Mental Health Construction Act of 1963 authorized grants of $150 million to states for constructing community mental health centers, which emphasize the new approach to the care of the mentally ill, centered on care and treatment in the patients' home communities. . . . The Maternal & Child Health and Mental Retardation Planning Amendments of 1963, along with the Mental Health Construction Act of 1963, authorized a broad program to prevent, treat, and ameliorate mental retardation. . . .

The National Institute of Child Health & Human Development, authorized in 1962, is now supporting research and training in eight major areas. The National Institute of General Medical Sciences, also authorized in 1962, gives recognition to the significance of research training in the sciences basic to medicine. . . . A $2 million Radiological Health Grant Program was established in 1962 to provide matching grants to assist states in assuming responsibility for adequate radiation control and protection. . . .

. . . The Report of the Surgeon General's Advisory Committee on Smoking & Health was released in January 1964, calling attention to the health hazards of smoking. An information clearinghouse and a public education program directed toward preventing young people from acquiring the smoking habit are being developed.

Goldwater's Republican platform pledged as "the Republican alternative": "full coverage of all medical and hospital costs of needy elder people financed by general revenues through broader implementation of federal-state plans, rather than the compulsory Democratic scheme covering only a small percentage of such costs, for everyone regardless of need"; "tax credits and other methods of assistance to help needy senior citizens meet the costs of medical and hospital insurance; continued federal support for a sound research program aimed at both the prevention and cure of diseases."

The three national TV networks, CBS, NBC and ABC, had refused Sept. 7 to sell time to the American Medical Association for one-minute commercials attacking the Democratic administration's proposal for medical care for the aged through Social Security. The networks explained that their general policy precluded the sale of one-minute (but not longer) time segments for controversial issues. The AMA charged them Sept. 8 with censorship. ABC relented Sept. 10 and agreed to accept revised one-minute AMA commercials on the issue.

The AMA's policy-making House of Delegates Dec. 2 authorized a renewal of the AMA's fight against Congressional enactment of the Administration's Medicare proposal. The action was taken at the House's semi-annual meeting in Miami Beach, Fla. Nov. 30-Dec. 2. AMA President Donovan F. Ward told the 228-member assembly Nov. 30 that "the battle must go on" despite the overwhelming Administration victory in the recent Presidential election. This view, plus Ward's endorsement of the Kerr-Mills Act, was approved by the delegates Dec. 2. The delegates Dec. 2 also rejected compromise proposals on the matter suggested by the District of Columbia and Michigan delegations. The proposals: (1) a combination of federal tax credits and subsidies to encourage coverage by private health insurance (Michigan's proposal); (2) Congressional development of a medicare plan for the elderly in cooperation with Blue Cross-Blue Shield and other private insurance companies (the District of Columbia plan). Neither plan would have been financed under Social Security.

The AMA Jan. 9, 1965 proposed an "eldercare" health insurance program for elderly poor persons as an alternative to the Administration's program. Under the AMA plan, persons more than 65 years old would enroll in Blue Cross-Blue Shield or a commercial insurance plan and, if their incomes were below a certain level (to be set by law), part or all of the cost of the premiums would be paid by the states from state and federal funds provided under the Kerr-Mills Law. Benefits could be provided under such a plan for hospital, nursing home, medical, surgical and drug costs. It would be administered by private insurance companies. Ward, in announcing the plan, said it would accomplish "far more" than the Administration program "with none of the attendant evils of unpredictable expense, invasion of medical practice by the federal bureaucracy or disruption of the private health-insurance industry by the government." The AMA plan was incorporated in a bill introduced in the U.S. House of Representatives by Reps. Thomas B. Curtis (R, Mo.) and A. Sidney Herlong (D, Fla.). Ward led a three-man AMA delegation supporting "eldercare" in testimony before the House Ways & Means Committee Feb. 8. The AMA also used TV and radio commercials to promote its plan.

Two alternative programs were announced by Republicans Jan. 11 and 28. The first was introduced by Sen. Leverett Saltonstall (Mass.) with five cosponsors—Sens. Hugh Scott Jr. (Pa.); George D. Aiken (Vt.), Winston L. Prouty (Vt.), Thruston Morton (Ky.) and Norris Cotton (N.H.). It (1) would be financed through general Treasury revenues and contributions from states and participating individuals, (2) would be administered by the states, (3) would defray some doctors' fees and drug expense outside of hospital service, (4) would limit eligibility to single persons over 65 years earning $3,000 or less and to married couples that age with a combined income of $6,000 or less, (5) would make charges ranging from $10 annually (to persons earning $1,000 or less) to $10 monthly (for those earning $3,000 annually). The Jan. 28 plan, made public by Rep. John W. Byrnes (Wis.) and endorsed by House minority leader Gerald R. Ford (Mich.), (a) would establish a National Health Insurance Fund financed about two-thirds by appropriations from general federal tax revenues and about one-third by individual voluntary participants in monthly premiums ranging from $4 to $11.50, (b) would provide payment of the first $1,000 for hospital and nursing home room and board, 80% of additional room and board charges, 80% of other hospital, surgical and medical expenses exceeding $50. (The Byrnes proposal was rejected by 236-191 House vote April 8.)

Johnson's initial proposals for the creation of a "Great Society" were made in his 1965 State-of-the-Union message, which he delivered in person before a joint session of Congress Jan. 4. In this address, Johnson again called for "hospital care [for the elderly] under Social Security."

Three days later, Johnson Jan. 7 sent to Congress a special health message in which he asserted that it was the nation's "first concern . . . to assure the availability of and accessibility to the best health care for all Americans, regardless of age or geography or economic status." The President's proposal for providing hospital insurance for the aged under Social Security received top priority. The message also called for better health services for children and youths, for those afflicted with mental illness, for the disabled and for the mentally retarded. Johnson also proposed the establishment of a national network of 32 "multi-purpose regional medical complexes," the modernization of health facilities and measures to encourage increased manpower for health services.

Johnson said Congress "should" enact the health plan for the aged in 1965. He asked that the program "provide protection against the costs of hospital and post-hospital extended care, home nursing services, and outpatient diagnostic services." He also proposed "similar" protection for those not currently covered by Social Security; the costs, to be paid from the administrative budget, would be $10 million in fiscal 1966, $45 million in fiscal 1967. A final recommendation was that the states provide "adequate" medical assistance under the existing Kerr-Mills program for the aged unable to pay non-insured costs.

The message proposed that the projected multi-purpose regional medical centers be used "for an all-out attack" on heart disease, cancer, stroke and other major diseases. Lauding his Commission on Heart Disease, Cancer & Stroke for originating the suggestion in its December 1964 report, Johnson recommended that Congress enact a five-year program of project grants for development of the program. He proposed that the grants—$50 million in fiscal 1966, $75 million in fiscal 1967—be used primarily for personnel and not for construction costs. The personnel would not be federal employes. The centers would make available to physicians the latest techniques and specialized knowledge. They would be affiliated with medical schools, teaching hospitals and medical centers and would be supported by diagnostic services in community hospitals. They would provide diagnosis and treatment of patients and would permit clinical trials of advanced techniques and drugs.

Johnson proposed that Congress: (a) increase authorizations for maternal and child health and crippled children's services (funds would be earmarked for project grants to provide health screening and diagnosis for children of pre-school and school age and treatment and follow-up care services for disabled children and youths); (b) broaden the public assistance program to permit federal sharing of costs of medical and dental care for children in medically needy families; (c) extend grant programs for family health services and clinics for domestic agricultural migratory workers and their children and for community vaccination assistance.

In his message, The President urged a 5-year program of grants for the initial cost of personnel to man community mental health centers offering comprehensive services. Johnson also asked Congress to extend for 2 years the authorization of grants to help states develop programs to prevent mental retardation and to care for the mentally retarded. In a section on rehabilitation, Johnson asked Congress to authorize (a) project grants to help states expand these services, (b) federal matching funds to expand such services to a greater number of the mentally retarded and other seriously disabled individuals and (c) construction and modernization of workshops and rehabilitation centers.

The message requested funds for "a greatly increased hospital modernization effort as well as for expansion in the number and quality" of nursing homes. It called for a program of direct loans and loan guarantees to assist voluntary associations in the construction and equipping of facilities for comprehensive group medical practice. Johnson asked Congress to provide grants to medical schools (a) to help cover their costs of expansion of capacity and of "equality" of programs and (b) to enable them to experiment in education methods. He requested the authorization of scholarships for medical and dental students otherwise unable to take such training. The Health-Education-&-Welfare Secretary was directed to develop a long-range health manpower program. The message said the U.S. had 290,000 physicians. To meet the need for 346,000 within a decade, it said, the U.S. would have to increase graduations of new physicians by 50% by 1975 and of dentists by 100%. Johnson urged Congress to extend (for five years) and increase the authorization of the Health Research Facilities Act providing research facilities to universities and other nonprofit institutions. He also recommended increasing the federal share of defraying costs of specialized research facilities of a national or regional character.

Early versions of the Medicare bill—which financed medical insurance for the elderly through Social Security—were passed by 313-115 House vote April 8, 1965 and by 68-21 Senate vote July 9. The rival bills then went to Senate-House conference committee. The Administration-backed compromise bill that emerged July 21 was passed by the House July 27 and by the Senate July 28. Johnson flew to Independence, Mo. July 30 to sign the bill in a ceremony honoring Harry S. Truman, 81, the first President to propose federal health insurance under Social Security. Johnson, signing the bill, said, "We marvel not simply at the passage of this bill but that it took so many years to pass it."

The final vote for passage of Medicare in the House was 307-116 (237 D. and 70 R. vs. 68 R. and 48 D.). In the Senate the vote was 70-24 (57 D. and 13 R. vs. 17 R. and 7 D.). The bill, as finally agreed on by the Senate-House conferees, was expected to cost about $6½ billion in 1967; $4½ billion of the cost would be defrayed by increased payroll taxes for the basic health insurance program; $1.4 billion of the increased Social Security benefits would come from general revenue, and $600 million of the increased benefits would come from premiums paid by participants in the voluntary supplementary medical care plan. Under the bill, the annual maximum wage subject to Social Security tax would be increased from $4,800 to $6,600, and the total tax rate paid by both employes and employers would rise in seven steps to 11.3% in 1987. Currently, it was 7¼% and under previous legislation was scheduled to rise in two steps to 9¼% in 1968. The rate under the bill would be 8.4% in 1966, 8.8% in 1967-68, 9.8% in 1969-72, 10.8% in 1973-75, 10.9% in 1976-79, 11.1% in 1980-86, 11.3% thereafter.

The new Medicare law would provide health insurance for persons over 65 years old under a basic and a supplementary plan, the latter being optional; both plans were scheduled to start July 1, 1966. The basic plan covered everyone of that age except certain aliens and federal employes eligible for government health insurance under other law. The new law also extended Social Security coverage to self-employed physicians and to hospital internes.

Under the *basic plan,* each patient was entitled to 60 days of hospital care for each period of illness with the patient paying the first $40 of costs (covering room and board, prescribed drugs and services except private duty nursing and services of physicians other than interns or residents in training); he would also be entitled to an additional 30 days of such care, for which he would have to pay $10 a day. (Christian Science sanatoriums and psychiatric hospitals would be included, but there would be a lifetime limit of 190 days in psychiatric hospitals.) Each patient also would be entitled to: 100 days of nursing home care for each illness but would have to pay $5 a day after the first 20 days; 100 home health-care visits after hospitalization; diagnostic services provided by hospitals, with the patient paying $20 of the cost of each test and 20% of costs above $20.

Under the *supplementary plan,* enrollees would pay $3 monthly premiums, which would be matched by the federal government from general tax revenues. Coverage would include service of physicians, radiologists, anesthesiologists, pathologists and psychiatrists (whether performed in or out of a medical institution) and supplies such as surgical dressings and prosthetic devices, ambulance service, 100 home nursing visits each year in addition to those allowed under the basic plan and without requirement of prior hospitalization. Each patient would pay the first $50 of his annual costs and 20% of all annual costs above $50.

Under the Medicare law, the Kerr-Mills medical assistance program was consolidated with five related programs and was scheduled to end as a separate program Jan. 1, 1970. This consolidation resulted in a major expansion of the voluntary Kerr-Mills and similar programs of state aid to the "medically needy." The state-aid health-care program, which soon became known as "Medicaid," authorized the states to expand, with federal matching funds, public health-care assistance to persons, regardless of age, whose personal resources were deemed insufficient to pay for needed health care.

The AMA, meeting in New York June 20-24, had rejected resolutions urging non-participation in Medicare. Nine resolutions urging various forms of non-participation were submitted by state medical societies to the AMA House of Delegates. But a five-doctor committee June 23 recommended deferring consideration of any non-participation policy until the then pending Administration bill was enacted. The committee instead endorsed resolutions urging the federal government (a) to seek AMA advice on medical care legislation and (b) to appoint doctors to advisory panels for federal health-care programs. The committee's proposals were adopted with

minor amendments and little debate by the AMA delegates June 24.
The delegates changed a resolution "petitioning" Johnson for an
audience prior to final Medicare enactment to a resolution "restat-
ing" an AMA "offer to meet with the President." It was felt that
the AMA's action left individual doctors free to cooperate or refuse
to cooperate with Medicare without retribution from the AMA. The
delegates sanctioned the initiation of an "active campaign" to in-
struct members on conflict between Medicare and the AMA policy
that doctors could refuse to "dispose" service against their medical
judgment or "be a willing party" to a program "detrimental to the
public welfare."

Dr. James Z. Appel, 58, of Lancaster, Pa., installed as AMA
president June 20, told the House of Delegates: "Without the cooperation of the physicians of this nation, the intent of the [Medicare]
law cannot be carried out. Such lack of cooperation would be a vio-
lation of intent, would disparage respect for law and would stimulate retaliatory regulatory legislation." Appel indicated firm opposition to Medicare but denounced "unethical tactics such as boycott,
strike or sabotage." He urged "contain[ing]" Medicare through a
program "based on reason, logic and education" and utilizing "existing legal and parliamentary procedures that are a part of a representative democracy." "Political philosophy," he said, should not
influence a doctor's patient care. "If the law works badly, a doctor
must call this to the attention of his patients," he said.

(The Association of American Physicians & Surgeons, Inc. disclosed June 18 that it had sent doctors an appeal "to individually
and voluntarily pledge nonparticipation" in the Medicare program.)

The AMA House of Delegates in Chicago Oct. 3 adopted a report stating that individual doctors could ethically and legally refuse
or limit participation in Medicare, subject to "overriding ethical
considerations." The report was adopted at a special session held
Oct. 1-3. Resolutions calling for an organized boycott of Medicare
and for a campaign to repeal the program were defeated. AMA legal
consultant A. Leslie Hodson told the 236 delegates that a non-
participation resolution would violate the Sherman Anti-Trust Act.
AMA President Appel said at a news conference that he planned to
treat patients covered by Medicare.

Progress & Problems

Government Programs

THE SOCIAL SECURITY AMENDMENTS of 1965 set in motion a program that provided these two forms of Medicare financing not only for the aged but ultimately for the disabled and those suffering from kidney disease: (1) Hospital insurance, financed largely through Social Security, which pays for inpatient hospital care and subsequent skilled nursing home and home health benefits. (2) Supplementary medical insurance, financed by premiums and general tax revenues, which pays the bills for doctors and other outpatient services. Both forms of insurance are handled primarily through private insurance companies under contract with the Social Security Administration.

In addition, the non-insurance health program called Medicaid was authorized and began operating, effective Jan. 1, 1966. Medicaid ultimately provided federal funds to supplement state programs financing medical services to families with dependent children receiving public assistance and to most aged, blind and disabled persons who were eligible for supplementary income payments. States were also given the option of financing, with federal assistance, medical services for the "medically needy"—people whose incomes were slightly above the public assistance level but who were unable to pay their medical expenses.

A bill extending from March 31, 1966 to May 31, 1966 the deadline for enrollment in the voluntary medical insurance part of the Medicare program was passed April 6, 1966 by 387-0 House vote and Senate voice vote. President Lyndon B. Johnson, who had requested the change March 31, signed the bill April 8. The extension was granted to accommodate an estimated 1,300,000 eligible persons 65 years old or older (before Jan. 1) who had not either accepted or rejected the program. It was estimated that about 16,800,000 elderly persons had signed up and that a million had declined to sign up.

A $280 million health research bill backed by the Johnson Administration had been passed by the Senate July 26, 1965 and House July 27. Johnson signed the bill Aug. 9 in a ceremony at the National Institutes of Health. He said "a staggering era for medicine has begun" and announced his intention to name a task force "of the great experts of this nation" to "tell me and tell America where we are going, and how we are going to get there." He said the panel would "advise us how best to reach . . . the goals we will set for education, for heatlh . . . and for happiness for all of the children of not only our land but what we can do to help others." The bill extended through fiscal 1969 the Public Health Service (PHS) program for construction of health research facilities and authorized $280 million for the program. The bill also authorized the PHS to contract during fiscal 1966-68 for research, authorized increasing from 3 to 6 the number of Health, Education & Welfare Assistant Secretaries and abolished the post of Special Assistant to the HEW Secretary for health and medical affairs.

An Administration-supported bill to provide federal aid for staffing community mental health centers and to train teachers of handicapped children was passed by Senate voice vote July 26, 1965 and by 414-0 House vote July 27 and was signed by Johnson Aug. 4. The bill authorized a new 7-year program for staffing mental centers under grants to public or non-profit organizations. It authorized $19½ million in fiscal 1966, $24 million in fiscal 1967, $30 million in fiscal 1968 and unspecified sums in fiscal 1967-72 for centers that had received initial staffing grants. The bill also: (a) Extended through fiscal 1969 the program of grants to states for training teachers of mentally retarded and other handicapped children. (b) Extended through fiscal 1969 the grant program to states and public and private colleges and universities for research to improve educational opportunities for handicapped children. (c) Authorized grants to colleges and universities for building, equipping and operating facilities for the above research.

An Administration bill extending the grant program for vaccination of pre-school children and extending certain other health service programs was passed by the Senate July 26, 1965 and House July 27 and was signed by Johnson Aug. 5. As he signed the measure, the President cited as a "feasible" goal an increase in American life expectancy from 70 years to 75. Programs extended under the bill included: (Through June 30, 1968) the program of grants to states and local communities to buy vaccine to immunize all pre-school-age children against polio, diphtheria, whooping cough, tetanus and measles; (through June 30, 1968) the program of grants to public and nonprofit private bodies for health services to domestic migrant workers; (through June 30, 1967) the matching grant program with the states to provide general public health services; (through June 30, 1966) the program of grants to states, local communities and nonprofit private organizations for research on new methods of out-of-hospital care.

A bill authorizing a three-year aid program for the establishment of regional medical programs to combat heart disease, stroke, cancer and related diseases was passed by the House Sept. 24, 1965 and Senate 29 and was signed by Johnson Oct. 6. The federal aid, in the form of grants, was to go to medical schools, research institutions and hospitals for regional cooperative arrangements for such programs. The programs were to make the latest techniques of combating these diseases available to doctors and patients. Patients could gain admittance at such programs only by reference from a practicing physician. The federal aid could not be used for construction of new buildings but only for repair or remodeling of existing buildings. Planning grants were also authorized. (Johnson Nov. 29 named a 12-member National Advisory Council on Regional Medical Programs. Dr. J. Willis Hurst of Atlanta, Johnson's own heart specialist, was appointed to head the council. The new body was to work with Surgeon General William H. Stewart on plans for implementing a bill to establish regional centers to study heart disease, stroke and cancer.)

A bill authorizing appropriations of $105 million over fiscal 1966-70 to help build nonprofit medical library facilities and provide aid for related programs was passed by the House Oct. 1, 1965 and Senate Oct. 12 and was signed by Johnson Oct. 22. $40 million was authorized over fiscal 1967-70 for the construction aid. The other programs were five-year programs and included help for training personnel and for research.

A bill providing for two new programs and expanding other programs of aid for education in the health professions was passed by the Senate Sept. 30, 1965 and House Oct. 11 and was signed by

Johnson Oct. 22. The new programs were: (1) A four-year program of grants to help non-profit schools of medicine, dentistry, osteopathy, optometry and podiatry improve their educational quality. (2) A four-year program of scholarship grants to schools in the same health fields plus pharmacy. Extended and expanded under the legislation were programs (a) of grants for construction of teaching facilities for training medical personnel; (b) of loans for medical students (to be phased out by fiscal 1972). The bill also extended improvement grants and student-aid provisions to accredited nursing schools.

Johnson sent to Congress March 1, 1966 a special message calling for improved federal health services and increased aid to education. He said his "ambitious goals" included "good health for every citizen to the limits of our country's capacity to provide it." Only $41 million was requested to finance the new health proposals for the first year. This request was part of $4.67 billion proposed in the fiscal 1967 budget for federal health programs (the total was an increase of $1 billion over fiscal 1966 expenditures). (There was an additional $3 billion in Social Security trust funds for Medicare.)

Among the message's major proposals: (a) Modernization of obsolete hospitals by using federal money to finance planning followed by the federal guarantee of 90% of the value of mortgages and federal payment (over a 10-year period) of up to 40% of the amount guaranteed. (b) A five-year federal grant program for research and demonstration projects to improve health services' organization, financing, and use. (c) Development of comprehensive public health services in states and communities by giving states federal planning grants, followed by a matching-grant program for communities and a separate grant program for states, communities, medical schools and hospitals to meet specific health problems. (d) A three-year grant program to train personnel in the "critically understaffed" health services. (e) A center in the Public Health Service for research on alcoholism and for treatment of "this affliction." (f) Appointment of a committee on mental retardation "to assess our progress" and "seek out new and better ways to cope" with it.

Medicare Starts

The Medicare program went into effect July 1, 1966. Dr. William H. Stewart, U.S. Surgeon General, reported at a press conference that 94% of the nation's general hospitals (containing 95.9% of all hospital beds suitable for Medicare patients) were in compliance with laws governing hospital standards and provisions against discrimination. Failure to comply with anti-discrimination standards was statutory cause for depriving a hospital of the right to participate in Medicare. The only states with substantial percentages of their general hospitals ineligible for Medicare on civil rights grounds were Mississippi, where only 23.6% of hospitals were in compliance, and Louisiana, were 67.6% were in compliance. As of noon July 1, 6,600 U.S. hospitals had applied for participation in the Medicare program and had qualified on medical standards, but 327 of them had not been cleared on civil-rights grounds. One hundred hospitals had not applied for participation.

A group of black doctors and dentists from Atlanta charged July 6, in a statement issued following a meeting with Health, Education & Welfare Department officials, that only one of Atlanta's 10 major hospitals had complied with desegregation requirements although nine of the hospitals had been certified by the Public Health Service (PHS). Eight civil-rights groups in Atlanta had issued a statement June 16 charging that the government was about to certify Atlanta hospitals in which segregated practices were being maintained. The organizations signing the statement included the Atlanta branch of the National Association for the Advancement of Colored People (NAACP), the Atlanta Urban League, the American Friends Service Committee, the American Civil Liberties Union and the Georgia Council on Human Relations. The NAACP had sent a telegram of protest to the PHS June 21, charging that the Americus Sumpter Hospital in Americus, Ga. had tricked PHS investigators into believing that the hospital had been desegregated. The telegram alleged that during the inspection tour, "Negro employes were placed by the hospital in beds on white wards" and "one white patient was moved to the Negro section."

President Johnson had said in a statement released June 30 that "more extensive preparation [had been made] to launch this program than for any other peaceful undertaking in our nation's history." He said "Medicare will succeed" if hospitals "accept their responsibility under the law not to discriminate against any patient because of race," if doctors "treat their patients with fairness and compassion as they have in the past" and if patients "cooperate in scheduling treatment and do not demand unnecessary hospital and medical services." Johnson had held a meeting on Medicare at the White House June 15 with about 250 physicians, hospital administrators, dentists and other health profession leaders. At the meeting he had appealed to hospitals for compliance, to Medicare patients for curbing unnecessary requests for special privileges and to "the responsible medical societies and professional leaders to take the lead in trying to help us prevent unreasonable costs for health services."

A report recommending that doctors bill Medicare patients directly "under ordinary circumstances" had been adopted June 29 by the House of Delegates of the American Medical Association during the AMA convention, held in Chicago June 26-30. The delegates also approved a resolution recommending that doctors "not accept any assignment form" of billing, the second method permitted under Medicare (this method authorized the patient to sign over his Medicare benefit claim to the doctor, who could apply to the insurance company for reimbursement; this reimbursement was subject to the Medicare reimbursement schedule). Under direct billing, the fees were not subject to limitation and would be paid by the patient, who would then apply for reimbursement. The AMA delegates June 29 also authorized a drive to establish direct billing under the state medical assistance programs for the needy (Medicaid) established under the Social Security amendments of 1965. In two other resolutions adopted June 29, the delegates (1) expressed their willingness to "provide a full measure of constructive leadership" in the operation of Medicare but stated their opposition to any further extension of the program, and (2) tentatively approved "utilization review committees" that would review the need for long-term hospitalization of Medicare patients.

Dr. Charles L. Hudson, 62, of Cleveland was installed as new AMA president. In his inaugural speech June 28, Hudson called Medicare "unwanted" and "unnecessary" but urged physicians not "to belabor the past" and instead "to make the most, for our patients and our colleagues, of this new program—and to prevent extension of it, without demonstrated need, toward a national health service." He told the delegates June 30: "We must guard against falling into the trap of denying the federal government its rightful responsibilities. There are many services that are the natural province of government. . . . We must strike a balance, in supporting government action where it is constitutionally and logically needed, and opposing it only when it goes beyond those bounds." Dr. James Z. Appel of Lancaster, Pa., outgoing AMA president, had warned in his opening speech June 26 against increasing fees or obstructing reimbursement of Medicare patients. The aim of Medicare, he said, was to "conserve the ability" of a Medicare patient to meet financial obligations, and he reminded the delegates that a physician's "first concern" was the patient. Dr. Milford O. Rouse of Dallas was elected president-elect of the AMA June 29. Rouse told newsmen June 30 that he would continue direct billing of his patients, and "if they don't want to cooperate, I'll just tell them to go down the hall" to another doctor. He said he did not intend to "clutter my brain" with Medicare regulations and would send patients confused over reimbursement procedures to the Social Security office. (Rouse urged the AMA June 20, 1967 to combat the "threat" to the private practice of medicine from government planning. The government, he warned, was "making its moves into areas where, to its own satisfaction at least, it is able to demonstrate unfilled needs for health care or health care planning." AMA member doctors, Rouse said, "oppose the basic social welfare philosophy of the so-called Medicare law as unnecessary and detrimental to the best interest of maintaining high quality medical care." Rouse said June 26 that the AMA recognized Medicare "but does not support or endorse it." An attack on his statement had been made by Dr. Quentin D. Young, chairman of the Medical Committee for Human Rights, Dr. John L. S. Holloman Jr., president of the National Medical Association, and Dr. Lytt I. Gardner, chairman of the Physicians Forum.)

Congressional Quarterly reported Aug. 5, 1966 that of 304 organizations that had reported lobbying spendings in 1965 to influence legislation in Congress, the top spender was the AMA, which reported spending $1,155,935.30 in its unsuccessful campaign to defeat Medicare.

More than $3.2 billion was paid in Medicare's first year of operation to cover 10 million doctor's bills and five million hospital bills, it was disclosed Oct. 24, 1967. The first-year statistics were reported by Mrs. Dorothy P. Rice, chief of the Social Security Administration's Health Insurance Research Branch, at the American Public Health Association convention in Miami Beach. Other data reported: (a) Two-thirds of the 10 million persons enrolled in Medicare utilized its services, (b) $2½ billion was paid in hospital insurance, $700 million in supplemental medical insurance; (c) there were five million Medicare admissions of four million persons to almost 7,000 hospitals for an average stay of 17 days; (d) the average per capita payment was $175 for every person in Medicare; the average reimbursement was $481 for an in-patient hospital claim, $71 for a medical bill; the average daily charge for general care hospitals was $46, the average operation cost $180 for physician's services.

Medical Care in New York & Elsewhere

Gov. Nelson A. Rockefeller, of New York April 30, 1966 had signed a state Medicaid bill to provide medical aid to any family of four with a net income of less than $6,000 a year. Financed by state and federal funds, the program would offer aid for services of physicians, dentists, nurses, optometrists and podiatrists and for care in hospitals, nursing homes and for the cost of drugs, glasses, dentures, laboratory and X-ray work.

A highly critical report on New York State's non-profit health insurance plans had been issued Oct. 1, 1962 to the state's health and insurance departments by the Columbia University School of Public Health & Administrative Medicine. The report, based on a study begun in 1958, covered 10 New York State health plans— seven Blue Shield plans, the Health Insurance Plan of Greater New York, Group Health Insurance, Inc. and Group Health Dental Insurance, Inc. The study was headed by the school's director, Dr. Ray E. Trussell, and an associate professor, Frank van Dyke. Among its findings: (1) Subscribers were often subjected to inferior medical care, including unnecessary surgery by unqualified physicians. (2) New York City's Blue Shield did not pay bills in full as promised. (3) Extra fees were wrongly charged by some doctors. (4) Medical societies that controlled Blue Shield ignored the fallacies of the plans. Among the report's recommendations: (1) Qualified physicians should replace the unqualified in substandard hospitals. (2) Benefits should be broadened, particularly by Blue Shield, to provide full payment of bills for at least 75% of its subscribers. (3) Plans should be controlled by laymen rather than doctors.

A similarly critical study of hospital and medical care in New York City had been released by the Columbia unit May 10, 1962. The study had been requisitioned by 13 New York metropolitan area International Brotherhood of Teamsters (IBT) locals as an investigation of the effectiveness of the Teamsters' current Blue Cross insurance program. The study covered 406 union members and their wives and children over a two-year period. Its findings: (a) 40% of the patients had received inadequate medical care; (b) 20% of the hospitalizations had been unnecessary; (c) unnecessary operations were performed; (d) 20% of surgical cases had unjustifiable operating delays; (e) medical care was particularly inadequate in hospitals without training programs and accreditations; (f) surgeons' fees were almost twice the amount allowed by the insurance; (g) 92% of the patients felt—largely without justification—that they had received the best care. The IBT announced May 13 that it was using the report as the basis of a new five-year program to improve its hospital and medical care coverage. The program, financed by its welfare funds at an estimated cost of $3,675,000, was to provide: (1) a center to advise patients concerning doctors and hospitals; (2) a special surgery unit at Montefiore Hospital for brain, chest and genito-urinary operations, cancer radio-therapy and diagnosis; (3) a 20-bed hospital unit to experiment in better care and lower costs; (4) a continuing sample "audit" of the quality of hospital and medical care given members.

A United Hospital Fund survey, reported by the *New York Times* Feb. 24, 1966, found serious inadequacies in New York's hospitals. The report said: "There is not a single institution in the city which does not require costly modernization"; 47 of the city's 130 general hospitals were so obsolete that they required replacement; 24 required major modernization and 59 partial renovation.

Rockefeller Jan. 16, 1968 submitted to the State Legislature a record $5.494 billion budget for fiscal 1968-69. The increase of $856 million over the fiscal 1967-68 budget was the largest increase in the state's history. To balance the budget, Rockefeller decided, among other steps to drastically reduce the Medicaid program to produce an estimated saving of about $200 million while disqualifying 600,000 of the 5.7 million persons eligible for the aid (3½ million were enrolled).

Gov. Ronald Reagan of California Feb. 5, 1968 submitted to the California Legislature a record $5.699 billion budget for the fiscal year 1968-69. The increase of $629 million (12%) from the $5.07 billion budget Reagan had signed in June 1967 made the budget the largest for any state. Reagan's proposals for "Medi-Cal," the program of medical aid to the indigent, called for an increase of $62 million (22.6%) in state support (raising spending to $336 million).

President Johnson had announced Jan. 20, 1968 a new federal-private program for Washington to provide health and housing facilities for the poor, particularly the elderly poor. The program was sponsored by the National Medical Association (NMA), 97% of whose members were black, in cooperation with the federal government, the District of Columbia and Howard University. Dr. Lionel F. Swan, NMA president, said that the project would be started with a $60,550 planning grant from the Health, Education & Welfare Department. The plans were to use a 335-acre site near Howard University to build facilities for group medical practice, a nursing home, a medical office building, housing for the elderly, social care facilities, a neighborhood service center for the elderly and a job-training center in health posts. Plans were to be developed for similar projects in other urban areas.

Johnson Program

In a "Message on Older Americans," submitted to Congress Jan. 23, 1967, Johnson recommended: (a) Extension of Medicare to the disabled who were under 65 and currently covered by Social Security or railroad retirement benefits; (b) extension of Medicare coverage to non-routine foot treatment; and (c) a study of the feasibility of including the cost of prescription drugs under Medicare.

In his budget for fiscal 1968, submitted to Congress Jan. 24, 1967, Johnson proposed a $1.2 billion annual increase in spending on health programs. More than $5 billion in fiscal 1968 expenditures was requested for Medicare and Medicaid. Total trust fund payments under Medicare were estimated at $4 billion in fiscal 1968 ($2.7 billion for hospital and nursing home benefits, $1.3 billion for physicians' services). $907 million of these payments was to come from administrative budget transfers to the Medicare trust funds to cover costs for eligible aged persons not covered by Social Security or railroad retirement and for matching monthly premium payments in the supplementary medical insurance program. Johnson proposed legislation: (a) to increase the authorization for grants to control specific diseases; (b) to reimburse federal hospitals for services to the aged, to extend Medicare to the disabled under Social Security and railroad retirement, to assure that reimbursements to hospitals for depreciation under Medicare go into replacement of facilities and equipment; (c) to improve the Medicaid system); (d) to improve health care (including dental care) for children; (e) to help the staffing of centers for the mentally retarded; (f) to improve state laboratory diagnostic services.

A major health bill, the Partnership for Health Amendments of 1967, was passed Nov. 21, 1967 by Senate voice vote and 347-3 House vote and was signed by Johnson Dec. 5. The legislation authorized $589 million in fiscal 1968-70 for grants to the states for health services and planning. $40 million of the authorization was to be allocated for rat-control projects. The rat-control provision was added by the House Sept. 20 in accepting an amendment by Reps. Henry S. Reuss (D, Wis.) and Charles McC. Mathias Jr. (R, Md.). The vote was 159 D. and 68 R. vs. 110 R. and 63 D. The vote and the serious level of debate reversed a July 20 House action rejecting consideration of an Administration rat-control bill. The measure adopted also provided for a new program for the federal licensing of clinical laboratories dealing in interstate commerce. A survey of the extent of serious hunger and malnutrition in the U.S. was also authorized.

Johnson sent Congress March 4, 1968 a health message in which he proposed measures to deal with the high cost of medical care, the high infant mortality rate and the growing need for more doctors and other health personnel. To reverse the "unacceptable increases in medical costs," Johnson suggested a revision of the systems used to figure federal payments for hospital care and drugs under Medicare, Medicaid and child-health programs. He also asked Congress to authorize the publication of a U.S. "Compendium of Drugs," to be prepared by the Heatlh, Education & Welfare Department in cooperation with pharmaceutical manufacturers—"who would bear the cost of its publication"—and physicians and pharmacists. It would provide complete data on prescription drugs—"use and dosage, warnings, manufacturer, generic and brand names, and facts about their safety and effectiveness."

Johnson asked Congress to authorize the HEW Secretary "to establish a reasonable cost range" to be used when federal reimbursement for drugs was made under government-aided programs. Such reimbursement would apply to all cases except "where hospitals and other health care institutions have established effective and reliable systems for cost and quality control." Citing data that the retail price for 30 tablets of 12 drugs of the same type ranged from $1.25 to $11, Johnson said: "The taxpayer should not be forced to pay $11 if the $1.25 drug is equally effective. To do this would permit robbery of private citizens with public approval."

In his message, Johnson stressed the necessity of exploring "ways ot prevent unnecessary hospitalization" and of testing "incentives designed to control the cost of hospital care." The HEW Department was ordered by the President to begin testing the effectiveness of such incentives "immediately." For child-health care, Johnson requested a $58 million increase in funds—to $237 million in fiscal 1969—for prenatal and postnatal care for "needy" mothers.

Johnson announced that he had ordered the HEW Secretary to establish a Center for Population Studies & Human Reproduction "to give new energy and direction" to research in the fields of birth control and human fertility. "As we move to expand our knowledge of population and human reproduction, we must make that knowledge available to those who want it," he said. "Last year, the federal government helped to bring information and counseling . . . to more than 500,000 women. But there are millions more who want help." He called for "an increase in funds from $25 million in fiscal 1968 to $61 million in fiscal 1969 so that 3 million women can have access to family planning help."

In his March 4 message, Johnson proposed a Health Manpower Act of 1968 "to train more health workers and to train them better and faster." This act was to be an extension and improvement of five current programs due to expire in 1969—the Health Educational Act of 1963, the Nurse Training Act of 1964, the Health Personnel Training Act of 1966, the Health Research Act of 1965 and the Graduate Health Training Act of 1964. One improvement suggested was larger grants to medical schools that expand enrollment. The message also proposed action "to lower the shocking toll of deaths caused by accidents in America" and "to launch a nationwide volunteer effort to improve the health of all Americans." "The compelling need in the case of accidents," the President said, "is for modern, effective rescue systems to give immediate attention to accident victims." He said a Cabinet-level study would be made for "a test program to help our states and communities develop effective rescue systems to fit their own needs." To spur the volunteer effort, Johnson announced the formation of a new Council on Physical Fitness & Sports headed by Vice President Hubert H. Humphrey. Johnson also asked Congress to consider passing a new Health Service Personnel Act to attract career workers into government health service.

The Health Manpower Act of 1968 was approved by the House Aug. 1, 1968 and Senate Aug. 2 and was signed by Johnson Aug. 16. It provided two-year extensions of four existing health laws— the Public Health Service Act of 1944, the Health Research Facilities Act of 1956, the Health Professions Educational Assistance Act of 1963 and the Nurse Training Act of 1964. Another health law—the Allied Health Professions Personnel Training Act of 1966—was extended for one year. Among the programs continued were grants to medical and nursing schools for construction of new facilities, rehabilitation of current facilities, curricula improvements and development of new teaching methods. Scholarship and loan programs in the health professions were extended and enlarged, and a new nursing scholarship program was granted.

A bill extending (for two years) federal aid programs for regional medical projects and other specialized health programs was passed by the Senate Sept. 27, 1968 and House Oct. 1 and was signed by Johnson Oct. 15. The regional medical programs were for heart disease, cancer and stroke. Other aid programs extended included those for health care for migratory workers and for providing facilities for narcotics addicts. The legislation also authorized a two-year program of rehabilitation of alcoholics.

Political Developments

The national health-care problem was one of the major issues taken up during the 1968 election campaign.

The late Sen. Robert F. Kennedy, then campaigning for the Democratic Presidential nomination, said at Indiana University Medical Center in Indianapolis April 26, 1968: "Billions of dollars of new money went into the health industry, yet "the national systen of health care has failed to meet the most urgent medical needs of millions of Americans." What was required was revision of "the existing system under which people are cared for in the costliest of institutions, the hospital, by the costliest of manpower, the doctor." One revision would be to hire and train non-professionals to "dispense a wide variety of simple medical care." Another would be to decentralize health care with supplementing hospitals and neighborhood health centers.

The 1968 Republican platform, adopted in Miami Beach Aug. 7, included a health plank that said: "The inflation produced by the Johnson-Humphrey Administration has struck hardest in the area of health care. Hospital costs are rising 16% a year—four times the national average of price increases. We pledge to encourage the broadening of private health insurance plans, many of which cover hospital care only, and to review the operation of government hospital care programs in order to encourage more patients to utilize non-hospital facilities. Expansion of the number of doctors, nurses, and supporting staff to relieve shortages and spread the availability of health care services will have our support. We will foster the construction of additional hospitals and encourage regional hospital and health planning for the maximum development of facilities for medical and nursing care. We will also press for enactment of Republican-sponsored programs for financing of hospital modernization. New diagnostic methods and also preventive care to assure early detection of physical impairments, thus fostering good health and avoiding illnesses requiring hospitalization, will have our support. Additionally, we will work with states and local communities to help assure improved services to the mentally ill within a community setting and will intensify research to develop better treatment methods. We will encourage extension of private health insurance to cover mental illness. While believing no American should be denied adequate medical treatment, we will be diligent in protecting the traditional patient-doctor relationship and the integrity of the medical practitioner. We are especially concerned with the difficult circumstances of thousands of handicapped citizens who daily encounter architectural barriers which they are physically unable to surmount. We will support programs to reduce and where possible to eliminate such barriers in the construction of federal buildings.''

The 1968 Democratic platform, adopted in Chicago Aug. 28, said: "As it promoted better education, so did Democratic leadership promote better health for all. The program of mercy and justice known as health care for the aged which President Truman originally proposed and Presidents Kennedy and Johnson fought for finally became law in the summer of 1965. Because of it, more than seven million older citizens each year are now receiving modern medical care in dignity—no longer forced to depend on charity, no longer a burden on relatives, no longer in physical pain because they cannot afford to pay for the healing power of modern medicine. Virtually all older Americans, the well and the sick alike, are now protected, their lives more secure, their afflictions eased. To deal with other aspects of the nation's health needs, measures were enacted in the Democratic years representing an almost fourfold increase in the government's investment in health. Programs were enacted to cope with the killing diseases of heart, cancer and stroke; to combat mental retardation and mental illness; to increase the manpower supply of trained medical technicians; to speed the construction of new hospitals. . . .

"Medical care for the aged should be expanded to include the costs of prescription drugs.

". . . The best of modern medical care should be made available to every American. We support efforts to overcome the remaining barriers of distance, poverty, ignorance, and discrimination that separate persons from adequate medical services. During the last eight years of Democratic administrations, this nation has taken giant steps forward in assuring life and health for its citizens. In the years ahead, we Democrats are determined to take those final steps that are necessary to make certain that every American, regardless of economic status shall live out his years without fear of the high costs of sickness.

"Through a partnership of government and private enterprise we must develop new coordinated approaches to stem the rise in medical and drug costs without lowering the quality or availability of medical care. Out-of-hospital care, comprehensive group practice arrangements, increased availability of neighborhood health centers, and the greater use of sub-professional aides can all contribute to the lowering of medical costs.

"We will raise the level of research in all fields of health, with special programs for development of the artificial heart and the heart transplant technique, development of drugs to treat and prevent the recurrence of heart diseases, expansion of current task forces in cancer research and the creation of new ones including cancer of the lung, determination of the factors in mental retardation and reduction of infant mortality, development of drugs to reduce the incidence of suicide and construction of health research facilities and hospitals. We must build new medical, dental and medical service schools, and increase the capacity of existing ones, to train more doctors, dentists, nurses, and medical technicians.

"Medical care should be extended to disabled beneficiaries under the Old Age, Survivors and Disability Insurance Act to the same extent and under the same system that such care is available to the aged.

"Thousands of children die, or are handicapped for life, because their mothers did not receive proper pre-natal medical attention or because the infants were unattended in the critical first days of life. Maternal and child health centers, located and designed to serve the needs of the poor, and voluntary family planning information centers, should be established throughout the country. Medicaid programs administered by the states should have uniform standards so that no mother or child is denied necessary health services. Finally, we urge consideration of a program comparable to Medicare to finance pre-natal care for mothers and post-natal care for children during the first year of life."

Rising Medical Costs

The costs of medical care rose between World War II and the early years of Medicare at a faster rate than did the general Consumer Price Index (CPI), according to a study in the November 1968 issue of the Department of Labor's *Monthly Labor Review.* Among the findings of this Bureau of Labor Statistics (BLS) study:

On the . . . [CPI] index base of 100 for 1957-59, the index of medical care prices advanced from 49.4 in 1935 to 136.7 in 1967, a rise of nearly 177 percent.

Average Annual Percent Changes of Consumer Price Indexes Medical Care & Medical Care Elements 1952–67

U.S. City Average & Selected Metropolitan Areas

Item	U.S. city average	Atlanta	Baltimore	Chicago	Detroit	Los Angeles-Long Beach	New York	Philadelphia	St. Louis	San Francisco-Oakland
1952–64										
Medical care	3.2	2.6	3.9	4.3	4.2	2.9	2.4	3.6	3.0	3.4
Medical care services	3.6	3.0	4.3	4.9	4.7	3.2	2.9	3.9	3.3	3.6
Physicians' fees	3.0	3.5	2.9	4.0	2.7	3.0	2.6	1.9	2.8	2.8
Dentists' fees	2.4	2.6	1.5	3.0	2.6	2.5	1.5	3.6	2.4	2.2
Hospital daily service charges	6.1	4.5	7.4	6.4	4.8	5.9	7.1	5.6	6.2	5.8
Drugs and prescriptions	.7	.5	1.3	.8	–.1	1.0	–.2	1.4	.5	2.3
1965										
Medical care	2.8	2.0	3.1	2.1	2.7	1.9	3.5	3.2	4.4	3.1
Medical care services	3.5	2.1	3.9	2.7	3.0	2.1	4.2	4.4	4.5	3.6
Physicians' fees	3.8	4.4	3.8	2.2	3.8	1.6	5.5	4.5	5.7	3.2
Dentists' fees	2.6	.9	4.3	2.0	2.0	3.3	1.3	2.8	6.5	1.8
Hospital daily service charges	6.6	1.8	6.8	4.7	5.2	4.7	10.2	8.3	7.7	8.8
Drugs and prescriptions	0	1.5	.3	–.2	.6	.4	1.0	–1.4	–.3	.5
1966										
Medical care	6.6	7.1	5.0	5.0	9.1	7.7	6.8	6.3	7.4	7.4
Medical care services	8.1	9.0	5.9	6.6	10.0	9.9	7.5	8.2	9.2	9.1
Physicians' fees	7.8	5.8	5.5	4.9	8.6	7.1	9.5	4.2	11.3	8.0
Dentists' fees	4.6	4.1	4.9	3.9	6.7	5.6	1.2	8.2	4.7	7.9
Hospital daily service charges	16.5	22.3	14.9	11.0	15.1	29.2	13.1	20.4	11.0	18.6
Drugs and prescriptions	.2	–.6	.8	–1.1	2.2	–2.4	3.6	–.9	–.6	–1.1
1967										
Medical care	6.4	3.6	8.2	8.1	6.7	5.1	6.7	7.0	4.0	4.3
Medical care services	7.9	7.6	10.5	10.0	7.9	5.3	7.9	8.4	5.4	5.4
Physicians' fees	6.1	6.3	9.1	8.3	8.5	5.3	7.3	6.0	4.4	2.4
Dentists' fees	5.1	5.2	8.0	5.6	2.2	2.0	6.9	5.0	–.8	
Hospital daily service charges	15.5	15.1	20.1	19.9	11.4	8.2	11.4	14.3	13.6	11.6
Drugs and prescriptions	–.2	–2.2	–1.7	.3	–1.2	3.5	1.8	.3	–1.2	–1.3

[1] Based on data for December of each year; data for 1952–64 calculated as geometric average.

The bulk of the increase occurred in the period since 1946. . . . Since wartime price controls were lifted, medical prices have advanced at a rate half again as fast as that for consumer prices as a whole. Because the medical care index is composed chiefly of services (except for drugs and prescriptions), medical care prices fully participated in the "catch-up" movement of all consumer service prices in the postwar period. However, the cost of medical care services has risen even more rapidly than have the prices of other services. During the past 21 years, prices for medical care services increased nearly 2½ times, while all services doubled.

One of the major factors contributing to the upward trend in medical prices has been the increased demand for medical care services in the face of continuing shortages of skilled manpower. A recent BLS report on health manpower found about 3.7 million workers employed in the medical and health services industry in 1966. This was nearly a third more than the 2.8 million employed in 1960. Yet shortages of health personnel were still acute in 1966 with at least 144,600 urgently needed to staff hospitals and extended care facilities. Not included in this figure are physicians and other medical practitioners. . . .

In addition to the demand created by population growth, changes in medical technology, in education, in the income of patients, in the age distribution of the population, and in urbanization have all contributed to increased demand for medical care services. In the Health, Education & Welfare Department's [1967] report to the President on medical care prices, the following points were made on increased demand for physician services in the period 1950 to 1965:

"(1) Because of the advance in medical science and the improvement in medical education, the public's faith in the power of the physician, in his equipment, and in drugs has increased. This has caused more people to seek physicians' care.

"(2) In addition to the increased size of the population there have been changes in the characteristics of the population that have tended to increase demand. 'Women go to doctors more than men; urban people more than rural people; educated people more than uneducated people, and old people more than the rest of the population.'

"(3) By 1964, 86 million more people had surgical expense insurance than in 1950. In addition, the number of persons covered by regular medical expense plans with benefits for nonsurgical physicians' fees increased from 22 milloin to 109 million. Studies have shown that persons with health insurance tend to be hospitalized for surgery more often than persons without insurance, thus increasing the demand for physician and hospital services."

The increasing demand for hospital services has forced hospitals to expand both their facilities and their staffs, pushing costs upward. To attract competent personnel, hospitals have had to offer higher wages than the traditionally low pay associated with service industries. In 1966, for example, 90% of all hospital employees received increases averaging 8.1%. . . .

. . . Per capita expenditures for all medical care items, roughly adjusted for price change . . . , rose by more than 70% between 1946 and 1966, about the same rate as did "real" per capita expenditures for physician services. Expenditures for drugs gained by nearly 170% during the same interval, but the increase for hospital services was only 30%.

Hospital daily service charges have been increasing faster than any other component of the medical care price index. The postwar increase for hospital room rates, as shown in the CPI, was 441%, compared with 71% for all consumer prices, 125% for all medical care prices, and 107% for physicians' fees. The average annual rate of increase for hospital room rates has thus been more than 3 times that of the overall CPI. . . .

Physicians' fees have not advanced as rapidly as hospital charges, but they have more than doubled in the past 10 years. . . . Doctors have tended to attribute their higher fees in recent years to the general economic conditions and the higher cost of doing business. Nevertheless, some charges clearly reflect the shortage of doctors. With an overload of patients, physicians in some cases have tried to discourage the practice of making house calls by raising the rate for such a service to a level that few patients are willing to pay. The postwar emphasis on medical specialists has also helped to boost physicians' fees since general practitioners have become scarce and specialists, with their extra training, are able to command higher fees. . . .

Despite the obvious similarities, dentists' fees have not increased with the same rapidity as have physicians' fees. They have been faced with the same inflationary pressures. . . . However, in 1966 when physicians' fees rose 7.8%, dentists' fees rose by only 4.6%. One possible reason for the disparity is the fact that few consumers have health insurance covering dental care while over 80% of the population has some kind of coverage for physicians' fees. . . .''

Health-Care System Criticized, Wider Programs Urged

As Medicare and Medicaid continued in operation, complaints of alleged failures and inadequacies of the U.S. health-care programs became increasingly common.

Dr. George W. Graham, president of the American Hospital Association, testified before the House Ways & Means Committee Oct. 28, 1969 that AHA ''studies indicate that the administrative and general man-hours in hospitals increased 15% during the first year of Medicare. Many additional employes . . . were added because of the administrative complexity of the Medicare program. It is our estimate that costs required to comply with the current Medicare reimbursement regulations amount to more than $150 million a year in the hospitals alone. . . . In addition, there are significant claim review and auditing costs borne by the intermediary, which bring the total cost of administering the program to well over one-quarter of a billion dollars a year without including the government's own administrative costs. Much of this, we believe, is completely unnecessary and wasteful. It is the single most frustrating and disturbing element to providers of [Medicare] service.''

Dr. John L. S. Holloman Jr. of New York, chairman of the Physicians Forum, told the House Ways & Means Committee in a prepared statement Oct. 30, 1969 that although the U.S. spent about $60 billion for health purposes during fiscal 1969, with approximately $18 billion of the total ''coming directly from the federal government, . . . large segments of the population are deprived of adequate medical care services, and wide discrepancies persist in the quality of present services. Millions of the poor receive only emergency type care. We rank 14th in infant mortality among industrial nations and 18th in male life expectancy." (By 1974 the U.S. had dropped to 20th in infant mortality and 28th in life expectancy of males aged 45. In the early 1950s the U.S. had been the industrial nation with the lowest rate for mothers dying in childbirth, but by 1974 its rate was seventh. At the same time, the U.S. had dropped to 12th place in life expectancy for females.)

According to Hollomon, "the Medicaid program . . . has been most discouraging. (1) It has not helped to eliminate the dual system of medicine which is still practiced. In fact, the application of a means test for obtaining care has aggravated and accentuated the degrading and unequal system of charity medicine. (2) Medicaid has exposed the hodge-podge of fiscal mechanisms without providing any overall administrative guidelines. (3) Medicaid, with its time formula for state participation, has not reached the poorest states where it is most urgently needed, and in those states which have set up a program it has failed to cover all persons for whom medical care costs are burdensome. In addition the program has raised public expectation concerning health services and now instead of increased services most programs face curtailment."

Holloman reported that "the Medicare program has functioned more smoothly than Medicaid, but it still has serious problems. (1) Financial barriers to necessary services are still present. (2) There is an over-emphasis on custodial forms of care and an under-emphasis on prevention of illness and rehabilitation in the aged. (3) There are uncoordinated Social Security administrative patterns in operational responsibility. (4) There are separate financing and eligibility mechanisms."

Hollomon held that "current methods of financing health care make it impossible for all people to afford adequate health care. Effective preventive care is not widely available, and especially not to the most vulnerable groups in our society, impoverished families in urban and rural slums. 92% of our $60 billion health expenditures are directed toward the treatment of disease and disability. Only 8% of that sum finds its way into preventive medicine. In this light perhaps we should call it a 'sickness-care delivery system' rather than a health care delivery system. Our present method of delivery of health care is archaic and grossly inefficient and therefore we, of the Physicians Forum, call for the creation of a national health system that will stimulate and encourage the practice of preventive as

Life Expectancy

(In years, at various ages, by race and sex,
for various periods)

Age, sex, and race	1900–02 [1]	1929–31	1939–41	1949–51	1955	1959–61	1969
All classes							
At birth	49.2	(NA)	63.6	68.1	69.5	69.9	70.5
0 to 64 years [2]	44.4	(NA)	55.9	58.7	59.5	59.7	59.9
65 years	11.9	(NA)	12.8	13.8	14.2	14.4	14.8
75 years	7.1	(NA)	7.6	8.4	8.7	8.7	9.3
White Male							
At birth	48.2	59.1	62.8	66.3	67.3	67.6	67.9
0 to 64 years [2]	43.7	52.9	55.8	58.2	58.8	59.0	59.3
65 years	11.5	11.8	12.1	12.8	12.9	13.0	13.0
75 years	6.8	7.0	7.2	7.8	8.0	7.9	8.2
White Female							
At birth	51.1	62.7	67.3	72.0	73.6	74.2	75.1
0 to 64 years [2]	45.7	54.9	58.0	60.5	61.1	61.4	61.6
65 years	12.2	12.8	13.6	15.0	15.5	15.9	16.6
75 years	7.3	7.6	7.9	8.9	9.2	9.3	9.9
Negro and Other Races Male [3]							
At birth	32.5	47.6	52.3	58.9	61.2	61.5	60.7
0 to 64 years [2]	30.6	44.4	47.9	53.1	54.6	54.9	54.6
65 years	10.4	10.9	12.2	12.8	13.2	12.8	12.5
75 years	6.6	7.0	8.2	8.8	10.4	8.9	10.4
Negro and Other Races Female [3]							
At birth	35.0	49.5	55.6	62.7	65.9	66.5	68.4
0 to 64 years [2]	32.5	45.7	49.9	55.1	56.8	57.3	58.3
65 years	11.4	12.2	13.9	14.5	15.5	15.1	15.7
75 years	7.9	8.6	9.8	10.2	12.0	10.1	12.2

NA = not available.

[1] Original Death Registration States (10 States and the District of Columbia).

[2] Average years of life lived between birth and age 65, computed by the formula $(T_0 - T_{65}) \div l_0$.

[3] Negro population only, for 1900–1902, 1929–1931, and 1939–1941.

Source: National Center for Health Statistics, U.S. Public Health Service reports presenting United States life tables for indicated years.

well as curative medicine, organize the use of existing health resources and establish a national health care financing agency to be supported completely out of the general treasury. . . ."

As another indication of dissatisfaction with Medicare and Medicaid, a Committee of One Hundred for National Health Insurance had been announced in November 1968 by Walter Reuther, president of the United Auto Workers. Members of the committee included Dr. Michael E. deBakey, president of Baylor College of Medicine; Mrs. Mary Lasker, president of the Albert and Mary Lasker Foundation, and Whitney M. Young Jr., executive director of the National Urban League. Although he recognized the advances in health-care made by other nations, Reuther said he did "not propose that we borrow a national health insurance system from any other nation. No nation has a system that will meet the peculiar needs of America. I am confident that we have in America the ingenuity and the social inventiveness needed to create a system of national health insurance that will be uniquely American—one that will harmonize and make compatible the best features of the present system, with maximum freedom of choice, within the economic framework and social structure of a national health insurance system."

Thomas J. Watson Jr., chairman of International Business Machines Corp., declared in an address at the Mayo Foundation at Rochester, Minn. Nov. 19, 1970 that, because of "shocking" failures of the U.S. medical-care delivery system, the time had come to "overhaul the system" and make the "only . . . choice before us that will work: some very new form of national health insurance." Watson said he had come to this decision despite "that old taboo—'socialized medicine.' " Watson recalled that in 1945-49, when President Truman's call for national health was rejected, he (Watson) had accepted the arguments against the proposal. "But . . . I cannot accept it in 1970," he declared. In the two decades since Truman's national-health-insurance plan was defeated, the U.S. "has dropped from seventh in the world to 16th in the prevention of infant morality," Watson said, "has dropped in female life expectancy from sixth to eighth, has dropped in male life expectancy from 10th to 24th, and . . . bought itself this unenviable trend by spending more of its gross national product for medical care—$1 out of every $14—than any other country on the face of the earth."

In an April 1973 report, the Research & Policy Committee of the Committee for Economic Development, with some exceptions, made three major conclusions about the U.S. health-care system:

First, faulty allocation of resources is a major cause of inadequacies and inequalities in U.S. health services that result today in poor or substandard care for large segments of the population. While manpower, facilities, and services are lacking in some areas, . . . they are in excess in others. There is also functional as well as geographical maldistribution, causing most notably the nearly nationwide inadequacy in primary care while medical specialties often exceed requirements. The market mechanism works imperfectly in meeting needs for health care; there is a distortion in incentives and pricing, and functions are poorly organized and often inefficient. Nor has there been an adequate effort at overall planning. What confronts the United States is an essential industry—the nation's third largest in the numbers of people employed—that delivers vitally important services at a level far below its potential capability.

Second, the task of assuring all people the ability to cope financially with the costs of health care has been made realizable by the substantial base of coverage now provided by both private and public insurance plans. The dramatic alteration in the patterns of financing health care over the past quarter of a century or more is illustrated in several ways. Between 1950 and 1972, direct payments by individuals as a share of personal health expenditures were reduced from 68% to 35% of the total, as private insurance and public expenditures increased. However, . . . direct payments have increased substantially despite the greater coverage, rising from approximately $7 billion to $25 billion. Other statistics show that about 50% of the cost of hospital care is now paid for by some unit of government and private insurance pays for another 35%; government pays for 25% of the cost of physicians' services, private insurance for 35%. For those people covered by private health insurance, the carriers pay for about 70% of consumer outlays for hospital care and nearly 50% of outlays for physicians' services. . . . There now exist large-scale, functioning mechanisms for the financing of health care in the United States. These can provide a firm base for further—and much needed—improvement and extension of the system so that it covers the entire population.

Third, unless step-by-step alterations are made in the means of delivering services and paying providers, closing the gaps in financing would overburden an inadequate system and offer little prospect of materially improving the quality and quantity of medical services or the health of the American people. The very programs intended to help people meet rising costs have contributed unintentionally to further increases in cost. For example, the most prevalent kind of health-insurance coverage is hospital care, whereas ambulatory-care benefits still are scantily insured; this has contributed to the overuse of expensive hospital facilities at the same time that it has discouraged the development of badly needed ambulatory-care services. Likewise, reimbursing providers of care by tolerating the passthrough of costs has reduced or eliminated incentives for economy. To pour large amounts of money into the present system through the expanded benefits of a national health-insurance plan would undoubtedly create further distortions in demand, pricing, incentives, and resource allocation without markedly improving services. We cannot stress too much the importance of scheduling benefits only when they can be delivered in care. We caution that whatever national health-insurance program is finally enacted will have to contain some provision for phasing to an adequate level of benefits by steps—not all at once.

The criticism of the U.S. health-care system increased through the mid-1970s.

Sen. Abraham A. Ribicoff (D, Conn.), as secretary of health, education and welfare in the Kennedy Administration, had headed a task force to draft a Medicare bill. He told Congress Feb. 8, 1975 that "the 23 million Medicare beneficiaries are paying more of their own money out of pocket for medical expenses than they were before Medicare was enacted [in 1965]. Since Medicare was enacted, premium and coinsurance rates have shot up 110%. . . . The average out-of-pocket [medical] payment for Americans aged 65 and over has grown from $234 in 1966 to $311 in 1973. . . ." According to the Health Insurance Institute, the average American aged 65 or older had health expenses totaling $1,218 during 1974. Of this, nearly two-thirds was paid by government, private health insurance, philanthropy, industry or other third parties, and $415 came out of the patient's own pocket. (About 12 million Americans 65 or older had private health insurance to supplement their Medicare benefits.) Ribicoff commented briefly April 17, 1975 on Medicare's background, failings and prospects as a basis for a national health insurance program. He said in a statement in the *Congressional Record:*

"Medicare was a major breakthrough in assuring a measure of health protection for one segment of the population. Because it was a new concept, however, Congress limited its coverage. It was, in fact, a financial program to help meet some of the costs of short-term and acute medical care. Since its enactment in 1965 we have found that the program should be improved and expanded. . . . Since 1965 we have expanded Medicare to cover all disabled persons, those who have chronic kidney conditions, and many more. Its services have likewise been expanded to cover a wider range of nonhospital items. At the same time we have found a need to curb costs and abuses under Medicare. Major oversight hearings which we held in 1969 led to improvements in the administration and cost control mechanisms of Medicare. . . .

"Much more needs to be done to improve Medicare. In fact, as the debate continues over national health insurance, we should look closely at Medicare. It provides a good working example of what should be done and what should be avoided in a national health insurance program. In fact, Medicare can serve as a pilot program for national health insurance. We know what must be done to improve Medicare.

"It must be expanded to provide a comprehensive range of services in all different medical settings—both in and out of the hospitals, in clinics, doctors' offices, HMOs, foundations, skilled nursing and intermediate facilities, and in the home. It must assure that the patient is not burdened with medical bills. It must run smoothly so that doctors, patients, and hospitals are not overcome by redtape. And it must be accomplished in a way which provides the patient with the maximum of freedom of choice.

"The capacity of the federal government to administer a health insurance program is limited. And the amount of tax money available to pay for a program is also limited. That is why we would do well to start with improving the Medicare program. Let us turn it into the national health insurance program that older Americans thought they were getting in 1965. If this works, then we can expand our health coverage programs in an orderly fashion. . . .

"It is time to change Medicare from a limited financial program to the program which we originally envisioned—comprehensive national health insurance for all older Americans. The Medicare program I envision is one which provides a range of care from preventative and diagnostic physician's services to the most acute hospital care. Nursing home, home health care, dental care, eye care, hearing care, prescription drug coverage are just a few of the areas which should be covered. In short, Medicare should be a balanced program which encourages the best kind of care with the greatest possible freedom of choice for the patient. And it should be a program that provides reasonably for all the providers in the system—hospitals, doctors and others and at the same time is efficiently administered at the smallest possible cost to the government. . . ."

The fragmented health-care system was attacked by the Congressional Black Caucus (made of black members of the House of Representatives and Senate) in a legislative agenda entered in the *Congressional Record* by Rep. Charles B. Rangel (D, N.Y.) March 10, 1975. According to the agenda, "Medicaid and Medicare reach only a minimal number of people and with a relatively low level of benefits. A large number of persons have no medical plan at all, and even those with medical plans frequently do not have regular preventive care. Basically, the problem is one of cost. Unfortunately, the medical industry and the country have forced us to choose between the high costs of comprehensive coverage and a gamble with our own health." The agenda listed these six principles "which must be incorporated in any [comprehensive health-care] bill finally passed: (1) It must set forth a positive health concept which includes preventive services, health maintenance and community education for personal and community health. (2) Health care must be recognized as a right, not merely as a privilege. (3) Health coverage must be comprehensive and include the full range of health care, preventive, diagnosis, treatment and rehabilitation regardless of one's ability to pay. (4) There must be progressive trust fund financing so that health care is insured of continuation as a permanent program. (5) Consumers, that is, the community residents, must be permitted and encouraged to participate in health-care-program operations. (6) Finally, the health care program must be reinforced with adequate financing for research, planning and administration.''

Casper W. Weinberger, then secretary of health, education and Welfare, had told the Senate Finance Committee May 21, 1974 that "inadequate health insurance can severely limit the life span of a person who cannot afford vital health services when they are needed, and there are many such in this country, and we think inadequate health insurance can severely limit the life potential of people who could not afford preventive or corrective health measures." Weinberger reported that "some 25 million Americans have no health-care insurance at all, and millions more have clearly inadequate health-care protection, protection that may become further eroded by inflation as we move into a period in which we have no statutory health-care cost controls for the first time since the middle of 1971. Less than half the people under 65 have protection against catastrophic health-care costs, and almost none of those over 65 have that kind of protection, and this at a time when, just for example, the costs of a terminal cancer can exceed $20,000, easily. Too many of the health insurance policies are sort of a standby kind of equipment, not furnishing protection until one is stricken and then protection only in the most expensive facility, a hospital.''

Leonard Woodcock, the late Walter Reuther's successor as president of the United Auto Workers and a leader in the movement for national, comprehensive health insurance, amplified Weinberger's complaint. He charged in a statement to the Senate Finance Committee May 22, 1974 that "the insurance industry has created a myth that almost all Americans already have health insurance which covers basic expenditures for care. The reality is that, even by the industry's own figures, the majority of Americans do not have adequate basic coverage. Thirty million Americans have no heatlh insurance at all. Half the population does not have coverage for such important basic services as visits to the physicians' office. Half are not covered at all unless hospitalized, creating unnecessary hospitalization. Twenty-six percent of all full-time workers in private industry do not have group insurance. In particular, those 100 million-plus Americans who have commercial health insurance policies lack good basic protection. . . . Many of the individual and family policies provide very low specified benefits such as $10 a day for hospital daily service charges that are currently averaging $120 a day. Of the 82 million Americans said to have group coverage from commercial companies, more than half have 'basic protection' only without 'major medical' supplementation. According to the industry, 27% of this group have 'coverage' of under $25 per day for hospitalization and the number of days is often very limited. Even for those with major medical policies in addition to basic coverage, half have hospital benefits of under $50 a day. . . .''

State Regulation

Officials and agencies of most states have taken at least some action to regulate the charges for health care and the expansion of health-care facilities and services. In 1973 the federal Department of Health, Education & Welfare (HEW) sponsored a 50-state survey by the firm of Lewin & Associates, Inc. "to investigate three principal issues: (1) how states are attempting to control cost increases in the rates of institutional care; (2) how states are using their regulatory power to control the expansion of health care facilities and services; (3) what states are doing to strengthen their regulation of health insurance companies." The data reported relate largely to conditions in March 1974. An HEW summary of the report's major findings highlighted the following facts:

A major approach to the task of controlling the costs of institutional care revolves around the issue of reimbursement. Traditionally, reimbursement to hospitals by public and private purchasers has taken several forms: (1) payment of reasonable retrospective costs; (2) payment of charges on an indemnity basis by private insurance carriers; (3) payment by individuals of the entire cost of care or as supplemental payments above insurance coverage. At present, the majority of states use retrospective cost reimbursement to pay for hospital services purchased by programs they administer. . . .

The most widespread departure from retrospective reimbursement is the broadly defined strategy of prospective reimbursement. This approach has a number of variations; however, rate review programs based on prospective reimbursement share certain common characteristics: rate decisions are not left to the exclusive discretion of the provider; predetermined levels of target costs or revenue requirements are based on an estimate of future costs and utilization; they feature a risk incentive factor; and retrospective adjustments are limited to defined factors and ranges.

Eight states have established public rate setting agencies that regularly approve or establish prospective rates and review requests for modification. In three of these states, commissions have been specifically established to perform these functions. In the remainder such power is vested in previously existing public agencies, such as a health department. In four states, the rate setting agency is also responsible for purchasing health care services.

Rate Setting Authorities for Prospective Reimbursement Systems

State	Type of Authority	Name of Agency
Arizona	State	Dept. of Health Services, Division of Administration & Industry Affairs, Phoenix
Colorado	State	Dept. of Social Services, Division of Medical Services, Denver
Colorado	Blue Cross	Colorado Hospital Service, Denver
Connecticut	State	Commission on Hospitals & Health Care, Hartford
Connecticut	Blue Cross	Connecticut Blue Cross, New Haven
Delaware	Blue Cross	Blue Cross & Blue Shield of Delaware, Wilmington
Hawaii	Blue Cross	Hawaii Medical Service Association, Honolulu
Indiana	Blue Cross	Mutual Hospital Service, Indianapolis
Kentucky	Blue Cross	Blue Cross Hospital Plan, Louisville
Maryland	State	Health Services Cost Review Commission, Baltimore
Massachusetts	State	Rate Setting Commission, Boston
Michigan	Blue Cross	Michigan Hospital Service, Detroit
Missouri	Blue Cross	Blue Cross of Kansas City, Kansas City
Montana	Association	Montana Rate Review System, Inc., Helena
Nebraska	Association	Nebraska Hospital Association, Lincoln
New Jersey	State	Department of Health, Trenton
New Mexico	Blue Cross	New Mexico Blue Cross & Blue Shield, Albuquerque
New York	State	Department of Health, Albany
North Carolina	Blue Cross	Blue Cross & Blue Shield of North Carolina, Durham
Ohio	Blue Cross	Blue Cross of Southwest Ohio, Cincinnati
Ohio	Blue Cross	Blue Cross of Northeast Ohio, Cleveland
Oklahoma	Blue Cross	Blue Cross & Blue Shield of Oklahoma, Tulsa
Pennsylvania	Blue Cross	Blue Cross of Western Pennsylvania, Pittsburgh
Pennsylvania	Blue Cross	Blue Cross of Northeastern Pennsylvania, Wilkes-Barre
Rhode Island	Blue Cross	State Budget Office, Dept. of Administration, Providence
Wisconsin	State	Associated Hospital Service, Milwaukee

In addition to the eight state rate review systems, Blue Cross plans sponsor 16 prospective reimbursement systems; in two states, such systems operate along with state programs. In two others states, nonprofit corporations have been established under the sponsorship of the state hospital associations to set prospective rates on a voluntary basis. There are thus 26 prospective reimbursement systems currently in existence in 22 states. These systems involve about 25% of the nation's hospitals. . . .

Substantial differences exist in the methods used to determine prospective rates and payments. Three general and overlapping methodologies have thus far been developed: (1) systems basis (including annual budget review, charge increase review, and annual formula increase); (2) determination of reasonableness (as measured by such indices as the institution's cost history, interinstitutional comparison, formulae applied to increases or normative standards; (3) unit of payment (based upon charges, inclusive per diem, preadmission rate, or allocation of budget costs). Most systems utilize budget approval and institutional comparisons and pay on the basis of charges. . . .

. . . Of the six [state] commissions specifying either provider or non-provider membership, five place purchasers, consumers and government officials in the majority. . . .

Typical costs to the rate setting agency for review tended to vary between $1,000 and $3,000 per hospital. The five state-administered programs for which information was available reported total budgets of about $3 million. Staffs varied from the equivalent of one to 20 full-time persons and budgets from $30,000 to over $1 million. In brief, prospective rate review systems for hospitals are currently quite limited:

• State rate review agencies exist in only eight states.
• Medicaid rates are determined prospectively in only five states.
• State-rates apply to all purchasers in only one state.
• Participation is statewide and mandatory in only 15 of the 26 prospective reimbursement purchasing systems operated by public and private agencies.

However, increased interest was identified in many areas. In 10 states, includ-

Rate Setting Methodology of Developed Prospective Rate Systems

System Basis	Number of Programs
Budget Approval	11
Charge Increase Review	11
Formula	4
Basis for Determining Reasonableness	
Institutional Comparison	14
Cost History Only	10
Formula	2
Normative Standards Only	0
Unit of Payment	
Charges	15
Per Diem	6
Budget Alloction	3
Per Admission	1
Experiments Testing Several Methods	1

ing four with existing Blue Cross prospective systems, plans were identified for more extensive rate review programs. Six of these cases may involve public rate setting agencies. . . . If the ten projected systems were established, and the existing ones continued, 55% of the nation's hospitals, housing 65% of the beds, would be involved in prospective rate review.

The study also investigated patterns of reimbursement for skilled nursing homes. Six of the eight states which set prospective hospital rates do the same for nursing homes. In four other states, the state Medicaid agencies set prospective rates for nursing homes. Altogether, 11 states have established such programs.

In about 85% of the physician reimbursement systems identified, including both Medicaid and Blue Shield, payment was made on the basis of usual and customary fees. Similarly, adjustments were usually based on actual changes in such fees. . . .

Discouraging or preventing the creation of facilities in excess of community need has been the goal of various methods of Capital Expenditure & Services (CES) controls. Such controls may take several forms. First, direct control may be exercised through statutory requirements that providers obtain prior approval from a designated agency for plans involving capital expenditures for health facilities and/or changes in services; state certificate of need statutes prevent a disapproved facility from obtaining a license to operate. Second, indirect controls may require that a change in facilities or services must obtain prior approval to qualify for reimbursement. . . . While indirect control does not prohibit construction, it does reduce the ability to recoup costs and therefore may affect efforts to enlist necessary financing. Still another form of indirect control is state capital financing programs that requires prior approval. Finally, CES controls also include voluntary compliance with public planning efforts; this was the original thrust of the "Partnership for Health" approach established by the 1966 amendments to the Federal Public Health Service Act.

CES controls are used extensively throughout the nation. Among the 50 states and the District of Columbia, all but one report some form of direct or indirect CES control. . . .

Twenty-four states have enacted Certificate of Need (C/N) laws. There is clear evidence that interest in direct controls is high among the states. Eleven of the C/N laws have been enacted within the past two years, and nine other states are reported likely to pass similar statutes within the next three years. The trend in more recent and proposed legislation is toward broader coverage.

Indirect controls are the most widespread method of CES regulation. Thirty-seven states are participating in the Federal "Section 1122" program. Under this program, a Designated State Planning Agency (DPA) reviews CES projects and recommends that HEW disallow reimbursement for capital costs from federal Medicare, Medicaid and Maternal & Child Health programs for facilities not in compliance with the DPA determination.

Many Blue Cross plans have also applied similar controls. In 15 non-C/N states, at least one Blue Cross plan requires approval of changes in facilities or services by designated areawide planning agencies in order to qualify for reimbursement. In four states with C/N laws, Blue Cross plans have applied more extensive requirements. Blue Cross plans in 42 states provide for prior approval as a prerequisite for reimbursement for capital expenditures. . . .

Participation by C/N states in the Section 1122 program is generally attributed to the desire for federal funding and also to compensate for gaps in the state's C/N statute. Among the five states that have enacted neither C/N statutes nor contracted for Section 1122 reviews, two experience CES controls by Blue Cross plans and two by voluntary CHP review. . . .

. . . Sanctions are generally uniform. In all but two of the 24 C/N states, a project that is not approved cannot be licensed to operate and, in some cases, can be denied a construction permit. . . .

The number of levels of review within the C/N process . . . reflects a serious concern for ensuring due process and maintaining a system of checks and balances. It is almost axiomatic that the more severe the potential regulatory action the more administrative processes (with attendant cost and delay) are likely to be required.

The relationship between rate review and CES control processes is of particular interest:

• the reimbursement denied by rate review agencies may be for operating cost as well as capital costs, which is a stronger sanction than is available under 1122 review programs and some Blue Cross reviews;

• the rate review agency could deny reimbursement for existing services it considers unnecessary;

• rate review agencies may or may not feel bound by the CES review agency recommendations (i.e., even if a Certificate of Need is granted, the rate review agency may choose to reduce reimbursement). . . .

Health insurance is regulated in every state. State programs were analyzed in terms of five consumer oriented goals: (1) to ensure that purchasers have advantageous choices and adequate and reliable information upon which to make decisions; (2) to assure prompt and fair treatment of claims and complaints by carriers; (3) to protect policy holders from loss of benefits because of the carrier's financial impairment; (4) to promote economy and efficiency in the provision of health insurance; and (5) to improve and expand the availability of health insurance coverage for all segments of the population. . . . [However], not all state insurance departments accept all of these goals as appropriate to their function. . . .

In general, there is a great deal of consistency among the states, particularly in the traditional functions of protecting the consumer from fraud and loss of benefits due to carrier insolvency. Only a small number of insurance departments, however, report authorities and activities beyond traditional regulatory areas.

In terms of ensuring that the consumer has adequate choices and information, the study revealed that virtually all states have authority to assure the clarity of policy language; far fewer review the appropriateness of the premium charged. . . .

State Actions to Ensure Clarity of Policy Language

Type of Policy	No. of States
Private insurance—individual	51
Private insurance—group	47
Blues—individual	47
Blues—group	47

State Agencies Reviewing Appropriateness of Premium

Type of Policy	No. of States
Private insurance—individual	32
Private insurance—group	18
Blues—individual	40
Blues—group	36

All states are reported to have enacted legislation to prevent the sale of unreviewed policies by unauthorized agents as well as to regulate marketing and advertising practices. Thirty-two states require grace periods for purchasers to reconsider their decisions, and 19 states are reported to have "consumer information programs," although only a few appeared to be extensive.

All insurance departments report the existence of sections to handle complaints by consumers; however, there was considerable variation in the types of action which the departments had undertaken. Most departments (39) investigated such complaints, some mediate (26) or require adjustment (24), and 11 states initiate court action on behalf of consumers.

To protect the consumer from loss of benefits because of financial impairment of their carrier, states set requirements for initial capitalization, impose reserve requirements and create insolvency funds. Private-insurance-carrier capitalization ranged from $150,000 to $1,500,000; "Blues" capitalization ranged from zero (15 states) to $400,000. "Blues" must maintain unearned premium and claims reserves in 14 states and meet less stringent contingency reserve or other requirements in 21 others. Eleven states reported that they had insolvency funds which included coverage of health insurance written by private life insurance companies. (Two of these funds also covered the "Blues" plans in the state.) These funds would ensure payment for claims already incurred for which an insolvent carrier has insufficient reserves, but they do not address the problem of continuity of coverage for the insured.

States which were pursuing the goal of promoting economy and efficiency in the provision of health insurance and, concomitantly, in the delivery of health care services (and some state officials questioned the appropriateness of this goal) limited themselves to regulation of Blue Cross/Blue Shield Plans. States generally have greater regulatory authority over service plans, and the service benefits of these plans offer greater leverage than the indemnity benefits of private companies.

Methods for achieving this goal include:

• Containing direct administrative costs of insurance carriers. Nineteen states reported regulation of the overall administrative or selling expenses of nonprofit health service plans. In addition, six states having statutory authority in this area did not report either the presence of this authority or its use.

• Mandating changes in benefits to encourage lower cost care. Only three states reported mandating such changes (one each for outpatient surgery, outpatient testing and home health). Many responded that regulation is unnecessary since an increasing number of policies are already including these benefits.

• Placing pressure on health care providers via regulated carriers. Eight states require private insurance carriers or Blue Cross Plans to reimburse hospitals on a prospective basis. In five such states, the insurance commissioner has a formal role in the rate setting process. In four states, the insurance commissioner reported current or planned use of his regulatory authority to compel cost containment activities by Blue Cross Plans.

Twenty-six states are reported to have eliminated the rights of health insurers to terminate the coverage of high risk clients prior to the renewal date. Only two states mandate renewal opportunities, and five require group policies to include provision for conversion to individual coverage. Four states had enacted state catastrophic insurance plans. In a further effort to expand the availability of coverage. one state requires the "Blues" to accept all individual applicants, and six states report that they mandate open enrollment periods; other states reported voluntary open enrollment periods by the nonprofit service plans. . . .

Staff & Budget for Health Insurance Regulation

	Number of domestic commercial carriers plus percent	Estimated full time equivalent staff		Estimated budget	
		Number	Ranking	Thousands of dollars	Ranking
1. Alabama	96	3	Low	60	Low.
2. Alaska	6	11	High	(1)	
3. Arizona	27	4	Low	(1)	
4. Arkansas	77	4	do	43	Low.
5. California	(1)	(1)		(1)	
6. Colorado	10	20	High	336	High.
7. Connecticut	42	6	Average	90	Average.
8. Delaware	8	1	Low	20	
9. District of Columbia	7	25	High	(1)	
10. Florida	67	(1)		1,250	High.
11. Georgia	34	10	High	(1)	
12. Hawaii	16	2	Low	30	Low.
13. Idaho	6	(1)		(1)	
14. Illinois	153	8	Low	750	Average.
15. Indiana	34	2	do	(1)	
16. Iowa	73	31	High	135	Low.
17. Kansas	25	6.5	Average	149	Average.
18. Kentucky	8	9	High	102	Do.
19. Louisiana	3	15	do	216	High.
20. Maine	2	1	Low	(1)	
21. Maryland	22	15	High	350	Do.
22. Massachusetts	2	5	Average	(1)	
23. Michigan	47	9	High	200	Do.
24. Minnesota	59	4	Low	(1)	
25. Mississippi	6	8	High	70	Average.
26. Missouri	65	6	Average	54	Low.
27. Montana	6	8	High	(1)	
28. Nebraska	40	6	Average	90	Average.
29. Nevada	1	5	do	(1)	
30. New Hampshire	2	1	Low	20	Low.
31. New Jersey	(1)	(1)		(1)	
32. New Mexico	10	(1)		(1)	
33. New York	170	49	High	1,590	High.
34. North Carolina	27	15	do	(1)	
35. North Dakota	13	2.5	Low	75	Average.
36. Ohio	84	10	Average	340	High.
37. Oklahoma	2	15	High	300	Do.
38. Oregon	9	5.5	Average	160	Average.
39. Pennsylvania	207	20	do	390	Low.
40. Rhode Island	11	2	Low	(1)	
41. South Carolina	77	5	do	150	Average.
42. South Dakota	12	2	do	18	Low.
43. Tennessee	24	(1)		(1)	
44. Texas	52	20	High	(1)	
45. Utah	2	8	do	(1)	
46. Vermont	1	3.5	Low	30	Low.
47. Virginia	36	3	do	(1)	Do.
48. Washington	79	10	High	(1)	
49. West Virginia	13	4	Low	(1)	
50. Wisconsin	52	5	do	165	Average.
51. Wyoming	3	2	do	(1)	
Total	49	45		28	

1 Not available.

Health Manpower Problems

A major and widely discussed health problem is the scarcity of doctors in rural and depressed urban areas.

A report by the AMA's Board of Trustees June 19, 1967 warned that the U.S. shortage of physicians was reaching "alarming proportions" and urged "an immediate and unprecedented increase" to meet the need. One step in that direction, the board recommended, would be for medical schools, whose enrollment had remained "static" for years, to "review their [admission] policies." The report also urged that schools of osteopathy be converted into medical schools and that osteopathic students transfer to medical schools. (Dr. John W. Hayes, president of the 13,000-member American Osteopathic Association, June 22 rejected any such "conversion.") A statement calling for large increases in the number of doctors trained in the U.S. and for extension of the opportunity to go to medical school to all qualified students was issued jointly March 5, 1968 by the AMA and the Association of American Medical Colleges. In the 1967-68 school year the nation's 94 medical schools had accepted 9,290 of 20,000 applicants.

According to findings of the Health Subcommittee of the Senate Committee on Labor & Public Welfare, 312 of the nation's 510 state planning areas had fewer than 100 physicians per 10,000 residents by 1975. The aggregate physician shortage in these 312 areas exceeds 22,000. Commenting on the subcommittee's findings about the distribution of doctors, Sen. Edward M. Kennedy (D, Mass.) told the Senate Dec. 5, 1975 that "more than 50% of the counties in the nation had fewer doctors in 1970 than in 1960; 35% of physicians now practicing in rural counties are over 55 years of age and are expected to retire within 10 years. This will increase the shortage of physicians in rural areas by an additional 8,000 doctors. Inner-city areas now have fewer than one-quarter of the physician supply of the affluent suburban areas. More than 10,000 additional physicians are now needed in inner-city areas. The supply of physicians in inner-city urban areas has declined continuously since World War II. The number of physicians in the inner-city area of one city, Chicago, declined by 30% between 1950 and 1970. There are not enough family practitioners and other primary care physicians. The American Medical Association has stated that 50% of new physicians should be in the primary care specialties. In the large prepaid group practices, 65% of physicians are in the primary care specialties; in Great Britain, the share is 75%. Only 38% of physicians in the United States are now practicing in the primary care specialties. And fewer still, only 31% of physicians now in training, are in the primary care specialities. . . . One-third of the interns and residents in the country are graduates of foreign medical schools. In 1973, in 13 states, more than 50% of new physician licenses went to foreign medical graduates. The quality of care provided by many foreign trained physicians is suspect, at best. Only 20% of foreign medical graduates entering the country can pass parts I and II of the National Boards Examination. Many do not speak good English. . . ."

Kennedy had discussed the disproportionate distribution of doctors and other rural health problems in April 1975 at the First National Conference on Rural America. "Throughout the nation, there is one physician for every 665 people," he said. "In rural areas, however, the figure is less than one physician for 1,250 people. . . . And the problem is getting worse. Between 1960 and 1970 half of the counties in the states of Alabama, Missouri, Nebraska, Pennsylvania and Texas lost physicians. And almost two-thirds of the counties in the states of Arkansas, Iowa, Indiana, Illinois, Kansas, Mississippi, Minnesota, Oklahoma and Ohio saw the physician-population ratio decrease. As the physicians who have been practicing in these areas since the '30s, even the '20s, retire, no one is taking their place." The other main health problem in rural areas, as elsewhere, was cost, Kennedy declared. "We hear a great deal about people in the United States who cannot afford health care," Kennedy said. "It is all true. Health care now costs Americans an exorbitant amount of money. On the average, each American now pays—as insurance premiums, out-of-pocket payments, and taxes—more than $490 a year for health care. An average seven-day stay in the hospital now costs more than $990. The delivery of a child costs more than $950. An appendectomy, more than $2,000. Last year, more than 22% of American families experienced health care costs in excess of $1,000. To meet these large expenses, most Americans have some form of health insurance; but this health insurance is diluted with sizeable deductibles and co-payments. And 25 million Americans have no health insurance at all. The high cost of health care strikes rural residents especially hard. First, many rural residents face the risk of health care without health insurance at all. While more than 75% of urban residents have health insurance protection, only 64% of rural non-farm, and 51% of farm, residents, have health insurance. The explanation of this deficit is not difficult. Rural populations are less readily enrolled in health insurance plans for administrative reasons. The great bulk of health insurance enrollment is done through organized groups of people—mainly the employees in a place of work. In small towns and agricultural regions, however, such organized groups are both fewer and smaller than in urban areas. Most rural residents work on the farm or in a small business—not for a large factory. Second, the income of rural residents is significantly less than that of other United States citizens. . . . Many rural families are . . . poor. . . . The combination of lack of health insurance and low income is the first major problem of health care in rural areas. Millions of rural residents put off visits to the doctor—endure needless suffering—because the bill would be too high. The retired farmer with arthritis, the middle-aged farmer with a bad back, the child of a young farmer with a fever: all wait. Maybe it will go away. The doctor's bill will be too much. . . .''

Problems of the nation's health-care system were analyzed by health officials of various Health, Education & Welfare Department agencies in a health-manpower legislative proposal dated Jan. 24, 1975. Among the findings of this HEW paper:

Delivery of personal health-care services to the nation's population is accomplished through a complex, pluralistic, largely private system involving several major components—consumers, product manufacturers, third party payers, state and local governments, education and training institutions, providers and provider institutions, and the federal government. A very broad national consensus has emerged during the last decade that the overall performance goal for this multifaceted system should be to provide access to adequate services at a reasonable cost for all persons, regardless of their socio-economic status. This consensus has been explicitly codified in the recently enacted National Health Planning & Resources Development Act of 1974.

There are generally recognized performance short-falls of the health-care system with respect to this overall goal: widely varying access to and utilization of services, uneven quality of available services and continuing escalation of service costs. Because the system is labor-intensive, it is not surprising that several major deficiencies and inefficiencies within the system that have been identified as directly related to these performance short-falls involve health manpower. The most pervasive of these problems are the following:

(1) Overall shortage and uneven geographical distribution of primary care services.* (2) Uneven geographical distribution of secondary and tertiary care (specialty) services, including apparent distortions (under- or over-supply in certain

---

*Working definition of primary care services: Provision of personal health services characterized by delivery of first contact health-care services; assumption of longitudinal responsibility for the patient regardless of the presence or absence of specific diseases; serving as referral entry point to specialized secondary and tertiary care services; and integration of physical, psychological and social aspects of health care to the limits of the capability of the practitioner.

specialties), in the national profile of specialty services. (3) High cost and uneven productivity of services delivery, associated in great measure with inefficient organization of service delivery systems. (4) Lack of uniform standards for assuring adequate levels of service quality.

These deficiencies and inefficiencies are persistent and interrelated *systemic conditions* of the health-care system which, through time, have grown more serious in nature. The conditions do not represent problems with just one component of the system (e.g., third party payors), but rather joint problems resulting from the structural and functional characteristics of the linkages among the system components, and of the components themselves. . . .

It is a generally accepted proposition that health manpower production systems must modify both their processes and outputs in order to contribute to a long-range attack on the four systematic conditions identified [above]. . . . Specifically, there is a broadly-based consensus that the following interrelated major changes in direction are needed:

(1) Improved Geographic Distribution of Manpower Output. (2) Increased Production Capacity and Output in Primary Care Manpower. (3) Increased Training in Team and Group Practice Modes. (4) Improved Specialty Profile of Manpower Output. (5) Standardization of Manpower Performance Qualifications. (6) Extension of System Capacity to Support Continued Competence. . . .

The necessity for the federal government to participate, indirectly or directly, in the health-care system in order to assure achievement of national health-care goals, has been historically established. In addition to direct operation of limited special purpose service delivery systems (*e.g.,* Department of Defense, Veterans Administration, Indian Health Service) and public health programs (*e.g.,* disease control and hazardous product protection), the federal government has conducted and fiscally supported biomedical research on a large scale.

The federal government's involvement in health-services delivery on a broader base has included financing the costs of health-care facilities, primarily hospitals, partial financing of health-care services for major segments of the population, and more recently, partial, sometimes total, financing of health planning and service agencies (*e.g.,* Neighborhood Health Centers). For over a decade, now, health-manpower development also has been partially financed in a substantial amount by the federal government through student assistance, institutional support and special project and program support.

The basic rationale for the federal activities listed above includes two major dimensions: achievement of the end-results desired as a matter of national public policy are (1) beyond the jurisdiction or resource capacity of the separate states, and/or (2) the competitive market economy system is unacceptably inefficient or ineffective.

The objective of the federal role in health-manpower development is to assure an adequate supply and an appropriate mix and distribution of qualified health personnel for the nation's health care system so that it can achieve national health care goals most efficiently and effectively. . . .

. . . Federal health manpower programs of institutional support and of general student assistance for manpower production at the less than post-baccalaureate levels do not appear necessary, or justified, to assure desired changes in those production systems. . . .

Post-baccalaureate training institutions and programs, on the other hand, must be viewed as vital national resources. It is most difficult for state and local jurisdictions, and for private organizations, to generate the fiscal resources necessary for these institutions to respond to nationwide needs. Federal programs of institutional support and student assistance, as well as targeted discretionary programs, are justified to assure that desired changes in those production systems occur.

The health professional schools, particularly medical and dental schools, are vital national resources from other perspectives than just their role as producers of manpower needed nationwide: these institutions perform the bulk of federally financed biomedical research and development and deliver a substantial amount of the nation's hospital-based patient care, much of it federally reimbursed. Most of these activities, separately funded through different federal agencies with separate program, policy and funding priorities, must be performed jointly by the schools. Because of these interrelationships, changes in priorities, policies or fund flows from one federal sponsor have profound effects on these jointly performed activities and their other outputs. Institutional support, therefore, in the form of a stable capitation-based operating subsidy under the federal health manpower program for assuring manpower production changes, should be viewed more broadly as helping to assure the financial viability of institutions, with multi-purpose functions of critical national importance.

The principal conclusion following from this basic rationale for determining federal role relationships with the nation's post-secondary education and training systems producing manpower for the delivery of personal health care services is that federal institutional assistance programs should be limited to schools of medicine, osteopathy, dentistry, podiatry, and public health. Schools of veterinary medicine would not be included. . . . Neither would schools of pharmacy, nursing and allied health be included under institutional assistance, but targeted student assistance and discretionary program support are necessary to assure desired changes in direction of these manpower production systems. . . .

Historically, the nation's health manpower production systems have responded well to federal encouragement to change. The post-baccalaureate health professional institutions, for example, earlier expanded their biomedical research capacity dramatically during the '50s and '60s. During the last decade, they have equally dramatically expanded their manpower production capacity and output. This latter goal has represented the major priority of federal health manpower programs of the last decade, with the bulk of federal funds expended targeted to that general purpose—a quantum increase in the supply of health manpower.

Current projections of manpower supply indicate that the output capacity of the nation's manpower production system is approaching a level that assures an adequate supply for the range of manpower requirements that are likely to be obtained during the '80s and beyond. . . . This suggests that the major federal priority should shift from encouraging further rapid and massive expansion of capacity to more targeted efforts to assure the changes in direction of manpower production systems identified [above]. . . .

The need for the federal government to shift from a priority of assuring a rapid and massive increase in health professional supply is justified by explicit recognition of the non-validity of what may have been an implicit assumption partially embodied in that priority. . . . The belief may have persisted that massive increases in professional manpower supply—even oversupply—would satisfactorily address those problems [listed above] through operation of the competitive market for physician services.

Two essential characteristics of a truly competitive market, for this approach to be effective, are: individual sellers (or buyers) have no discretionary power over the price of the service in the market and changes in supply do not effect demand at a given market price (supply and demand are independently determined). . . . [These conditions] do not hold for most health professionals, particularly physicians and dentists. Physicians enjoy considerable discretion over the demand for services by their patients and within fairly wide limits can set prices to attain chosen income levels. For these reasons, physicians can continue to choose practice specialties, settings and locations which do not alleviate specialty or geographic maldistribution problems in the face of various supply levels—even with "oversupply." Given the high cost of physician production, federal policies should guard against encouraging an oversupply. . . .

It is a generally accepted proposition that highly trained health personnel are being used for the performance of tasks that can be performed with comparable, adequate quality by personnel with less formal training. Programs for increasing manpower output in mid-level occupational levels and for inter-disciplinary 'team' training are included in the proposed consolidated discretionary target authority as direct approaches to these problems of improved utilization and productivity of health professionals. The productivity of manpower production systems is the target of another provision of the consolidated discretionary target authority which supports programs of educational research and development designed to improve the effectiveness and efficiency of those systems. Finally, the overall approach of increasing the nation's primary care capacity impacts on these deficiencies by guiding the health-care system away from inappropriate utilization of specialists for providing general primary care. . . .

Nixon & the Developing 'Crisis'

Nixon Administration & the Health-Care 'Crisis'

Richard M. Nixon was elected President of the United States in November 1968. In mid-1969, during his first year in office, Nixon warned that the nation was menaced with a health-care "crisis," and he ordered deep cuts in federal spending on medical programs.

Hospital Aid. Health, Education & Welfare Secretary Robert Finch March 25 proposed a "radical redirection" of federal programs for building health facilities. In a statement to a House Commerce subcommittee, Finch suggested replacing the $254 million annual Hill-Burton Act grant program for hospital construction with a $500 million annual loan-guarantee program focused on modernizing existing hospitals.

Finch also proposed giving states up to $150 million in block grants to expand medical facilities such as "outpatient clinics, neighborhood health centers, skilled nursing homes and structures designed to increase efficient sharing of hospital resources." His proposal, Finch said, would provide for such "known needs" as 164,000 extended-care beds, 177 more rehabilitation facilities and 872 ambulatory-care facilities.

Finch cited a need to redirect the program from the "rural emphasis" under the Hill-Burton Act.

HEW Moves to Cut Health Costs. The Department of Health, Education and Welfare (HEW) announced two actions, effective July 1, 1969, for curtailing rising costs of federal medical care programs. One regulation, announced June 26, called for hospitals and nursing homes under the medicare program to specify all costs incurred in providing service to the aged. The automatic "cost plus" fee previously paid by the government would be discontinued. HEW Secretary Robert H. Finch said that "after three years of experience we believe the costs" under medicare "shouldn't be determined in the future by the application of a flat percentage which increases directly in relation to increases in total costs, but should be specifically identified and thus recovered."

The second move, announced June 30, restricted payments to doctors and dentists in most states under the medicaid program to the Jan. 1, 1969 level, at least until July 1, 1970. After that date, payments would rise according to a formula based on the consumer price index. Previously, states had been allowed to set their own maximums on payments under the federal-state program. Under the new regulation, if payments at the Jan. 1 level were lower than customary charges among three-fourths of the physicians in a locality, the state could request permission from HEW to raise payments to the local level.

During a Senate Finance Committee hearing on medicaid and medicare costs July 2, Internal Revenue Service Commissioner Randolph W. Thrower announced that a special audit would be made of the tax returns of an estimated 10,000 doctors who had each received payments totaling at least $25,000 from the government under the programs.

Social Security Commissioner Robert M. Ball announced Sept. 26 that, beginning Jan. 1, 1970, medicare patients would be required to pay the first $52 of a hospital bill instead of the $44 payment previously required. Patient contributions for hospital stays of longer than 60 days and for nursing home stays of longer than 20 days were also to begin Jan. 1.

Fight on Health Post. Robert H. Finch, secretary of Health, Education and Welfare, said June 27, 1969 that he was "reluctantly and regretfully" ending an effort to have Dr. John H. Knowles appointed as assistant secretary for health and scientific affairs, the top health post in the government. The appointment was opposed by the American Medical Association (AMA) and conservative Congressional leaders, notably Sen. Everett Dirksen (R, Ill.).

Finch nominated Dr. Roger O. Egeberg, 65, dean of the School of Medicine of the University of Southern California, for the job June 28. He said the Egeberg appointment had not been cleared with the AMA.

Finch, who had offered the post to Knowles Jan. 15, said he was dropping his sponsorship of the appointment because the controversy would have impaired Knowles' effectiveness in the position. Knowles, 42, general administrator of the Massachusetts General Hospital in Boston, had taken positions on many medical issues at odds with AMA positions—he had emphasized preventive rather than curative medi-

cine; he had criticized private medicine for not meeting the needs of the elderly and the poor; and he had supported Medicare, more federal aid for hospitals and more group practice.

Egeberg's record was similarly liberal: he had supported medical care for the aged, comprehensive health insurance and use of public funds to help defray medical costs for the poor. Egeberg said his major problem in his new post would be "the delivery of medical care" to many millions of people.

In announcing Egeberg's appointment, Finch also outlined HEW's health program goals. They would be to control the "inflation of medical costs," including "new approaches" to Medicaid; to seek new ways to organize and deliver health services; to increase the number of physicians; to "push an integrated attack on our environmental health problems"; and to review family-planning and population problems.

There were indications, specifically from Dirksen June 24, that Finch had won the argument and that President Nixon would nominate Knowles. But the issue remained officially unresolved June 26. Among the factors reportedly influencing the President, was fear that insistence on Knowles' appointment would cause loss of vital votes on extension of the surtax bill. There were reports that Sen. John G. Tower (Tex.) and Rep. Bob Wilson (Calif.) had cast influential votes with Mr. Nixon against Knowles. They were chairmen of the Republican Campaign Committees in their respective houses of Congress, and the AMA, through its political arm, the American Medical Political Action Committee, was a large contributor to House and Senate candidates ($680,000 in 1968).

President Nixon had heightened the element of uncertainty over the appointment by his remark at his news conference June 19 that he would support Finch's recommendation on the post.

Some discontent within the party had emerged June 27: Sen. Jacob K. Javits (R, N.Y.) expressed concern that the AMA would be "a dominant factor" in determining the Administration's health policies; Sen. Edward W. Brooke (R, Mass.) said Mr. Nixon had yielded to "outrageous pressures" and spoke of the consequences of "such blatant disregard for the public interest"; Sen. Charles E. Goodell (R, N.Y.) said the decision involved a choice "on the basis of merit or politics" and "politics won."

Goodell had spoken out in the Senate June 18 against Dirksen's opposition to the Knowles appointment. "No one organization, no one man, should be permitted to dictate or veto a Presidential appointment of one so eminently qualified . . . " he said, and if the nomination were lost "the public interest has suffered a grievous defeat."

'Crisis' in Health Care? President Nixon warned July 10, 1969 that the nation faced a "massive crisis" in health care. At a White House news conference called to present a Health, Education and Welfare Department health program, the President gave his "unqualified support" to a series of HEW measures designed to prevent what Mr. Nixon warned would become a breakdown in health care services.

HEW Secretary Robert H. Finch and Roger O. Egeberg, assistant secretary-designate, presented an eight-page report outlining a series of steps planned or already instituted by the department to curb inflated medical costs and to distribute resources more effectively in the nation's medical system. The report called on private medicine to initiate "revolutionary change in medical care systems."

The report sharply criticized the federal-state Medicaid program covering health costs for the poor as "badly conceived and organized" and warned that a four-fold increase in the program's cost could be expected by 1975. It announced a new Task Force on Medicaid to be headed by HEW Undersecretary John G. Veneman and Blue Cross Associations President Walter J. McNerney. The task force was to plan measures to halt spiraling costs and develop long-range goals for Medicaid.

Also planned was an HEW Office of New Careers to train medical corpsmen returning from Vietnam to help relieve the medical manpower shortage.

Another committee was to be established to study ways of expanding industry's role in health programs for workers. The report called on the health insurance industry to develop wider and more effective coverage, and it urged medical schools to find ways of increasing enrollment and shortening training time.

Dr. Dwight L. Wilbur, president of the American Medical Association, July 10 pledged AMA cooperation in solving the nation's health care problems. He commended Finch for "seeking no easy but demoralizing way out through reducing the quality of care. . . . "

AMA Convention. The American Medical Association (AMA) opened its annual meeting in New York July 13 with 60 delegates angrily walking out of the association's House of Delegates session. They left after a coalition of young doctors and their radical supporters interrupted the meeting to denounce the AMA. Dr. Richard Kunnes, representing an alliance of liberal organizations of health professionals, told delegates that the "AMA is really the American Murderers Association." Kunnes, 27, was a senior resident in psychiatry at the Albert Einstein Hospital in New York.

When the meeting was resumed after a recess, Dr. Roger O. Egeberg, assistant secretary for health and scientific affairs in the Health, Education and Welfare Department, suggested that the delegates be patient with the demonstrators.

The AMA presented its "tax credit insurance" plan July 14, designed to nullify the medicaid program and prevent enactment of a national compulsory health insurance system. Under the AMA proposal, every citizen would be guaranteed optional health care through insurance company policies. Those who could not pay for policy coverage would be credited with benefits according to the amount of income tax they pay.

The AMA installed Dr. Gerald D. Dorman of New York City as its new president July 16 after police were summoned to prevent a threatened disruption by a coalition of radicals and liberal health groups. The delegates called in the police after they denied the demonstrators' request to address the 244-member House of Delegates during the installation ceremony. Kunnes said the planned demonstration was canceled because "of the incredible police power that had been summoned."

Governors for Compulsory Health Insurance. At the 61st annual National Governors Conference, held in Colorado Springs, Colo. Sept. 1–3, 1969, the nation's governors approved a resolution advocating a national compulsory health-insurance program. The proposal was drafted by a committee headed by Gov. Nelson A. Rockefeller (R, N.Y.).

The health-insurance resolution called for a program handled by private companies and financed through payroll deductions levied on employers and employes. Among the few dissenters were Govs. Ronald Reagan (R, Calif.) and Stanley K. Hathaway (R, Wyo.), who favored an amendment on behalf of the American Medical Association to make the program voluntary.

Health Research Funds Cut. A prospective 10% reduction in grants for medical research was announced Sept. 12 by top government health officials. Funds for continuing projects faced a 5% cut. The reductions, made necessary by budget cuts and inflation, were announced by Dr. Roger O. Egeberg, assistant secretary of health, education and welfare, and Dr. Robert Q. Marston, director of the National Institutes of Health.

The announcement followed reports Sept. 9 and 10 that NIH research grants up for renewal were being cut 20% and that 19 medical research centers across the country were expected to be closed because of a shortage of federal funds.

Egeberg said Sept. 12 the 19 centers probably would be closed.

Medicare Premium Hike Announced. Health, Education and Welfare Secretary Robert H. Finch said Dec. 26, 1969 that the $4 a month premium for Medicare would go up to $5.30 a month July 1, 1970. He said the $4 rate, set in December 1968, was "too low to cover costs during the current premium period" and that the solvency of the program should have been protected by increasing the premiums in December 1968.

Study scores Medicare waste. A staff study released by the Senate Finance Committee Feb. 9, 1970 criticized the fiscal administration of the Medicare and Medicaid programs and recommended legislation to set limits on fees paid to doctors. Copies of the 322-page report on abuses under federal health care programs had been made available Feb. 4. The committee had held hearings in July 1969 on preliminary findings of the study group.

The study said carriers under the Medicare program—private insurance groups such as Blue Shield that served as intermediaries between the federal government and doctors receiving payments—often paid more for Medicare patients than they ordinarily paid for their own subscribers. In allowing these payments, the study said, the Social Security Administration abandoned the provisions of the Medicare statute and "the clear Congressional intent" of the law and contributed to "enormous inflation" of doctors' costs under the program. (Medicare costs had doubled since the law went into effect in 1967 and Medicaid costs had quadrupled. In the fiscal year ending June 30, Medicare costs were predicted at about $8 billion and Medicaid costs at $5 billion.)

The report also contained statistics on thousands of doctors and groups of doctors who had received $25,000 a year or more in Medicare and Medicaid payments in 1968. To curb spiraling Medicare costs, the study group recommended that regional advisory groups be empowered to establish maximum fees for services covered under the program. The group also suggested that Medicaid fee schedules be established and that a new Medicaid fraud and abuse unit be set up to monitor state programs.

Administration comment—In testimony before the Finance Committee Feb. 25, Health, Education and Welfare Undersecretary John G. Veneman said the Nixon Administration favored renegotiation of Medicare and Medicaid fee schedules. He said that fee ceilings might have to be set for payments to doctors and hospitals. Veneman said that the statutes, which allowed "reasonable and customary charges" under the programs, had not "provided opportunity for major cost control efforts."

Higher spending budgeted. Nixon Feb. 2, 1970 submitted his budget for fiscal 1971.

Nixon requested that health funds be increased by $1.7 billion in 1971 to a total of $15 billion. $1.5 billion of the rise was to cover increases in the Medicare and Medicaid programs. For Medicare, spending was expected to rise $1.3 billion to $8.8 billion. To finance the program a rise in the Social Security payroll tax financing the program was recommended, as was an increase from $4 to $5.30 in the monthly premium paid by individuals for insurance for physicians' fees.

For Medicaid, outlays of $2.9 billion ($244 million higher) were requested. Legislation was to be submitted to limit the federal share of Medicaid costs in an attempt to direct the program more into preventive and acute medical treatment programs.

Family planning services were to be funded at a $92 million level ($34 million more).

Also increased were outlays for medical research, manpower training and construction of health facilities—to a $2.2 billion level.

The hospital construction program under the Hill-Burton Act was put at a $305 million outlay level with focus on out-patient and ambulatory care rather than on general buildings.

Expanded health care proposed. The Nixon Administration proposed March 25, 1970 to expand health-care services for elderly and poor Americans. The new proposal, outlined in a statement by Health, Education and Welfare Secretary Robert H. Finch and explained to reporters by HEW Undersecretary John G. Veneman, would offer persons covered by Medicare and Medicaid an optional preventive care program.

Finch said that "we're not getting our money's worth from Medicare and Medicaid." He contended that the new program, designated Medicare Part C, would provide better care at essentially the same cost. Finch said the plan was designed: "To see that all possible steps are taken to prevent illness, such as periodic examinations and appropriate immunizations; to treat illness as soon as possible to prevent it from becoming more serious; to avoid unnecessary hospitalization; and to provide a full range of services from a single source in a coordinated, efficient manner."

Under the new proposal, preventive care would be provided through prepaid group health programs currently available in about a dozen cities. Veneman said that the "Part C option could be designed to encourage the growth of medical maintenance organizations to serve not only older Americans under Medicare, but Medicaid and private consumers as well."

Hospital aid veto overridden. President Nixon's veto of the Hill-Burton hospital aid bill June 22, 1970 was overridden by Congress June 30. The bill thus became law. Authorizations for the Hill-Burton program, which since 1946 had aided 10,382 construction and modernization projects with the federal share of costs totaling about $3.5 billion, were due to expire June 30.

The House voted 279-98 June 25 to override the veto, the vote 27 more votes than the two-thirds majority of those present and voting required for override. The 212 Democrats voting to override the veto were joined by 67 Republicans. Only three Democrats—Reps. William M. Colmer (Miss.), John O. Marsh Jr. (Va.) and O. C. Fisher (Tex.)—voted to sustain the veto.

The Senate acted June 30, voting 76–19

to override the veto, or 12 more than the number required. Twenty-three Republican senators joined the 53 Democrats in the majority, while the 19 votes supporting Nixon were cast by Republicans.

Sen. Ralph W. Yarborough (D, Tex.), who had helped to draft the bill, summed up the outcome: "It shows that the nation's priorities must be reordered and . . . that the Congress is interested in reestablishing itself as a coequal branch of the government."

The bill, originally approved by Senate voice vote June 8 and 377–0 House vote June 10, authorized through fiscal 1971–73 $1.29 billion for categorical grants and $1.5 billion for federally guaranteed or direct loans.

Nixon had called this a "long step down the road of fiscal irresponsibility." The direct grant authorization was more than $350 million higher than the Administration request for fiscal 1971. The Administration also had proposed replacing the categorical grant program with other forms of aid—direct grants, direct loans and guaranteed loans. The direct grants it proposed to be used primarily for outpatient facilities and ambulatory care centers.

Health care reorganization urged. A Nixon Administration task force said June 29 that "new options, new goals and new attitudes" were needed to provide the nation with a workable health care system.

In a report to Health, Education and Welfare (HEW) Secretary Elliot L. Richardson, the panel said: "There isn't enough money and there aren't enough doctors to provide the needed care just on a fee-for-service basis." Rather than relying on private, individual practice, the panel recommended the country turn towards pre-paid health care plans, group practice and eventually, some form of national health insurance.

The 27-member panel, called the Task Force on Medicaid and Related Programs, echoed an earlier Administration proposal to supplement the government's health care services with a preventive care program.

The task force, headed by Blue Cross Association President Walter J. McNerney, said while more money was needed to upgrade health services already offered by the government, that "money alone will not guarantee either capacity or effectiveness to the system."

The panel said: "For two decades programs financing medical care, whether public or private, have been reinforcing traditional ways of providing service." To develop a more effective system, the group proposed that at least 5% of all Medicaid and Medicare funds—currently $11.6 billion a year —be devoted to development and implementation of new health care plans. The task force also asked Richardson to appoint a new study panel to devise a long-range plan to finance health care. In introducing the report at an HEW news conference, McNerney said the task force thought that national health insurance for all Americans was "desirable" but had not decided what form it should take.

In a discussion of the failures of Medicaid, the panel estimated that only one-third of the 30 to 40 million eligible persons actually received services under the program and that the cost of serving this fraction exceeded earlier estimates of funds needed to serve all those who were eligible.

The panel said: "The promise of Medicaid that some care, at least, would be available to all who needed it has vanished into the obscurity of state determinations of eligibility and the parsimony of state determinations of solvency." One of the key recommendations was that the federal government pay for all the basic Medicaid services, rather than funding on a state-federal matching basis as in the current program. The panel cautioned against relying on Medicaid indefinitely as a primary approach to health care for the poor.

U.S. health insurance proposed. A bipartisan Senate group introduced legislation Aug. 27, 1970 to create a comprehensive national health insurance plan by 1973 at a cost, based on current estimates, of $40 billion a year. The bill would replace federal health programs, such as Medicare and Medicaid, with a plan that would serve all Americans, regardless of age or income.

The bill, called the Health Security Act, was based on a plan proposed July 7 by the 100-member Committee on National Health Insurance, a panel set up by the late Walter P. Reuther and chaired by Reuther's successor as president of the United Automobile Workers, Leonard Woodcock. Members of the Reuther committee included Sen. Edward M. Kennedy (D, Mass.), who introduced the legislation, and three of 14 other senators co-sponsoring the bill. Other Reuther panel members were Houston heart specialist Dr. Michael E. DeBakey and National Urban League Executive Director Whitney M. Young Jr.

In introducing the legislation, Kennedy said: "Until we begin moving toward national health insurance, neither Congress nor the medical profession will ever take the basic steps that are essential to reorganize the system." The bill was designed to improve the way health care was delivered by encouraging group medical services and preventive medicine, setting national standards for hospitals and doctors, supplementing health manpower training programs and providing for the development of a national health policy.

Kennedy said the bill would not set up a European-style national health service, with facilities owned and doctors employed by the government. He said the bill's sponsors sought a "working partnership" in health care between public and private sectors of the economy.

Under the proposed legislation, a Health Security Trust Fund, similar to the Social Security Trust Fund, would be set up to receive an annual $24 billion in income and payroll taxes to finance 60% of the system. The remaining $16 billion of the $40 billion annual cost would come from general federal revenues, $6 billion of which was the current annual contribution to federal health programs to be superseded by the new plan.

All services "required for personal health" would be covered under the proposal except for long-term institutional care, psychiatric and dental care and some drugs and medical appliances. Kennedy said the exceptions were "dictated by inadequacies in existing resources or in management potentials." Other areas not covered would be the cost of nonprescription drugs and personal items such as toothbrushes. It was estimated that the public would have to pay $16 billion a year for health service not covered under the plan.

In addition to Kennedy, the Democratic sponsors of the bill were Sens. Ralph W. Yarborough (Tex.), George

SELECTED INDICATORS OF HEALTH STATUS (annual rates)			
	1950	1960	1970
Birth rate (per 1,000 population)	24.1	23.7	18.4
Death rate (per 1,000 population)	9.6	9.5	9.5
Average life expectancy at birth in years	68.2	69.7	70.9
Infant mortality rate (deaths under 1 year of age per 1,000 live births)	29.2	26.0	20.0
Leading causes of death (per 100,000 population):			
Diseases of the heart	355.5	369.0	362.0
Cancer	139.8	149.2	162.8
Cerebrovascular disease	104.0	108.0	101.9
Accidents	60.6	52.3	56.4
Tuberculosis, all forms	22.5	6.1	2.6
Kidney diseases	16.4	6.7	3.7
Diabetes	16.2	16.7	18.9
Cirrhosis of liver	9.2	11.3	15.5

S. McGovern (S.D.), Walter F. Mondale
(Minn.), Claiborne Pell (R.I.), Philip
A. Hart (Mich.), Alan Cranston (Calif.),
Harold E. Hughes (Iowa), Birch Bayh
(Ind.), Lee Metcalf (Mont.), Eugene
J. McCarthy (Minn.), Edmund S.
Muskie (Me.) and Stephen M. Young
(Ohio). The two Republican sponsors,
who along with Yarborough and Ken-
nedy served on the Reuther panel, were
Sens. John Sherman Cooper (Ky.) and
William B. Saxbe (Ohio).

Medical school reforms urged. The Car-
negie Commission on Higher Education,
in a report that took it three years,
said Oct. 29, 1970 that the traditional
"biological research" emphasis of medical training in the U.S. was "no longer
adequate" to meet the nation's health
care needs in the 1970s.

The report, issued in Los Angeles during a meeting of the Association of American Medical Colleges, urged medical
schools to also concentrate on delivery of
health care services and to rely more on
other segments of universities to train
medical students in the sciences and other
disciplines.

The 19-member commission, headed
by Dr. Clark Kerr, said medical education over the last 60 years was formed
largely on a model developed in a classic
report by Dr. Abraham Flexner in 1910.
The Flexner Report, the commission
said, had great influence in upgrading the
level of medical education by emphasizing
scientific research and concentrating on
the quality of teaching. But the panel
said the Flexner model "largely ignores
health care delivery outside the medical
school and its own hospital."

The commission said "Americans deserve and can afford better health care."
"Although the best medical care in this
country is as good as any in the world,"
the report said, "many Americans receive
inferior care." In mortality rates, the
commission said, the U.S. ranked low
among 22 industrial nations—19th in
male, 6th in female and 15th in infant
life expectancy. The report also cited
"weaknesses" in the U.S. system of private health insurance—inadequate cov-

erage for outpatient, dental and psychiatric needs; "overutilized" hospital services and coverage "poorly designed to
encourage" preventive care.

The panel said "the most serious shortages of professional personnel in any major occupational group in the United
States are in the health services." Claim-
ing that there were more qualified students than places to train them, the commission asked for more medical schools
and shortened time requirements for
medical training from eight to six years
for doctors and from four to three years
for dentists.

The commission urged medical schools
to provide more opportunity for women
and for students from minority groups.
The panel said the nation also needed better training for paramedical workers to
qualify them to perform services now
done by physicians.

The commission said a federal investment of $1 billion by 1980 would be
needed to upgrade medical training. The
report also called for an equilization of
the financial burden among states and between states and the federal government.
The panel urged uniform tuition fees in
medical and dental schools.

Among other recommendations, the
commission asked that a National Health
Manpower Commission be established,
that a voluntary health services corps be
created to serve low income and rural
areas in the U.S. and that health education centers with medical school affili-
ations be developed throughout the country to better relate medical training to
health care delivery in the community.

Ghetto clinics supported. Dr. Walter
C. Bornemeier, president of the American Medical Association (AMA), called
on the AMA Nov. 29, 1970 to provide
technical assistance and help doctors
obtain financing so they could establish
private clinics in the nation's ghettos.
Bornemeier said such clinics would
serve to give the poor access to medical
care "on the same basis as the most
affluent citizens."

He also urged the AMA to reverse
its long-standing policy and encourage

individual physicians to seek and accept federal loans or grants to help them finance such clinics in poverty neighborhoods.

(In the past, the AMA had opposed acceptance of financial assistance from the federal government in connection with the practice of medicine.)

Bornemeier said the AMA should take steps to assure that the proposed neighborhood medical facilities would be controlled by the medical profession. Unless those steps were taken, he said, "medicine will default to hospitals, to government, and to social service agencies who even now vie for the control of the mechanisms which deliver medical care."

Bornemeier asked his association to "formulate and implement" a program to help the doctors establish the ghetto clinics. He said the service should include "assistance with architectural drawings, site requirements, management and operational plans, staffing requirements, equipment schedules and suggestions for obtaining financing from local banks."

Family practice. The House Dec. 8, 1970 and the Senate Dec. 10 approved a bill authorizing $225 million over a three-year period for grants to medical schools and hospitals to provide departmental training in family medical prac-

tice. The bill, designed to help relieve a shortage of doctors in general practice, also would provide grants for development and planning of such programs, and a study of malnutrition problems was to be made with a view toward establishing courses at medical schools. But President Nixon announced Dec. 26 that he had "pocket" vetoed the measure during Congress' six-day Christmas recess.

The veto, however, was ruled invalid Aug. 15, 1973 by U.S. District Judge Joseph C. Waddy in Washington, and the U.S. Court of Appeals for the District of Columbia upheld Waddy's ruling Aug. 14, 1974.

Waddy held that "the short recess" of Congress did not prevent the bill's return for reconsideration, therefore, the veto was invalid and the bill had became law without the President's signature.

Sen. Edward M. Kennedy (D, Mass.), a co-sponsor of the bill and plaintiff in the suit, acted as the attorney of argument in the case.

Family planning bill passed. A bill authorizing $382 million for fiscal 1971–73 for family planning services and population research activities was approved by the House Dec. 8, 1970 and Senate Dec. 10. It called for the establishment of an Office of Population Affairs within the Health, Education and Welfare Department.

LIFE EXPECTANCY BY SEX AT SELECTED AGES, BY SELECTED COUNTRIES: 1970

Country	Age in years					
	35		55		65	
	Male	Female	Male	Female	Male	Female
Sweden	39.8	44.0	21.9	25.6	14.4	17.2
Canada	37.8	43.6	20.5	25.4	13.7	17.4
France	37.2	43.9	20.2	25.7	13.4	17.4
Italy	37.5	42.7	20.0	24.3	13.0	16.1
United Kingdom: England and Wales	36.6	42.2	18.9	24.1	12.0	16.0
Germany: Federal Republic	36.2	41.3	18.9	23.1	11.9	15.0
United States:						
Total	36.0	42.4	19.5	24.8	13.1	17.0
White	36.5	43.0	19.6	25.0	13.1	17.1
Other	32.5	38.5	18.5	22.7	13.3	16.4

Gross Enrollment & Estimated Total Net Enrollment Under Private Insurance Plans 1940–70

Hospital Benefits Enrollments

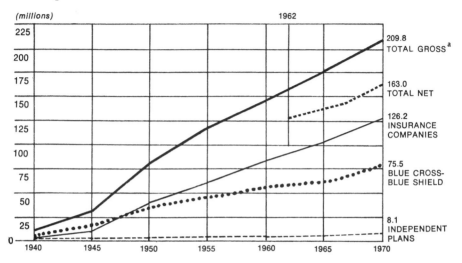

Surgical Benefits Enrollments

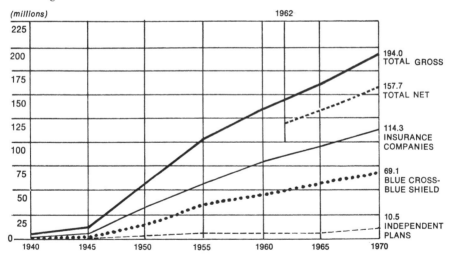

a/Gross enrollment contains duplication because of multiple coverage of individuals through supplementary plans and policies. The net number of different persons covered (which eliminates duplication) is estimated for 1962 and 1967 by the Social Security Administration on the basis of household surveys. The 1970 estimate is derived by applying HIAA percentage increase in net enrollment to the 1969 estimate (not shown).

Source: U.S. Social Security Administration, *Social Security Bulletin,* Vol. 35, No. 2 (February 1972), p. 8.

From Committee for Economic Development

It also required development of a five-year plan for extension of family-planning services to all persons desiring them, for research programs and for training of personnel. Grants to state agencies were authorized to help provide family planning services. Low-income families were to have priority in receiving cost-free family planning services.

Personnel aid for poor areas. The Emergency Health Personnel Act was passed by the House Dec. 18, 1970 and by the Senate Dec. 21 and was signed by Nixon Dec. 31. The measure authorized the government to assign personnel, including doctors, to areas with critical medical manpower shortages. The bill was sponsored by Sens. Warren G. Magnuson (D, Wash.) and Henry M. Jackson (D, Wash.).

The assignment of personnel would be made by the Public Health Service, and the salaries of the personnel would be paid by the federal government, which also had the options of setting no fees for the services performed or of setting fees and having them paid directly to the federal treasury or paid through Medicare or Medicaid programs.

Funding for the program was authorized at the $10 million level for fiscal 1971, $20 million in fiscal 1972 and $30 million in fiscal 1973.

Nixon's Health Program

President Nixon in 1971 proposed a major restructuring of the U.S. health-care system—a "new National Health Strategy." The program was announced in a special message Feb. 18 after Nixon, in his State-of-the-Union message, had given advance notice of his plan.

Plan previewed. A brief outline of the forthcoming Nixon health plan was made public by the President Jan. 22, before a joint session of Congress, in his 1971 State-of-the-Union address.

Nixon said that Congress would be offered "a far-reaching set of proposals for improving America's health care

and making it available more fairly to more people." This would include: (a) "a program to insure that no American family will be prevented from obtaining basic medical care by inability to pay"; (b) "a major increase in and redirection of aid to medical schools to greatly increase the number of doctors and other health personnel"; (c) incentives to improve the delivery of health services to send medical care into areas lacking adequate services, to make greater use of medical assistants and to slow the "alarming rise" in medical care costs; and (d) programs "to encourage better preventive medicine."

In requesting an additional $100 million appropriation for an effort to find a cancer cure, Nixon urged a national commitment similar to those that "split the atom and took man to the moon."

Nixon for 'new National Health Strategy.' Nixon Feb. 18 submitted to Congress a 17-page message outlining his proposals for "a comprehensive national health insurance program, one in which the public and the private sectors would join in a new partnership to provide adequate health insurance for the American people." The insurance program was part of an overall plan that Nixon described as "a new National Health Strategy."

The new plan proposed:

■ A National Health Insurance Standards Act, under which employers and employes would be required to share the costs of basic health insurance to cover all workers and their families.

■ A Family Health Insurance Plan to cover poor families not included under the National Health Insurance Standards Act. Expanded insurance would be coupled with an increasing use of prepaid health centers, called Health Maintenance Organizations (HMO).

(The Administration's proposals were designed to cover private sector workers and welfare families. However, it would exclude Armed Forces personnel and civilian federal employes, who "would continue to have their own insurance programs," and the elderly, who would "continue to have Medicare.") .

Proportion of Consumer Health-Care Expenditures
Met by Private Health Insurance 1950–70

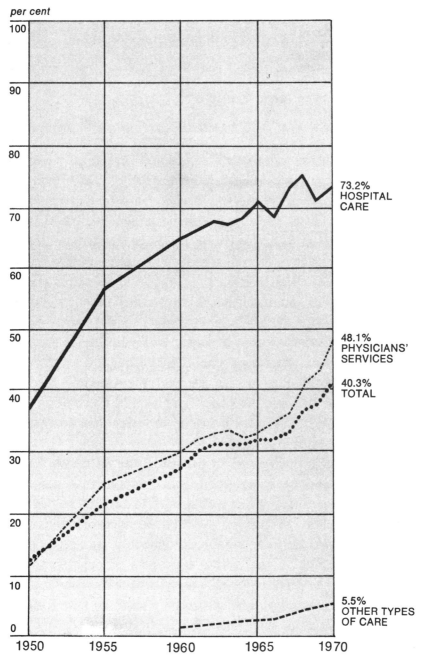

Source: U. S. Social Security Administration, Social Security Bulletin, Vol. 35, No. 2 (February 1972), p. 19.
From Committee for Economic Development

Nixon preceded his proposals with a brief review of recent developments in health-care and with an assessment of the current situation. He said:

"In the last 12 months alone, America's medical bill went up 11%, from $63 to $70 billion. In the last *ten* years, it has climbed 170%, from the $26 billion level in 1960. Then we were spending 5.3% of our Gross National Product on health; today we devote almost 7% of our GNP to health expenditures. This growing investment in health has been led by the federal government. In 1960, Washington spent $3.5 billion on medical needs—13% of the total. This year it will spend $21 billion—or about 30% of the nation's spending in this area.

"But what are we getting for all this money? For most Americans, the result of our expanded investment has been more medical care and care of higher quality. A profusion of impressive new techniques, powerful new drugs, and splendid new facilities has developed over the past decade. During that same time, there has been a 6% drop in the number of days each year that Americans are disabled. Clearly there is much that is *right* with American medicine.

"But there is also much that is wrong. One of the biggest problems is that fully 60% of the growth in medical expenditures in the last ten years has gone not for additional services but merely to meet price inflation. Since 1960, medical costs have gone up twice as fast as the cost of living. Hospital costs have risen five times as fast as other prices. For growing numbers of Americans, the cost of care is becoming prohibitive. And even those who can afford most care may find themselves impoverished by a catastrophic medical expenditure.... For some Americans— especially those who live in remote rural areas or in the inner city—care is simply not available. The quality of medicine varies widely with geography and income. Primary care physicians and out-patient facilities are in short supply in many areas, and most of our people have trouble obtaining medical attention on short notice. Because we pay so little attention to preventing disease and treating it early, too

many people get sick and need intensive treatment...."

Nixon said that his "new National Health Strategy," which "will marshall a variety of forces in a coordinated assault on a variety of problems, ... should be built on four basic principles": (1) Assuring equal access; (2) balancing supply and demand; (3) organizing for efficiency, (A) emphasizing health maintenance, (B) preserving cost consciousness; (4) and building on strength.

Among major elements of the message:

National Health Insurance Standards Act—Passage of the act would require all employers, beginning July 1, 1973, to provide "basic health insurance coverage for their employes." The minimum coverage, which would substantially exceed most programs currently in effect, would "pay for hospital services—both in the hospital and outside of it—for full maternity care, well-baby care (including immunizations), laboratory services and certain other medical expenses." Chronic psychiatric or extended nursing home care would not be included.

Each employe and each member of his family would be covered for a minimum of $50,000 over the life of the agreement—far above the upper limits of most existing insurance policies. After the $50,000 had been exceeded, a patient could still collect benefits of at least $2,000 yearly, or, if healthy, accumulate $2,000 yearly in future credits. Premiums and deductibles would vary according to circumstances and geographical regions and workers would be allowed to purchase membership in a Health Maintenance Organization (HMO) under the insurance plan.

The insurance plan would be paid for by employers and employes. "A ceiling on how much employes could be asked to contribute would be set at 35% during the first 2½ years of operation and 25% thereafter," according to the Administration proposal.

Family Health Insurance Plan—This plan, to be "fully financed and administered by the federal government," would cover "all poor families (with children) headed by self-employed or unemployed persons whose income is below a certain level. For a family of four persons, the eligibility ceiling would be $5,000." Charges would be based on income—for the poorest there would be no charges, and as "family income increased beyond a certain level ($3,000 in the case of a four-person family) the family itself would begin to assume a greater share of the costs."

The plan, which would also go into effect July 1, 1973, would cost about $1.2 billion in additional federal funds in the first year. "Since states would no longer bear any share of this cost, they would be relieved of a considerable burden," Nixon said. He added that as an encouragement to states "to use part of these savings to supplement federal benefits, the federal government would agree to bear the costs of administering a consolidated federal-state benefit package."

In addition, the message added that the "federal government would also contract with local committees to review local practices and to ensure that adequate care is being provided in exchange for federal payments. Private insurers, unions and employes would be invited to use these same committees to review the utilization of their benefits if they wished to do so."

Under the Family Health Insurance Plan, the parts of the current Medicaid program designed to help most welfare families would be eliminated; the Medicaid provisions covering the aged poor, the blind and the disabled would continue.

Other details of the overall program— Each state would be required to establish "special insurance pools which would offer insurance at reasonable group rates to people who did not qualify for other programs: the self-employed, for example, and poor risk individuals who often cannot get insurance."

Nixon proposed a change in Medicare regulations to allow beneficiaries to join HMOs and to "consolidate the financing of Part A of Medicare—which pays for hospital care—and Part B— which pays for outpatient services provided the elderly person himself pays a monthly fee to qualify for this protection." Nixon proposed that this monthly

fee be paid for by an increase in the Social Security wage base. Other Administration-proposed Medicare changes included a rise in the current $50 deductible for Part B and an increase in the amount the elderly would have to pay for hospitilization.

Nixon rejected a nationalization of the health insurance industry on the grounds that there was no need for such action and that it could be dangerous by denying people "the right to choose how they will pay for their health care," and removing "competition from the insurance system—and with it an incentive to experiment and innovate."

The program proposed extension of planning grants, totaling $45 million in the 1972 budget, to potential HMO sponsors, as well as loan guarantees to finance HMO initial capital requirements up to a total of $500,000 per HMO. In addition, the plan proposed that HMOs hold direct federal contracts as a means of overriding partial or total legal barriers against contract practice or practice by non-doctors in more than 20 states.

The program recommended creation of new federally-financed family health centers in urban and rural areas with a scarcity of medical care; the centers would be linked to hospitals or HMOs for comprehensive care. "Health education centers," for the training of doctors and other medical workers, were also proposed for scarcity areas.

To encourage increased medical school enrollment and shorter courses, the plan proposed that medical, dental and osteopathic schools be given $6,000 in federal aid annually for each student graduated—called "capitation grants."

The plan proposed creation of a "National Health Service Corps, made up largely of dedicated and public spirited young health professionals who will serve in areas which are now plagued by critical manpower shortages."

Nixon also recommended that the nation's "allied health personnel training programs be expanded by 50% over 1971 levels, to $29 million, and that $15 million of this amount be devoted to training physicians' assistants."

Nixon pledged the creation of a special commission to study the increasing problem of malpractice suits against doctors.

Mixed reaction to plan. The Nixon National Welfare Rights Organization and the National Council of Senior Citizens, both charging that it would provide the needy and the elderly with less federally paid health care than they currently receive under Medicaid and Medicare programs.

The American Medical Association (AMA) supported the program. AMA President Walter C. Bornemeier described the package Feb. 21 as "neither monolithic nor inflexible," and one which "preserves the many things that are good about our present health care system."

Sen. Edward Kennedy (D, Mass.), chairman of the health subcommittee of the Senate Committee on Labor and Public Welfare, Feb. 18 called the family health insurance plan "poorhouse medicine" and the employer insurance plan "wasteful and ineffective." He added that the proposals would give private insurors "a windfall of billions of dollars annually." Kennedy had earlier introduced legislation which would create a national health insurance system operated totally by the federal government.

Sen. Abraham Ribicoff (D, Conn.), a former secretary of health, education and welfare, Feb. 19 praised the Administration for being the first to seriously propose "a program to improve the health care of all Americans whatever their income and wherever they live." But he added: "If private health insurance is to survive, it must change its basic philosophy and act as an advocate on behalf of those in need of medical care and not as a neutral independent conduit which simply distributes money throughout the system."

Dr. H. Barry Waldman of the State University of New York at Stony Brook noted in the November–December 1971 issue of Medical Care, however, that "a national health insurance program which did involve common carriers was established in

Great Britain, in 1911, and was discarded in 1946." He suggested that "the lessons ... from the 35 years of experience with this program should be of value" in U.S. deliberations. Waldman cited Lord Beveridge's summary of findings in 1942 of "the major disadvantages of the approved society [insurance company] system": "(1) Lack of continuity when the individual changed his employment. (2) Conflicts of interest between different administrative authorities. (3) Different procedures for determination of claims, appeals and decision-making. (4) Additional administrative costs. (5) The impossible task the individual faced when attempting to select the most worthwhile society."

Kennedy plan attacked. Addressing the American Medical Association convention in Atlantic City June 22, President Nixon urged doctors to join the Administration's fight against drug abuse and assailed a proposal for "nationalized compulsory health insurance." The latter, a reference, confirmed later by a White House spokesman, to a plan offered by Sen. Edward M. Kennedy (D, Mass.), was "the most expensive" plan under discussion, Nixon said, and "would actually do the most to hurt American health care."

"The Administration's health insurance partnership would build on the strength of the present health care system," he said. "Nationalized health insurance would tear that system apart."

Nixon attacked the Kennedy plan, which he did not refer to by name, on the grounds it would triple the average family's federal tax costs for health programs and would lead to "complete federal domination of our medical system." Kennedy's proposal, which had a bipartisan liberal backing in Congress and was endorsed by organized labor, was a comprehensive plan underwriting almost all medical expenses for everyone through general tax revenues and a payroll tax earmarked for health care.

The Administration's health care plan was based on private insurance paid through payroll contributions by the employer and employe. Coverage for poor families would be financed from federal funds. The plan would not cover an estimated 15 million persons who were neither employed nor poor.

The AMA was backing its own plan providing income tax credits for the purchase of private health policies.

The AMA adopted a declaration June 23 saying that every doctor had the right "to choose whom he will serve and the conditions under which" he would serve them. Some doctors indicated that the declaration served notice that AMA members might withhold their services if they disliked the terms of a national health insurance policy system.

Programs Checked, Government Action

HEW moves to curb Medicaid fraud. The Department of Health, Education & Welfare issued final rules March 26, 1971 to prevent fraud by doctors, dentists and other dispensers of medical services under Medicaid. The regulations had been published in proposed form in 1969, following hearings by the Senate Finance Committee on charges of fraud in the Medicare and Medicaid programs.

Under the regulations, states would have to spot-check clients from among the 17 million participants in the $6 billion Medicaid program to determine whether reported services had actually been received. States would also have to file annual information returns with the Internal Revenue Service showing amounts paid to providers of Medicaid service, who would be identified by name, address and Social Security number. The regulations also provided for state and federal prosecution for Medicaid fraud.

(John D. Twiname, administrator of HEW's Social and Rehabilitation Service, said Feb. 16 that the department had ordered state agencies to make annual reviews of Medicaid patients in nursing homes and mental institutions to see that proper care was being given. Twiname said, "We are simply not going to permit Medicaid patients to be put into human warehouses and forgotten.")

Programs for aged assessed. The Senate Special Committee on Aging, in a report released April 4, 1971, said that housing, health and retirement income programs for older Americans continued to be "fragmented" and "haphazard."

Noting that the cost of premiums for the part of Medicare paid for by the elderly had nearly doubled since the program began in 1965, the report recommended that Medicare be entirely financed through payroll taxes and general revenues. The report also supported automatic cost-of-living rises in Social Security benefit levels.

A federal advisory council, in a report issued April 3, also recommended that the entire Medicare program be paid for through payroll taxes and federal revenues and that Social Security laws be changed to permit automatic cost-of-living adjustments. The 13-member council, headed by former Health, Education and Welfare Secretary Arthur S. Flemming, had been named in 1969 to review Social Security and Medicare as required by a provision of the Social Security Act.

The panel asked that Medicare be expanded to cover partial payment of prescription drugs for out-of-hospital use. It urged that Medicare be extended to persons receiving disability benefits under Social Security. The report also recommended extended Medicare coverage at a lower cost for persons with long illnesses.

President Nixon June 25 urged a national effort to improve the low status of many nursing homes for the elderly in America.

Deploring the "tragic isolation and shameful neglect of older Americans," the President cited substandard nursing homes that were "unsanitary and ill-equipped, overcrowded and understaffed." He made his appeal before a joint meeting in Chicago of the National Retired Teachers Association and the American Association of Retired Persons.

Nixon suggested the possibility of withholding federal funds from substandard homes. Medicare and Medicaid funds, he said, should not go to such homes and "subsidize them."

While many nursing homes were "outstanding institutions," he told the gathering, too many were considered "little more than warehouses for the unwanted, dumping grounds for the dying" and served "mainly to keep older people out of sight and out of mind, so that no one will notice their degradation and despair."

Notice should be taken, Nixon said, and he was confident "that our federal, state and local governments, working together with the private sector, can do much to transform the nursing home." He said this was the Administration's goal.

Consumer advocate Ralph Nader and six recent graduates of Miss Porter's School in Farmington, Conn. said Dec. 17 that the federal government should take steps to improve conditions in nursing homes since federal money paid half the homes' bills. The group's 12-week study entitled "Nursing Homes for the Aged: The Agony of One Million Americans" related the experiences of the six young women in their investigation of 24 Eastern nursing homes.

A federal district court judge in Washington ordered the HEW Department to produce (for the press) Medicare inspection reports on any of several thousand nursing homes receiving Medicare payments (reported Sept. 10, 1972). The order ended a three-year fight by newsman Mal Schechter against HEW's contention that the information was covered by the secrecy provisions of a 1939 law.

Schechter had requested records of inspections at 14 homes in the Washington area, and at a Marietta, Ohio home where 32 persons died in a 1970 fire.

Child care ordered. The Department of Health, Education and Welfare Nov. 9, 1971 ordered the 48 states in the Medicaid program to provide routine medical screening of all needy children, and to treat all hearing and eye defects and some dental problems uncovered in the tests. (Alaska and Arizona were not participants in Medicaid.)

The order, which would aid about 13 million children up to age 21 by 1974, would cost $200 million, 54% in federal and 46% in state funds. Congress had mandated that the regulations be effected by July 1, 1969, but HEW Secretary Elliot Richardson said state budgetary problems had caused the two-year delay.

A spokesman for the HEW announced Nov. 22, 1972 that 13 states and the Virgin Islands faced cutbacks in federal Medicaid assistance because they had failed to begin preventive medical and dental screening programs for the children of Medicaid-eligible parents, as required by the 1967 Social Security Act.

In addition, the states faced losses of 1% in AFDC payments under a provision of the 1972 Social Security Act requiring states to inform welfare recipients that the screening programs were available.

Some seven million children annually will be given medical exams by 1974, according to HEW, at a cost of $200 million, on a basis of 54% federal-46% state funds.

Health personnel training. Two health personnel training bills were given final Congressional approval by the Senate Oct. 19, 1971 and the House Nov. 9 and were signed by President Nixon Nov. 18. The bills, which authorized $3.7 billion over three years, were designed to raise the number of practicing physicians by 30% (to 436,000) by 1978, and the number of nurses by over 50% (to 1,100,000).

The bills provided construction grants for new and expanding medical, dental, veterinary, pharmacy and osteopathic schools. Schools expanding their enrollment would also get per capita yearly grants of $2,500–$4,000, with further incentives for allowing students to graduate in three years.

Professional schools would receive $1,000 for each student training as physicians' assistant or dental therapist, and nursing schools would receive a total of $885 million.

The bill included incentives to make more doctors available for family practice and for service in rural and central city areas. Increased enrollment of minority and disadvantaged students would be encouraged, and sex discrimination

Personal Care Expenditures by Source of Funds

$10.4 Billion, 1950 | $71.9 Billion, 1972

Left bar — $10.4 Billion, 1950:

Percent	Category
100%	
20.2%	$2.1 BILLION PUBLIC
3.0%	$0.3 BILLION
8.5%	$0.9 BILLION INSURANCE PAYMENTS
68.3%	$7.1 BILLION DIRECT PAYMENTS
0%	

Right bar — $71.9 Billion, 1972:

Category	Percent
100%	
$8.4 BILLION MEDICARE	11.6%
$7.3 BILLION MEDICAID	10.2%
$11.1 BILLION OTHER PUBLICa/	15.4%
$1.0 BILLION	1.4%
$19.0 BILLION INSURANCE PAYMENTS	26.4%
$25.1 BILLION DIRECT PAYMENTS	34.9%
0%	

INDUSTRIAL SERVICES

a/ Includes workmen's compensation medical benefits, general hospital and medical care (primarily mental and charity hospitals), Defense Department hospital and medical care, veterans hospital and medical care, maternal and child health services, school health, O.E.O. neighborhood health centers, medical vocational rehabilitation, and temporary disability insurance.

Note: Some numbers do not total, due to rounding.

Sources: U. S. Social Security Administration, *Social Security Bulletin*, Vol. 35, No. 1 (January 1972), p. 13; newly released data for 1972 were obtained from U. S. Social Security Administration, Office of Research and Statistics.

From Committee for Economic Development

would be prohibited in recipient schools.

The Administration, which originally asked for a much smaller program of guaranteed loans, supported the House bill on which the final bill was based. But Rep. Paul G. Rogers (D, Fla.) author of the bill, reported Nov. 9 that the Office of Management and Budget was planning to spend only half of the authorized funds.

Nixon said that the enactment of the Comprehensive Health Manpower Training Act of 1971 was a "first step" toward balancing the supply of health care with a growing demand for medical services.

Fiscal '73 budget. Nixon submitted his fiscal 1973 budget to Congress Jan. 24, 1972. Among health items included:

The year's outlays for research by the National Institutes of Health were to increase by $177 million to a total of $1.4 billion. Major initiatives were planned for cancer research, with a $335 million funding, up $57 million, and for heart and lung disease research, which was allotted $221 million, a $30.6 million increase.

Medicare outlays for health insurance for the aged would rise from $9 billion to $10.4 billion, and the Administration planned some changes in the Medicare program, to provide health benefits for the disabled and to eliminate the monthly premium for coverage of doctor bills.

Another increase was budgeted for Veterans Administration health care spending, a rise of $254 million to a $2.5 billion total.

A major reduction was planned for the Medicaid program of health care for the poor—from a $4.4 billion level to $3.4 billion. But the reduction was offset by an accounting change shifting some outlays into an earlier fiscal year (1972) and enabling a $1 billion advance payment in matching funds to be paid states for Medicaid and welfare cash grants.

The Administration also envisioned a shift of emphasis in the program away from costly hospital treatment to less-expensive outpatient care.

Health industry curbs sought. The Nixon Administration Feb. 10, 1972 submitted to Congress proposals to regulate the private health care delivery system, as amendments to its 1971 national health insurance plan.

Health insurance companies, including Blue Cross and Blue Shield plans, would be required, under strict state supervision, to clarify to consumers all rates, benefits, and alternate policies available. Rates would have to be approved by the states, which would also conduct public annual audits. The federal government could take over regulation two years after passage of the bill if a state proved ineffective.

The federal treasury would assume the obligations of insolvent companies, and recover the funds from other companies in the state.

Doctors, hospitals and nursing homes would be required to provide price lists to consumers, a practice temporarily required by the Price Commission over American Medical Association objections.

To encourage regional planning of health facilities, insurance premiums and federal funds would be denied to hospitals or nursing homes built or expanded without approval of state or regional planning bodies.

Free hospital care ordered. Health, Education and Welfare (HEW) Secretary Elliot L. Richardson announced new rules April 18, 1972 to enforce requirements that all hospitals and health care facilities that have received federal aid provide a minimum amount of free services to poor people.

Under the rules, which took effect in 30 days, any institution that had ever accepted funds under the Hill-Burton Act would have to provide free services to poor people equivalent to at least 5% of its operating cost and at least 25% of its net income, or face penalties ranging to revocation of its license. Institutions in financial difficulties, or in areas with few poor people, would be exempted.

The order was issued after five class action suits were filed against HEW, mostly by poverty lawyers working with

Office of Economic Opportunity funds, in the District of Columbia, West Virginia, Florida, Louisiana and Colorado. Nationally, 3,608 non-profit hospitals and 2,700 other facilities were affected.

Health Service Corps inaugurated. The newly organized National Health Service Corps assigned its first 288 professional personnel May 23 to 122 communities with inadequate services in 39 states and the District of Columbia.

The volunteers, who would be fulfilling their draft obligation, would be paid with federal money, with doctors receiving $12,000–$15,000 annually. The 152 doctors, 72 nurses, 20 dentists and 44 other personnel included in the first assignment would begin serving in rural and urban slum areas in July.

Patients would be billed according to ability to pay.

U.S. certifies homes. HEW Undersecretary John G. Veneman announced July 19 that 6,200 of the nation's 7,000 nursing homes had been certified to receive full Medicare payments.

Half the 30,000 patients at the 606 decertified homes were residents of 11 homes for the mentally retarded in New York state. These homes were reclassified as intermediate care facilities, and would receive payments, but at a 30% lower rate.

Some 4,700 of the approved facilities were given six-month certifications, pending removal of "correctible deficiencies" in buildings or staff. Action had not been completed on over 200 other homes.

Medicare-Medicaid changes. Under a compromise Social Security-welfare bill cleared by Congress Oct. 17, 1972 and signed by the President Oct. 30, Medicare coverage was extended to 1.5 million people receiving disability benefits for at least 24 months and Medicare payments were provided for some chiropractic and kidney dialysis treatments. The bill also set up

doctor "peer review" groups to hold down Medicare and Medicaid inefficiencies. Senate-House conferees, however, had eliminated a disputed proposal to extend Medicare to cover some drugs for non-hospital patients and glasses, dental and podiatric devices.

U.S. blood system urged. President Nixon told Congress March 2 that he had called on the Department of Health, Education and Welfare (HEW) to draw up a plan for an "efficient nationwide blood collection and distribution system."

Nixon's request for the blood bank study was detailed to Congress in a 14-page message, which for the most part reiterated proposals made by him in 1971.

(Mentioned by Nixon in his message were his proposals for national health insurance, health maintenance organizations and reforms in the Medicare and Medicaid programs.)

HEW Secretary Elliot L. Richardson said the Nixon message "was a plea to Congress to get on with it and enact the proposals [made last year]."

Speaking on the blood bank question, Richardson said "the problem has been that there is no national system." There was a need, he said, for "developing a reporting system to identify supplies and needs" that would be "integrated with a computer data bank."

Sickle-cell program. Federal health officials July 20, 1972 outlined the basic format of a government program to fight sickle cell anemia, a blood disease that primarily affected young blacks.

Dr. Rudolph E. Jackson, coordinator of the National Institutes of Health's (NIH) sickle cell program, Dr. Robert Q. Marston, NIH director, and Marjorie A. Costa, head of the National Center for Family Planning Services, emphasized that the fight against the disease would be a difficult one.

Even with the new program, they said, not enough money was committed to the fight. Additionally, until new sickle cell treatment centers were opened, there were only a handful of centers across the U.S. At least 19 new screening and education clinics were to be opened under the federal program.

Sickle cell anemia was an inherited blood disorder which was reported to afflict one in every 500 black Americans, or about 50,000. Additionally, it was believed that 2.5 million more blacks were carriers of the sickle cell trait. At the present time there was no cure for sickle cell anemia.

Syphilis project revealed. Details of a U.S. syphilis study involving 600 Alabama black men that dated back to 1932 were made public July 25, 1972 in an Associated Press (AP) report.

According to AP reporter Jean Heller, the U.S. Public Health Service (PHS) conducted the study in which 400 black men with syphilis went untreated, even after a cure for the disease was known. The other 200 men, who had no syphilis, were monitored as a control group.

The study, Heller said, was organized to determine from autopsies what untreated syphilis did to the human body.

Dr. Merlin K. DuVal, assistant secretary of health, education and welfare for health and scientific affairs, said July 25 he would begin an investigation at once. Other federal health officials said they were giving whatever medical services they could to the project's survivors while they continued to chart the disease's course.

The experiment, known as the Tuskegee Study, was begun by the PHS in 1932 with 600 black men from Tuskegee, Ala. At that time, Tuskegee had the highest syphilis rate in the nation. The men were induced to join the program with promises of free lunches, free transportation, free medicine for any disease other than syphilis and free burial after autopsies were performed. Four hundred of the group had syphilis and never received deliberate treatment for it. The other 200 had no syphilis and received no specific therapy.

The study was begun 10 years before scientists found penicillin to be a cure for syphilis. But even after penicillin's healing qualities were known, the group of 400 with syphilis were not treated with it.

According to the AP report, a 1969 study by the PHS's Center for Disease Control in Atlanta found that seven men of the original syphilitic group of 400 had died of the disease. Another 154 died of heart failure that U.S. health officials said was not specifically related to syphilis.

The Justice Department Dec. 14, 1974 announced the tentative settlement of a class action suit brought by surviving participants of the study.

Under the terms of the settlement, syphilitic participants still alive would receive $37,500; nonsyphilitic participants still alive would receive $15,000; the estate of each deceased syphilitic participant would receive $15,000 and the estate of each deceased nonsyphilitic participant would receive $5,000.

U.S. emergency care criticized. A National Research Council report charged that "thousands of lives" were lost in the U.S. each year "through lack of systematic application of established principles of emergency care," it was reported Sept. 17, 1972. It also charged that the Department of Health, Education & Welfare and the Executive Office of the President had failed to mobilize existing resources to develop a nationwide emergency treatment system.

Some 110,000 Americans were killed each year and 400,000 permanently disabled in accidents, the report said, and inadequate facilities, poor training and makeshift operations had contributed to the toll.

The council asked the Executive Office of the President to organize implementation of a program including: establishment of a nationwide "911" emergency telephone number staffed by informed operators; replacement of 80% of the nation's 25,000 ambulences which were inadequate; establishing emergency communications centers and special radio frequencies; nationwide training of emergency personnel; classification of hospitals according to their specialized emergency resources; upgrading of hospital emergency staffs and an increase in emergency medicine residencies; giving more responsibility to nurses, and increasing research funds.

Long-term poverty funding asked. An American Public Health Association study panel concluded that long-term funding of health care centers in poor areas was necessary to improve stability and quality of care, it was reported Nov. 13, 1972.

The study had been requested by four U.S. senators, with the support of Mississippi Gov. William Waller, to investigate charges surrounding the Delta Health Center in Mound Bayou, Miss. Although "there were problems surrounding the operations of the Delta" center, the panel found, they were not "irreversible or unique," and resulted largely from the lack of long-term funds, leading to difficulties in staff recruitment, and from failure to recognize the specific problems of operating in poverty areas.

Office of Economic Opportunity (OEO) Director Phillip V. Sanchez had decided Sept. 17 to overrule Waller's veto of a $4.15 million nine-month grant to the center. It was the second Mississippi health center to receive OEO funds in 1972 over Waller's objections; the other was in Jackson.

Waller had charged that the Delta center had delivered insufficient care for the money spent, but Owen Brooks, Delta's board chairman, claimed that Waller's vetoes were prompted by opposition to community control.

Health facilities study. Billions of dollars could be cut from the costs of health care in the U.S. by better construction planning, more attention to preventive medicine and better use of current facilities, according to a General Accounting Office (GAO) study released Nov. 22, 1972.

Better construction planning was a major focus of the report, which cited the example of a new $17.9 million hospital that, with better design, according to consultants' estimates, would have cost $1.5 million less and saved $10 million in operating expenses over 25 years.

One of the GAO recommendations was for reuse of hospital designs rather than reaching for originality of architecture. Other proposals were for a central data bank for hospital planners to obtain information about construction techniques, operating systems and materials, adoption of a common set of new-construction requirements under federal building programs and use of systems analysis in design and construction.

The report also recommended a sharing of hospital services to reduce the demand for new facilities, expanded home health care programs and use of out-patient clinics and nursing homes to handle services provided generally in the hospital room. The study found that one of four patients was receiving more care than necessary in hospitals and that health insurance coverage promoted such unnecessary care.

It also found that the health care system was not "geared toward prevention" and, in fact, "may not be able to meet future health demands" if the situation persisted.

A deficiency in planning also was noted in the report, which said "less than 50% of the 163 health planning agencies responding to our inquiries . . . provided data showing that they had knowledge of 1972 needs for various types of inpatient, extended and ambulatory care facilities and beds."

Lead paint curbed. In separate actions taken in 1972, the Food & Drug Administration (FDA) and the Department of Housing and Urban Development (HUD) acted to curb the use of lead in paints.

The FDA March 10 ordered lead content in all household paints, for interior or exterior surfaces, toys and other articles limited to no more than .5% after Dec. 31, and to no more than .06% after Dec. 31, 1973. FDA Commissioner Charles C. Edwards said March 10 that the American Academy of Pediatrics had persuaded the agency that its earlier proposed limit of .5% would not protect children one to three years old.

Dr. Merlin K. DuVal, an assistant secretary of health, education and welfare, told a Senate subcommittee March 10 that 50,000–100,000 children a year required treatment for lead paint poisoning, which caused 200 deaths annually and could cause brain damage.

It was reported Jan. 8 that HUD had banned all paints containing over 1% lead by weight from all uses in all properties owned or insured by the department, as of Jan. 1.

Political Developments

Party platforms. Both political parties had relatively detailed health planks in their 1972 political platforms.

The Democratic platform, adopted July 12, included the following statements:

Good health is the least this society should promise its citizens. The state of health services in this country indicates the failure of government to respond to this fundamental need. Costs skyrocket while the availability of services for all but the rich steadily declines.

We endorse the principle that good health is a right of all Americans.

America has a responsibility to offer to every American family the best in health care wherever they need it, regardless of income or where they live or any other factor.

To achieve this goal the next Democratic Administration should:

■ Establish a system of universal National Health Insurance which covers all Americans with a comprehensive set of benefits including preventive medicine, mental and emotional disorders, and complete protection against catastrophic costs, and in which the rule of free choice for both provider and consumer is protected. The program should be federally-financed and federally-administered. Every American must know he can afford the cost of health care whether given in a hospital or a doctor's office;

■ Incorporate in the National Health Insurance System incentives and controls to curb inflation in health care costs and to assure efficient delivery of all services;

■ Continue and evaluate Health Maintenance Organizations;

■ Set up incentives to bring health service personnel back to inner-cities and rural areas;

■ Continue to expand community health centers and availability of early screening diagnosis and treatment;

■ Provide federal funds to train added health manpower including doctors, nurses, technicians and para-medical workers;

■ Secure greater consumer participation and control over health care institutions;

■ Expand federal support for medical research including research in heart disease, hypertension, stroke, cancer, sickle cell anemia, occupational and childhood diseases which threaten millions and in preventive health care;

■ Eventual replacement of all federal programs of health care by a comprehensive National Health Insurance System;

■ Take legal and other action to curb soaring prices for vital drugs using anti-trust laws as applicable and amending patent laws to end price-raising abuses, and require generic-name labeling of equal-effective drugs; and

■ Expand federal research and support for drug abuse treatment and education, especially development of non-addictive treatment methods.

■ Pending a full national health security system, expand Medicare by supplementing trust funds with general revenues in order to provide a complete range of care and services; eliminate the Nixon Administration cutbacks in Medicare and Medicaid; eliminate the part B premium under Medicare and include under Medicare and Medicaid the costs of eyeglasses, dentures, hearing aids, and all prescription drugs and establish uniform national standards for Medicaid to bring to an end the present situation which makes it worse to be poor in one state than in another.

(A party charter, the first ever adopted by a U.S. political party, was adopted by the Democratic Party Dec. 7, 1974. It included calls for a comprehensive, national health insurance plan.)

The Republican platform was adopted Aug. 22. It said:

Our goal is to enable every American to secure quality health care at reasonable cost. We pledge a balanced approach—one that takes into account the problems of providing sufficient medical personnel and facilities.

Last year President Nixon proposed one of the most all-inclusive health programs in our history. But the opposition Congress has dragged its feet and most of this program has yet to be enacted into law.

To increase the supply of medical services, we will continue to support programs to help our schools graduate more physicians, dentists, nurses, and allied health personnel, with special emphasis on family practitioners and others who deliver primary medical care.

We will also encourage the use of such allied personnel as doctors' assistants, foster new area health education centers, channel more services into geographic areas which now are medically deprived, and improve the availability of emergency medical care.

We note with pride that the President has already signed the most comprehensive health manpower legislation ever enacted.

To improve efficiency in providing health and medical care, we have developed and will continue to encourage a pluralistic approach to the delivery of

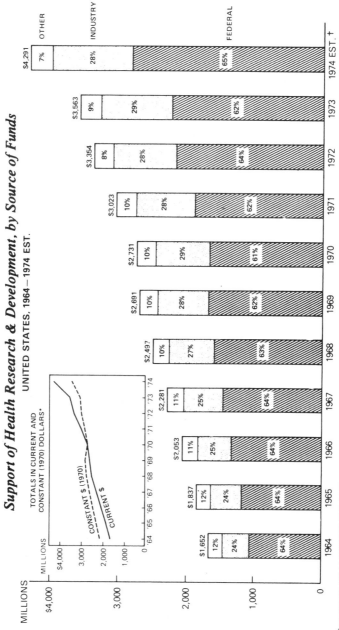

Support of Health Research & Development, by Source of Funds

UNITED STATES, 1964 – 1974 EST.

*CONSTANT DOLLARS BASED ON BIOMEDICAL R&D DEFLATOR (1970 = 100).   †INCLUDES FEDERAL FUNDS WITHHELD IN FY 1973 AND RELEASED FOR USE IN 1974.

quality health care including innovative experiments such as health maintenance organizations. We also support efforts to develop ambulatory medical care services to reduce hospitalization and keep costs down.

To reduce the cost of health care, we stress our efforts to curb inflation in the economy; we will also expand the supply of medical services and encourage greater cost consciousness in hospitalization and medical care. In doing this we realize the importance of the doctor-patient relationship and the necessity of insuring that individuals have freedom of choice of health providers.

To assure access to basic medical care for all our people, we support a program financed by employers, employes and the Federal government to provide comprehensive health insurance coverage, including insurance against the cost of long-term and catastrophic illnesses and accidents and renal failure which necessitates dialysis, at a cost which all Americans can afford. The National Health Insurance Partnership plan and the Family Health Insurance Plan proposed by the President meet these specifications. They would build on existing private health insurance systems, not destroy them.

We oppose nationalized compulsory health insurance. This approach would at least triple in taxes the amount the average citizen now pays for health and would deny families the right to choose the kind of care they prefer. Ultimately it would lower the overall quality of health care for all Americans.

We believe that the most effective way of improving health in the long run is by emphasis on preventive measures.

The serious physical fitness problem in our country requires urgent attention. The President recently reorganized the Council on Physical Fitness and Sports to increase the leadership of representatives of medicine, physical education, sports associations and school administrations. The Republican Party urges intensification of these efforts, particularly in the nation's school systems, to encourage widespread participation in effective physical fitness programs.

We have initiated this nation's first all-out assault against cancer. Led by the new National Cancer Institute, the drive to eliminate this cruel killer will involve Federal spending of nearly $430 million in fiscal year 1973, almost twice the funding of just two years ago.

We have also launched a major new attack on sickle cell anemia, a serious blood disorder afflicting many black Americans, and developed a comprehensive program to deal with the menace of lead-based paint poisoning, including the screening of approximately 1,500,000 Americans.

We support expanded medical research to find cures for the major diseases of the heart, blood vessels, lungs and kidneys—diseases which now account for over half the deaths in the United States.

We have significantly advanced efforts to combat mental retardation and established a national goal to cut its incidence in half by the year 2000.

We continue to support the concept of comprehensive community mental health centers. In this fiscal year $135 million—almost three times the 1970 level—will be devoted to the staffing of 422 community mental health centers serving a population of 56 million people. We have intensified research on methods of treating mental problems, increasing our outlays from $76 million in 1969 to approximately $96 million for 1973. We continue to urge extension of private health insurance to cover mental illness.

We have also improved consumer protection, health education and accident prevention programs. And in Moscow this year, President Nixon' reached an agreement with the Soviet Union on health research which may yield substantial benefits in many fields in the years ahead.

AMA campaign funds. The Washington Post reported Oct. 23, 1972 that the American Medical Association (AMA) and its political fund and affiliates comprised the largest single contributor to Congressional and state legislator races among business and professional groups. Since April 7, the AMA had donated $855,000 to various campaigns, including 43 incumbent GOP House and Senate candidates who received $130,400 and 25 Democratic incumbents who got $27,400. Among 33 GOP challengers for House and Senate seats, $104,500 was contributed by the AMA. Five Democrats who were not incumbents received $18,500.

The AMA money was directed at legislators who dealt with the health insurance issue. Since Aug. 31, the AMA had $635,000 in reserve for future campaign contributions, the Post reported.

(At its annual convention, held in San Francisco June 18–22, 1972, the AMA delegates had proposed June 20 that tax incentives be used to induce doctors to take their practices into the nation's inner cities and rural areas, places where they were needed most. Under the proposal, doctors leaving big city and suburban practices to practice elsewhere would be given federal and state tax credits.)

Health-Care System Under Continued Review

Budget seeks changes. President Nixon's fiscal 1974 budget, submitted to Congress Jan. 29, 1973, proposed several changes in federal health programs.

The 1974 budget made proposals for significant fund increases for Medicare, as mandated by Congress, and for research into cancer and heart disease, but reduced or eliminated programs of hospital construction and maintenance and

National Support for Health Research & Development, by Source & Performer

FISCAL YEARS 1950-1974 EST. (In millions of dollars)

Sector	1950	1955	1960	1965	1967	1968	1969	1970	1971	1972	1973	1974 est.
Total of A or B	$161	$261	$845	$1,837	$2,281	$2,497	$2,691	$2,731	$3,023	$3,354	$3,563	$4,291
A. BY SOURCE OF FUNDS												
Government	74	144	471	1,229	1,524	1,650	1,746	1,743	1,956	2,226	2,313	2,887
Federal	74	139	448	1,174	1,459	1,582	1,674	1,667	1,877	2,147	2,225	2,795
State & local	—	5	23	55	65	68	72	76	79	79	88	92
Industry	51	62	253	450	580	661	754	795	860	925	1,033	1,180
Private nonprofit	36	55	121	158	177	186	191	193	207	203	217	224
Foundations	11	14	40	42	46	50	47	47	57	53	60	54
Voluntary health agencies	10	17	36	46	54	57	61	61	63	63	70	82
Other	15	24	45	70	77	79	83	85	87	87	87	88
B. BY PERFORMER												
Government	35	64	138	356	433	486	542	576	659	708	753	853
Federal	35	64	138	305	369	403	458	489	568	609	628	692
State & local	†	†	†	51	64	83	84	87	91	99	125	161
Industry	55	69	280	483	653	725	813	828	889	964	1,042	1,217
Private nonprofit	71	128	427	936	1,120	1,199	1,242	1,240	1,363	1,566	1,612	2,042
Higher education	51	95	286	685	846	914	952	940	1,036	1,204	1,228	1,548
Other nonprofit	†	†	†	251	274	285	290	300	327	362	384	494
Foreign	†	†	†	62	75	87	94	87	112	116	156	177

†Breakdown not available, but data are included in column totals (line 1).

training of medical personnel, and called for a $700 million increase in payments by Medicare benificiaries.

Total Medicare payments would rise 20% to $12.1 billion, to cover care for 11.6 million people and hospitalization for about 5 million. The budget proposed changes in the Social Security law to require Medicare patients to pay 10% of hospital charges after the first day of hospitalization, at a total cost of $345 million. Officials of the Department of Health, Education & Welfare (HEW) said the change would help create "a cost awareness on the part of the medical care consumer which, besides its effect on over-utilization, should inhibit hospital price increases." Indigent patients could recover the costs through Medicaid, HEW said. Increased payments under the Medicare supplemental doctor's fee plan were also requested.

The 26-year-old Hill-Burton hospital construction act would be allowed to expire, since, the Administration said, hospital beds were already in oversupply, causing low occupancy rates and higher costs, and since hospitals received capital funds from depreciation payments under Medicare and Medicaid.

HEW planned to abandon the regional medical program for heart disease, stroke and cancer. HEW said the centers had failed to coordinate medical resources or disseminate research developments rapidly. HEW would continue to maintain some 515 community mental health centers, but would not expand the network to 2,000 centers as originally planned. Eight Public Health Service hospitals would be turned over to local control.

Training programs for doctors and dentists would continue to be fully funded because of shortages, but reductions were planned in training programs for nurses, pharmacists, veterinarians and other medical personnel. HEW said it would cease support for training research scientists, since federal aid had already increased their numbers massively, and since their earning potential enabled them to finance their own education. The program had previously cost $150 million a year.

Cancer research was budgeted for $445 million, up $91 million, and heart and lung research was scheduled for a $28 million increase to $250 million.

Hospital costs at new high—According to figures released by the American Hospital Association Jan. 14, the average daily charge for a day's stay in a hospital had nearly doubled in six years and had reached $105.30. The new figure was 11.6% higher than the year before but the percentage increase was the lowest since 1967. The figure, which included charges for rooms, meals, nursing care, and laboratory tests, was an average for a community hospital, with prices varying widely from institution to institution.

Handicapped aid veto sustained. A $2.6 billion vocational rehabilitation bill was vetoed by Nixon March 27, 1973 in his continuing battle against the "big spenders" in Congress. A vote in the Senate April 3 to override the veto was 60–36, four less than the two-thirds necessary to carry the program into the House for another test on the veto.

In his veto message, Nixon said "this bill is one of several now before the Congress which mask bad legislation beneath alluring labels."

The vocational rehabilitation bill was criticized by the President on the grounds it would divert aid to the handicapped from its original goal of training the employable, create "a hodgepodge" of new categorical grant programs, many of them overlapping, make efficient management impossible and would "cruelly raise the hopes of the handicapped in a way that we could never responsibly hope to fulfill."

Hailing the vote to sustain the veto in the Senate April 3, Nixon said, "Because enough senators had enough courage to stand up against the big spenders in defense of the average American's pocketbook, the tide in this battle of the budget is running in the people's favor."

The outcome of the Senate vote came about in large part because of the defection of five Southern Democrats who voted with 31 Republicans to sustain the veto. Ten Republicans joined 50 Democrats to override.

Federal Obligation for Health Research & Development, by Agency

FY 1950-1974 est.* (In millions of dollars)

Agency	1950	1955	1960	1965	1967	1968	1969	1970	1971	1972	1973	1974† est.
Total	$72.9	$138.9	$448.2	$1,174.2	$1,459.4	$1,581.9	$1,674.1	$1,666.6	$1,876.6	$2,147.3	$2,225.3	$2,795.5
Dept. of Health, Educ. & Welfare	36.1	69.7	310.7	826.2	1,051.2	1,139.0	1,191.4	1,177.0	1,316.0	1,584.3	1,609.9	2,075.9
National Institutes of Health‡	27.7	60.1	280.6	715.1	812.4	864.0	892.9	873.3	1,038.9	1,271.3	1,323.2	1,737.8
HSMHA	—	—	—	—	—	149.2	179.8	175.0	222.0	244.8	224.5	255.5§
Other PHS	7.7	8.2	20.5	66.8	200.0	80.0	70.1	73.1	25.7**	31.1**	30.2**	44.0**
Other DHEW	0.8	1.5	9.6	44.4	38.8	45.8	48.7	55.6	29.4	37.1	32.0	38.5
Atomic Energy Commission	18.3	28.6	50.3	84.6	95.9	95.0	97.9	104.2	104.9	102.7	110.6	126.5
Dept. of Defense	9.7	23.7	41.5	101.3	117.5	114.0	117.5	124.9	124.2	126.0	126.6	121.4
Dept. of Transportation	0.1	+	0.8	2.8	2.4	4.5	7.3	9.7	41.9	39.0	65.0	120.7
Veterans Administration	3.7	5.6	15.1	36.9	44.8	45.6	50.3	58.7	62.7	68.9	74.2	81.1
National Aeronautics & Space Admin.	—	—	0.9	60.0	81.6	108.6	116.8	85.9	74.9	50.3	42.3	80.2
Dept. of Agriculture	4.8	9.0	15.1	40.5	45.4	45.8	48.8	50.1	60.3	67.3	61.1	59.7
National Science Foundation	—	1.6	11.9	19.7	13.8	21.1	25.6	28.0	34.3	37.2	45.5	47.0
Dept. of Interior	0.1	0.3	0.7	0.6	2.0	2.7	4.4	12.4	22.6	34.9	33.3	33.3
Environmental Protection Agency	—	—	—	—	—	—	—	—	13.1	14.5	20.3	18.8
Dept. of State	—	—	0.8	0.8	2.2	2.7	8.7	10.8	15.2	15.1	16.3	10.3
Special Action Off. for Drug Abuse	—	—	—	—	—	—	—	—	—	—	11.9	10.0
Dept. of Commerce (NBS)	—	0.2	0.3	0.4	1.1	0.7	2.9	3.0	4.3	4.2	4.7	5.7
Consumer Products Safety Commission	—	—	—	—	—	—	—	—	—	—	—	4.3
Dept. of Justice	—	—	—	—	—	—	—	—	—	—	0.7	0.5
Tennessee Valley Authority	0.1	0.4	0.2	0.6	1.5	2.2	2.4	1.9	2.2	2.9	3.0	0.1

*Covers medical and health-related R&D (projects, resources, and general support), but not training or construction. †Includes funds withheld in FY 1973 but released for obligation in 1974. ‡As organized in the year specified. §Reorganized during FY 1974 into ADAMHA, CDC, HRA, and HSA (147.2, $40.6, $55.6, and $12.1 millions). **FDA only. ¶Less than $50 thousand.

Senate Democratic Leader Mike Mansfield (Mont.) referred to the massive vote-switching by Republicans in backing the veto. "Nothing's changed except their minds," he commented. "I just feel sorry for the handicapped, 10 million of them, our own people."

Funds authorized. Nixon June 19, 1973 signed a bill authorizing expenditures that he had opposed. The measure extended 12 expiring federal programs for one year with a total spending authorization of $1.27 billion. In his budget, Nixon had proposed to terminate five of the programs—the Hill-Burton hospital construction grants, regional medical programs, community mental health centers, public health and allied health training programs.

Under the bill, Hill-Burton programs were authorized $197,200,000, the regional medical programs $159 million, community mental health centers $234,-120,000, the programs for public health training $23,300,000 and for allied health professions $44,345,000.

Among the bill's other authorizations were $360,500,000 for comprehensive health planning services, $118,024,000 for family planning and population research and $41,750,000 for projects to aid those disabled by mental retardation or neurological disease from childhood.

By a 94–0 vote June 5, the Senate had cleared the bill by accepting House changes in the Senate's original version, which had been passed in March.

The principal change was a reduction in the total authorization from $2.2 billion to $1.27 billion. The House had passed its version by a 372–1 vote May 31.

Nixon indicated in his signing statement his continued opposition to many of the

PERSONAL CONSUMPTION EXPENDITURES FOR MEDICAL CARE

In the United States

(billions of dollars)

Year	Total medical care	Hospital services	Physicians' services	Medicines and appliances	Dentists	Net cost of health insurance	All other medical care
1948	$ 7.5	$ 1.6	$ 2.4	$1.9	$0.9	$0.3	$0.4
1950	8.5	2.0	2.6	2.2	1.0	0.3	0.5
1955	12.3	3.1	3.5	3.0	1.5	0.6	0.6
1960	18.6	5.1	5.3	4.4	2.0	0.8	1.0
1961	19.7	5.6	5.5	4.6	2.1	1.0	1.0
1962	21.4	6.1	6.0	4.9	2.3	1.1	1.1
1963	22.8	6.8	6.4	5.1	2.3	1.1	1.2
1964	25.2	7.7	7.1	5.4	2.6	1.2	1.2
1965	27.4	8.3	7.7	5.9	2.8	1.3	1.4
1966	30.4	9.3	8.4	6.7	3.0	1.4	1.6
1967	33.6	10.7	9.3	7.0	3.3	1.6	1.7
1968	36.8	12.3	10.0	7.6	3.5	1.6	1.9
1969	41.6	14.6	11.5	8.2	3.9	1.6	1.9
1970	46.3	16.9	12.9	8.7	4.3	1.4	2.1
1971	50.4	18.8	14.2	9.0	4.3	1.9	2.2
1972	55.7	20.5	15.3	9.8	4.6	2.8	2.6
1973	61.0	22.9	16.6	10.6	4.9	3.1	2.9

Note: The data exclude private expenditures in Federal, state, city and other government hospitals and nursing homes. In some cases the sum of the items does not equal the "Total medical care" shown, because of rounding. 1973 is the latest year for which data are available.

Source: U.S. Department of Commerce.

Table from Health Insurance Institute

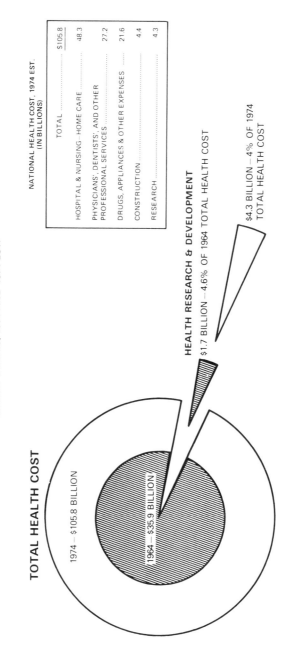

Health Research & Development as a Proportion of Total Health Cost

UNITED STATES, 1964 AND 1974 EST.

NATIONAL HEALTH COST, 1974 EST.
(IN BILLIONS)

TOTAL	$105.8
HOSPITAL & NURSING-HOME CARE	48.3
PHYSICIANS', DENTISTS', AND OTHER PROFESSIONAL SERVICES	27.2
DRUGS, APPLIANCES & OTHER EXPENSES	21.6
CONSTRUCTION	4.4
RESEARCH	4.3

HEALTH RESEARCH & DEVELOPMENT

$1.7 BILLION — 4.6% OF 1964 TOTAL HEALTH COST

$4.3 BILLION — 4% OF 1974 TOTAL HEALTH COST

TOTAL HEALTH COST

1974 — $105.8 BILLION

1964 — $35.9 BILLION

SOURCES: *SOCIAL SECURITY BULLETIN, VOL. 38, NO. 2, FEBRUARY 1975*
WITH ADJUSTMENT OF R&D, AND THEREFORE OF TOTALS, TO CONFORM WITH NIH DATA.

bill's provisions and based his approval on the short one-year duration.

Health funds impoundment reported.
The Nixon Administration during fiscal 1973 withheld more than $1 billion that Congress had appropriated for health programs, the House Commerce Committee reported July 26.

The amount impounded was more than 20% of the $4.759 billion allotted to the Health Services and Mental Health Administration and to the National Institutes of Health.

United Press International reported Aug. 26 that the Department of Health, Education and Welfare had withheld in fiscal 1973 a total of $1.8 billion in funds appropriated by Congress for social programs.

Among the cuts were $59 million from the National Cancer Institute, $44 million from the National Heart and Lung Institute, and $199 million from various mental health programs.

A federal district judge in Washington ruled Nov. 21 that the Administration must release $21.7 million in aid to nursing schools. Judge Thomas A. Flannery said the funding legislation had provided "mandatory grants" which left the Administration no discretion in their disbursement.

The President Dec. 19 ordered the release of approximately $1 billion in impounded funds for education and health programs. The order, which applied to money appropriated for fiscal 1973, included funds that had been the subject of lawsuits seeking their release.

Deputy White House Press Secretary Gerald L. Warren said Nixon wanted to "end the uncertainty" among potential recipients.

Nixon acted after he signed a bill appropriating $32.9 billion ($1.38 billion more than Administration requests) for fiscal 1974 for the Departments of Health, Education and Welfare (HEW) and Labor. Both houses had approved a conference committee version of the bill Dec. 5. In an attempt to meet Administration objections to the size of the bill, the conferees had accepted an amendment giving the President authority to withhold a total of $400 million from the appropriation as long as no single program was cut more than 5%.

Patients' rights. The American Hospital Association Jan. 8, 1973 released in Chicago a 12-point patient's bill of rights on behalf of its 7,000 member hospitals. The document was intended to "contribute to more effective patient care and greater satisfaction for the patient, his physician, and the hospital organization," the association said.

The New York Times summarized the 12 points Jan. 9:

The patient has the right to respectful and considerate care; the right to obtain from his doctor complete current information concerning his diagnosis, treatment and prognosis in terms the patient can reasonably be expected to understand; the right to receive from his physician information necessary to give informed consent prior to the start of any procedure and/or treatment; the right to refuse treatment to the extent permitted by law and to be informed of the medical consequences of his action; the right to every consideration of his privacy concerning his own medical care program; the right to expect that all communications and records pertaining to his care should be treated as confidential; the right to expect that within its capacity a hospital must make reasonable response to the request of a patient for services; the right to obtain information as to any relationship of his hospital to other health care and educational institutions insofar as his care is concerned; the right to be advised if the hospital proposes to engage in or perform human experimentation affecting his care or treatment; the right to expect reasonable continuity of care; the right to examine and receive an explanation of his bill regardless of the source of payment; and the right to know what hospital rules and regulations apply to his conduct as a patient.

Mental hospitals probed. A Stanford University psychologist reported in the January 1973 issue of Science that he and seven other people had successfully been admitted to 12 different mental hospitals, where they stayed up to 52 days without detection. Dr. David L. Rosenhan ran the experiment over a three-year period to determine whether mental hospitals could tell the sane from the insane. His conclusion was they could not, the New York Times reported Jan. 20.

The pseudo-patients resumed normal behavior after being admitted because they heard strange voices. Once admitted, anything they did was seen as an "aspect of pathological behavior," even pacing of the halls out of boredom and waiting outside the dining room before meals—the high point of the day for some of the patients. One nurse ascribed copious note-taking by one of the fakers to a crazy compulsion.

When each patient was finally discharged, it was with the diagnosis of "schizophrenia in remission," never a clean bill of health or a suggestion of misdiagnosis.

MD's and DDS's form union. Doctors and dentists meeting in Las Vegas, Nev. announced Jan. 29, 1973 that they were forming a union to fight interference in medical care by outside parties. Organizers of the American Federation of Physicians and Dentists said they had 8,000 signed members and 17,000 others pledged.

Union vice president Dr. Donald C. Meyer, a New York City dentist, said the federation's purpose was to fight encroachment on medical practice by the government, insurance companies, and hospital administrators. Dr. Sanford Marcus of San Francisco called the federation's primary goal one of upholding and improving the quality of patient care rather than the traditional union goal of winning economic benefits. President of the new group was Dr. Stanley S. Peterson of Springfield, Mo.

AMA faces conservative pressure. The American Medical Association (AMA), at its 122nd annual convention in New York June 24–28, 1973, faced increasing attack by its more conservative members who threatened to boycott a nationalized health system if it were established. The AMA decided to lift restrictions on investment in drug companies and rejected a plan to study the possibilities of unionization.

According to a survey of AMA membership made public June 24, one-third of the members would boycott establishment of a national health insurance system or would leave the practice of medicine

altogether if such a system were created.

AMA President Dr. Carl A. Hoffman said in his opening remarks June 24 that the Kennedy-Griffiths bill, providing for federal financing of medical care, was an "insidious threat" to the quality of medical care and would signal "the complete and total takeover of the entire health care delivery system by the government." (Recent reports showed that while the total number of doctors increased in 1972 by 12,000, AMA membership dropped by 338.)

In a speech June 27, Dr. Charles C. Edwards, assistant U.S. secretary for health, warned that the American people would not tolerate blind opposition by the nation's doctors to reformation of the national health care system. Dr. Edwards said an AMA "defensive position" against government reforms "would be seriously counter-productive."

The Washington Post reported June 25 that an AMA retirement fund investment portfolio showed that almost $10 million was invested in pharmaceutical firms. This was done after an AMA Judicial Council ruling that a physician's investment in drug companies was of questionable ethics and a potential source of conflict of interest.

However, AMA officials revealed June 26 that restrictions on the organization's investment in drug companies had been lifted, contending that continued restrictions would deprive the AMA's participation "in a long and well-recognized growth segment of the economy." The officials disclosed that the Judicial Council had decided June 24 to free the AMA's own corporate reserves totaling $22 million for pharmaceutical investment. Dr. Russell B. Roth of Erie, Pa., installed as the AMA's 128th president June 27, defended the council's action, stating that "considering the total amount of money, the percentage in pharmaceuticals is small [and] doctors exercise none of the proxies."

The AMA's house of delegates voted June 28 to postpone any attempt to set up a study committee on collective bargaining, seen as a move toward unionization. The delegates endorsed a statement that "physicians do not need to sacrifice their individual freedoms to obtain an effective socioeconomic organization."

Three former top AMA advisers had accused the AMA of being "a captive of and beholden to the pharmaceutical industry" in Feb. 6 testimony before the Senate Monopoly Subcommittee of the Small Business Committee. The advisers were the last two chairmen and a former vice chairman of the AMA's Council on Drugs, an independent group of scientists and doctors established by the AMA in 1905 to advise the medical profession on drugs. The council was abolished October 1972 in what the AMA called an economy move.

Dr. John Adriani, council chairman from 1968 to 1970, and Dr. Harry C. Shirkey, Adrian's successor, both of Tulane University, and former vice chairman Dr. Daniel L. Azarnoff, of the University of Kansas testified before the subcommittee. The following summary of their combined testimony was reported by the Feb. 7 Washington Post and New York Times:

The AMA had committed itself to publish a complete, unbiased guide to prescription drugs. Drawing on over 300 experts, the Council on Drugs completed the report in 1971 at a cost of over $3 million and readied the report for distribution to members. In January 1971, Max H. Parrott, chairman of the board of directors of the AMA, told the council that publication of the study would have to be delayed for a few months so the book could be reviewed by people he called "our friends,"—the Pharmaceutical Manufacturers Association (PMA). Actually the PMA had already been given draft copies. Although the council initially demurred, it later accepted. Soon after, the PMA submitted "three or four crates" of proposed revisions, which the council dealt with by making about 35 token revisions in areas such as dosage sizes and revised formulations. The council stood fast against any substantive revisions, especially against condemnations of heavily advertised drug combinations.

When the book appeared, Dr. Parrott attempted to tone down the report by adding a cover letter that said that some of the condemned combination drugs "may be justifiable."

A second clash came in September 1972, when the AMA board was given an advance look at the second edition of "AMA Drug Evaluations." Many medicines had been evaluated as "not recommended," a rating that board representative Dr. Richard Palmer asked be deleted. The council instead proposed that an explanation accompany each appearance of "not recommended," a compromise that was unacceptable to the board.

One month later the council was abolished and the task of completing the second drug manual was turned over to paid employes of the AMA.

Dr. Adriani testified that the "not recommended" designation left the AMA board with "no choice but to appease the pharmaceutical industry." The alternative he said, was to sacrifice ad revenues in the AMA Journal of Medicine.

MDs vs. peer review. The AMA House of Delegates Dec. 5, 1973 approved a resolution that urged the repeal of a federal law setting up cost and quality control procedures for federally financed health programs. The resolution, opposed by the AMA's leadership, reflected sentiment of doctors at the AMA's annual clinical convention in Anaheim, Calif.

The legislation opposed by the delegates would set up, beginning in 1974, local Professional Standards Review Organizations (PSRO) to oversee medical care dispensed under Medicare and Medicaid. The PSRO program, originally sponsored by Sen. Wallace F. Bennett (R, Utah), was intended to check the spiraling increases in Medicare and Medicaid costs, while insuring high quality of care.

The resolution for repeal was supported by an overwhelming majority of the doctors at the convention, although the AMA leadership had warned that there was no Congressional sentiment for repeal and that a campaign for repeal would damage the AMA's public image.

Medical aid to kidney patients. The Department of Health, Education and Welfare June 26, 1973 announced regulations that would extend Medicare coverage to people of any age who required kidney transplants or regular treatment with artificial kidney machines. The new benefits took effect July 1.

The authorized benefits covered most of the expenses for kidney transplant or long-term dialysis for 90% of the nation's kidney patients. Officials said participation in the program would be restricted to the approximately 750 kidney treatment centers in existence.

The rules announced June 26 were interim regulations. HEW officials said more time was needed to work out final regulations, to be issued by the end of the year.

The artificial kidney treatment, dialysis, cost $5,000–$24,000 a year, according to HEW figures. The total cost of a kidney transplant was estimated at about $20,-000.

Volunteer blood bank system. Health, Education and Welfare Department officials told a White House health seminar June 10, 1973 that the Administration would propose the creation of a nationalized, all-volunteer blood-supply system.

The department's deputy assistant director for health, Dr. Henry E. Simmons, said "for too long we have endured our present haphazard nonsystem of blood supply with its sporadic shortages across the country. Our investigation has determined that there is no overall shortage of blood, but widespread mismanagement of this vital national resource."

The Administration hoped that the private effort would come up with a unified and more effective system.

HEW Secretary Casper W. Weinberger said the new blood policy would lead to uniform federal regulation of blood banks and stimulate research for the collection and distribution of blood.

Emergency health bill enacted. A bill authorizing $185 million over three years for improving emergency medical services was passed by the Senate Oct. 30, 1973 and House Oct. 31 and signed by President Nixon Nov. 16. The President had vetoed an earlier version largely on the basis of a provision requiring continued operation of eight Public Health Service hospitals. The provision was deleted from the emergency health bill but was enacted as a rider to a defense procurement bill.

The Nixon Administration sought to phase out outpatient services at six of the hospitals and to close at least one of them. (A temporary restraining order barring any service cutback at the hospitals was issued by U.S. District Court Judge John

H. Pratt in Washington July 17. A preliminary injunction was granted July 27.)

The fund authorization would be utilized for grants to communities and public or private agencies for improvement of their emergency medical facilities and for training personnel.

Nixon's Aug. 1 veto of the original bill had been upheld when the House's 273–144 vote Sept. 12 to override it fell five votes short of the two-thirds majority needed to cancel a veto. The Senate's 77–16 vote to override Sept. 1 was 15 votes over the needed two-thirds margin.

In his Aug. 1 veto message, Nixon had asserted that the bill, which authorized spending of $185 million over a three-year period, "represents a promise of federal financial assistance that cannot be kept" since the funding was "far in excess of the amounts that can be prudently spent." He said the federal role in this area should be limited to such programs as a current demonstration program costing about $15 million in the year ending June 30, 1974.

Group health plan bill signed. President Nixon Dec. 29, 1973 signed into law the Health Maintenance Organization (HMO) Act authorizing the Department of Health, Education and Welfare (HEW) to spend $375 million over the next five years to help set up and evaluate prepaid health plans, under which subscribers for a flat fee would receive basic health services as they needed them.

The bill contained a provision enabling HEW to override laws in 40 states that had the effect of outlawing or hampering HMO's. The bill also required employers covered by minimum wage laws to give employes the option of having their company health care funds diverted to HMO's.

The bill had been passed despite a strong lobbying effort by the American Medical Association, which opposed legislation that would disturb the traditional doctor-patient fee system. HMO doctors would be salaried.

Price controls for health industry. The Cost of Living Council issued new price regulations for the health care industry Nov. 6, 1973, to take effect Jan. 1, 1974 after public comment.

The program's general aim was to reduce the 9% average annual increase in hospitals costs to 7.5% by limiting the overall annual increase in each patient's total bill. The current regulations had controlled price increases on individual hospital services, but there had been increases in the use of patient tests and in the use of more expensive equipment, the council said.

(Despite the 7.5% ceiling, Administration officials said exemptions to the regulations could bring the total increase to 9% and raise consumers' health care costs $5 billion annually.)

If the overutilization of hospital care were reduced, the Administration argued, the total cost of health care would also decline as unnecessary hospital admissions and the average patient's length of stay were cut back.

According to the plan: if a hospital had 1,000 patients with an average cost per stay of $1,000 in 1972, it could charge an average of $1,075 per stay and it could change its charges in order to earn $1,075,-000 in revenues in 1973, compared with $1 million in 1972. If admissions declined, average charges per patient could rise more than 7.5%; if there were increases in hospital admissions, the average charges would be less than 7.5%.

The American Hospital Association, which represented most of the nation's 7,-000 acute care facilities, criticized the plan, contending that economic incentives built into the program put a premium on short uncomplicated medical cases while causing an overall decline in the quality of services offered. Health care for patients requiring long term, intensive and expensive treatment would be impaired, the association charged.

Physicians and dentists would be permitted to increase their prices an average 4%, although no fee over $10 could be raised more than 10% in a single year and no fee under $10 could be raised more than $1. The medical lobby had sought a 5.5% increase. Previous controls had allowed a 2.5% increase in medical costs.

During 1972, physicians had raised prices 2.4% and dentists 2.8%.

A 6.5% limit was imposed on nursing homes' per diem costs. The outpatient departments in hospitals were allowed a 6% increase.

(Price controls for the health-care industry expired April 30, 1974 with the expiration of the Economic Stabilization Act of 1970.)

HEW shifts ethical drug buying policy. Casper W. Weinberger, secretary of health, education and welfare (HEW), announced Dec. 19, 1973 that HEW would start a policy whereby it would pay for prescription drugs covered by Medicare and Medicaid only at the lowest available market price. In effect, Medicare or Medicaid patients would be given generic drugs rather than generally more expensive brand-name equivalents.

In response to the HEW action, C. Joseph Stetler, president of the Pharmaceutical Manufacturers Association (PMA), warned that the government was taking a "huge gamble" in switching to cheap, equivalent drugs. Drugs containing the same active chemicals, he said, did not always have the same therapeutic value. Noting this objection, Weinberger commented that such instances were rare, and he said the proposed policy would be put into effect with assurance that patients would get safe and effective drugs.

Had the policy been in effect for all fiscal 1974, Weinberger said, HEW would have saved $28 million in Medicaid costs alone.

Psychosurgery barred. A Wayne (Mich.) County court ruled July 10, 1973 that state funds could not be used to finance experimental psychosurgery on persons confined against their will in state institutions, even when the patient's consent was formally obtained.

The court declared unanimously that even if an involuntarily detained patient were to agree to the surgery, the procedure would violate his First Amendment rights of free speech by damaging his ability to generate ideas. The decision, however, left open the possible use of psychosurgery (the destruction of some brain cells in an attempt to calm or improve behavior) when the procedure had advanced to the level where its benefits outweighed its risks. The court said that not enough was presently known about how the brain functions to permit the experimental surgery.

Biomedical research cuts criticized. Benno C. Schmidt, chairman of President Nixon's Cancer Panel, criticized the White House Nov. 30, 1973 for cutting the federal budget for biomedical research. "Neither the cancer program nor biomedical research generally can thrive" if the research budgets for the basic sciences and metabolic diseases were decreased, he said.

Schmidt singled out as his "biggest disappointment" the reduction in National Institutes of Health (NIH) training grants and fellowship programs to develop new research scientists. The White House Office of Management and Budget (OMB) originally had eliminated funding for research training grants, but after being pressured by Schmidt and the scientific community agreed to a $30 million program for fiscal 1974, $60 million for fiscal 1975 and $90 million for fiscal 1976. The total NIH budget—excluding cancer and heart research—fell from $878 million for fiscal 1972 to $767 million for fiscal 1974.

In a related development, Dr. Charles C. Edwards, assistant secretary of health, education and welfare for health, Nov. 20 called the war on cancer an administrative mistake. He contended that the secret to the success of the NIH had been maintenance of a proper balance among the different areas of medical research. Emphasis on one or two aspects of research would upset the balance, he said.

Ban on fetal research—The NIH April 17 had announced a ban on research by NIH-supported scientists on all live, aborted fetuses. The NIH had been studying guidelines, suggested in 1971 by an independent group of doctors, under

which research would be permitted if the aborted fetus were no older than 20 weeks, were no larger than 500 grams (1.1 lbs.), and no longer than 25 cm. (9.8 in.). The presumption was that such fetuses were incapable of surviving.

Nixon Administration Approaches Its End

Although Richard M. Nixon was unaware of it as the year started, 1974 was to be his last year as President, and many programs, the health programs among them, apparently lost ground as the President and the nation devoted increasing attention to the Watergate affair, the scandal that was to drive Nixon out of office.

Health care a major goal. In his 1974 State-of-the-Union message, delivered in person before a joint session of Congress Jan. 30, Nixon listed "10 key areas in which landmark accomplishments" could be possible in the year ahead. Itemizing the fourth key area, Nixon said: "We will establish a new system that makes high quality health care available to every American in a dignified manner and at a price he can afford." He also said:

The time is at hand this year to bring comprehensive high-quality health care within the reach of every American. I shall propose a sweeping new program that will assure comprehensive health insurance protection to millions of Americans who cannot now obtain it or afford it with vastly improved protection against catastrophic illnesses. This will be a plan that maintains the high standards of quality in America's health care and it will not require additional taxes.

Now I recognize that other plans have been put forward that would cost $80 billion and that would put our whole health care system under the heavy hand of the federal government.

This is the wrong approach. This has been tried abroad, and it's failed. It is not the way we do things here in America. This kind of plan would threaten the quality of care provided by our whole health care system.

The right way is one that builds on the strengths of the present system and one that does not destroy those strengths. One based on partnership not paternalism. Most important of all, let us keep this as the guiding principle of our health programs:

Government has a great role to play, but we must always make sure that our doctors will be working for their patients and not for the federal government.

Budget proposals. In his message for his 1975 budget, submitted Feb. 4,

1974, Nixon alluded to his plan for "basic reform in the financing of medical care," to bring "comprehensive insurance protection against medical expenses within reach of all Americans." But the proposed date was January 1976 so there were no funds for it in the fiscal 1975 budget.

The budget was dominated by the Medicare and Medicaid programs providing health care for the aged and poor, which absorbed 60¢ of every health dollar. The increase alone in Medicare spending was massive—$2 billion—which took the program to the $14.2 billion level. Medicaid spending followed with a $736 million increase to $6.6 billion.

The Administration made several proposals to try to hold down these costs. It suggested eliminating payments under Medicaid for dental care, and it planned tighter admission procedure for Medicaid patients proposed for elective surgery and an attempt to shorten hospital stays.

A $149 million increase was proposed for medical research spending at the National Institutes of Health, whose total budget would be $2 billion. But authorizations for all of the member institutes except those studying cancer and heart disease were decreased.

The health budget contained a new proposal for a $75 million program to finance regional health planning. The funds would provide for 200 regional health systems boards to plan facility sites and assist the states in regulation of rates and capital expenditures of hospitals and other health care units.

(The General Accounting Office had reported Jan. 11 that its collection of overcharges and other economy efforts in fiscal 1973 had produced recoveries of more than $5 million in the health field—including recovery of excessive payments to states of almost $4 million for Medicaid and $440 million for Medicare.)

Health care plan presented. President Nixon submitted his national health insurance plan to Congress Feb. 6, 1974 and urged its enactment "as soon as possible" so that the program could begin in January 1976.

The plan called for a basic insurance program to be available to all full-time employes; federally subsidized coverage for the poor, the unemployed, the self-employed and those with high medical insurance risk; and a revised Medicare program for the aged. The President said the program would cover the costs of catastrophic illnesses.

The basic program would be paid for by employers and employes. The subsidized program, which would eventually replace Medicaid, would be financed largely by federal and state governments. The increased Medicare coverage would be offset with increased charges. Nixon estimated that the program would cost an additional $6.4 billion a year in federal funds, an additional $1 billion in state funds.

The program was predicated on maximum use of the private health insurance industry. "Let us not be led to an extreme program," he warned, "that would place the entire health care system under the dominion of social planners in Washington."

(In an address to the American Hospital Association Feb. 5, Nixon urged support for his plan so that "a less responsible plan that would appeal to the demagogues" would not be enacted. "Let us not make the mistake," he said, "of destroying the best medical care system in the world that we already have.")

All three phases of his plan would be voluntary, Nixon told Congress, and one of the three would be available to every American and all would offer identical benefits. The benefits included physicians' care in and out of the hospital except regular check-ups for adults; outpatient prescription drugs; treatment for mental health, alcoholism and drug abuse within certain limits; eye, ear and dental care for children up to age 13; prenatal and well-baby care; family planning services; 100 days of nursing home care; home health services; blood and other services, such as X-rays and laboratory tests.

The states were to have the responsibility for reviewing insurance premium rates and physician charges and for setting hospital fees covered by the plan. Prior notice to the patients was required if doctors sent bills for charges above normal fees under the basic plan.

All full-time employes were to be offered the basic plan, or one supplementing the basic benefits, the latter requiring approval. The employer would pay 65% of the premium costs, the employe the remainder, for the first three years of the plan. These costs were put at $600 for a family and $240 for an individual. After three years, the employer share would rise to 75%.

A family would pay a deductible of $150 per person, up to a family limit of $450, and a separate $50 deductible for outpatient drugs, in annual medical expenses, plus 25% of medical expenses covered by the plan. If payments reached $1,500 in a year, the plan would absorb further costs that year.

The premium costs for small businesses and employers of low-wage workers would be federally subsidized for five years.

The plan for the unemployed and poor would replace most of the current Medicaid program. It would be operated under federal guidelines by the states, which would pay 25% of the increased costs of the program. The Medicaid program would be continued on an interim basis "to meet certain needs, primarily long-term institutional care," the President said. Eventually, it would be replaced with the "assisted health insurance" plan financed by the federal and state governments, contributions from employes and premium payments by patients.

Coverage would be extended to nonworking families with annual income below $7,500, all families with income below $5,000 and persons with high medical risk.

No premiums would be required for the families with income under $5,000 and individuals with income under $3,500, and their deductibles and copayments would be less than under the basic plan.

Medicare benefits would be expanded to cover outpatient drugs and mental health services.

In the program for the elderly, Medicare would be expanded to cover outpatient drugs and mental health services. A ceiling of $750 was set for the maximum annual cost to the individual, but the aged would have payments increased over the current program. Hospital and other care would require an initial $100 deductible, a separate $50 deductible for outpatient drugs and payment of 20% of all medical bills up to the $750 limit. Currently, Medicare patients paid $84 as the average cost of the first day of hospital care, then received 59 days of hospitalization free. A $90 annual premium also would be required from the aged.

Nixon offers compromise—Nixon May 20 stated his willingness to compromise with Congress in a national health insurance program in order to facilitate passage of the legislation in 1974. While advocating the Administration program, the President said in a radio address, "We are not ruling out compromise where compromise does not violate the basic principles of our proposals."

He cited three basic principles on which he would not compromise: freedom of the patient to choose a doctor; providing "all parties—consumers, providers, carriers and state governments—with a direct stake in making the system work"; and having the plan "build on the capacity and diversity of the existing system of health care rather than tear it down and seek to erect a costly, federally dominated structure in its place."

Nixon said his program was "the only major plan that offers extensive, uniform health coverage without raising your taxes; without severely damaging the effective private health insurance . . . and without establishing an enormous new federal bureaucracy."

The President said other major proposals—a plan offered by Sen. Edward M. Kennedy (D, Mass.) and Rep. Wilbur D. Mills (D, Ark.) and another by Sens. Russell B. Long (D, La.) and Abraham A. Ribicoff (D, Conn.)—had merit but he cited several objections. In his view, both were deficient because they involved direct administration by the federal government. He also objected to the Long-Ribicoff plan, restricted to coverage for catastrophic illnesses, because it would leave citizens "unprotected against many other substantial health costs."

Nixon cautioned that "there's a very real possibility of an unbridled increase" in the cost of health services because of the failure of Congress to enact mandatory price controls.

He urged the industry to restrain costs but said voluntary control was inadequate, that legislation must be enacted this year for protection against "prohibitive costs."

Under the Administration plan, employers would be offered health insurance policies from private companies, the cost being shared by employers and employes.

The Kennedy-Mills proposal offered generally the same coverage although the benefits would be somewhat more generous and the cost to employes somewhat less. The financing was different, however, from a 4% payroll tax (3% from the employer, 1% from the employe). It also would be compulsory and utilize the private insurance industry largely as an intermediary instead of as the policy seller.

Hearings on plans open—Hearings on national health insurance plans were opened by Mills' House Ways and Means Committee April 24. The opening witness was Health, Education and Welfare Secretary Caspar W. Weinberger, who urged enactment of the Administration program. He and Mills contested several points in their respective plans. Mills had reservations about the capability of state governments to police the program, as proposed by the Administration. Weinberger advocated a state role in control. Mills questioned the major role for private companies under the Nixon bill. Weinberger said this would save money and free the program from total federal control.

Both were cautious about cost estimates. Weinberger said it was "folly to make any estimates at all," but, pressed by committee members about financing, estimated the Administration program would cost about $60 billion annually in payments by employers, employes and the federal government.

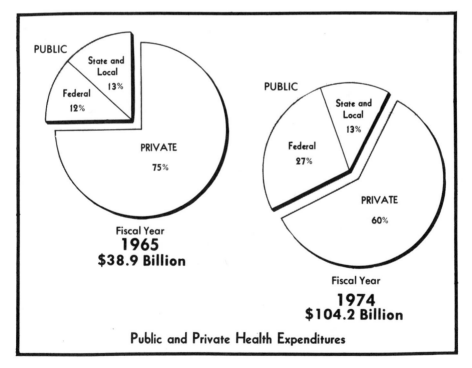

Public and Private Health Expenditures

Ribicoff and Long testified before the committee April 25. Ribicoff said: "Let's not do a program that's completely indigestible, but do a program one step at a time and see if it works. If you don't do it one step at a time, you are going to collapse not only what you are trying to do but the entire health care system."

The Long-Ribicoff plan, covering illnesses costing more than $2,000 a year, would be financed by a payroll tax and administered through the Social Security system.

Sen. Vance Hartke (D, Ind.), testifying May 22 before the Senate Finance Committee, repeated the frequently made observation that "the higher a person's income, the more likely he is to have hospital and surgical coverage. The higher a person's income, the more likely he is to be healthy." But he added the opinion that "we need health insurance for both the poor and the nonpoor. Both groups are suffering under the strain of the high costs of hospital and doctor care. Both groups have a right to quality health care, and both groups will benefit from national health insurance." Hartke listed this set of 15 widely accepted "basic principles for national health insurance":

"*First*, good health is the hope of every American, and access to quality health care is the right of every American. National health insurance must guarantee that right.

"*Second*, there are Americans who, because of income, employment status, or geographic location, do not have sufficient access to quality health care. National health insurance must guarantee that access.

"*Third*, national health insurance must cover the costs of preventive as well as remedial care.

"*Fourth*, it must cover the cost of hospitals and health-care practitioners.

"*Fifth*, it must cover the costs of both short-term illnesses and long-term sickness and debilitation.

"*Sixth,* it must cover the costs of home health care and mental health care.

"*Seventh*, it must allow patients to choose their own doctors.

"*Eighth*, it must provide a means to establish a system of health insurance cov-

erage for lower income individuals and families.

"*Ninth*, it must not differentiate between the scope of coverage afforded to the poor and the nonpoor.

"*Tenth*, it must not provide for any unnecessary governmental intervention in the health-care delivery or insurance system.

"*Eleventh*, it must seek to avoid unnecessary paperwork, regulations, or other complications which only serve to inhibit the provision of quality health care and heighten suspicion and frustration among the people.

"*Twelfth*, the extent of financial assistance provided by the federal government should be related in a rational and responsible manner to family income. In other words, those most in need should get the most financial assistance.

"*Thirteenth*, the means of financing the national health-insurance program should not add to the already burdensome and regressive payroll taxes but should be geared in a more progressive manner to income tax liability.

"*Fourteenth*, national health insurance must provide for expanded benefits for those 65 and older which are similar, if not identical, to those provided for people under 65.

"And *fifteenth*, it must include reasonable provisions for cost control and utilization review."

Dr. Michael D. Bromberg, in a statement on behalf of the Federation of American Hospitals, told the Senate committee May 22 that the federation had drafted a "health-care consumers' bill of rights" containing the following "elements":

"(1) *Access to health care*—Consumers must have equal access to health manpower and health care facilities, regardless of financial means.

"(2) *Quality care*—The consumer must have access to quality care.

"(3) *Reasonable cost*—Health care should be delivered efficiently and economically, consistent with the delivery of quality patient care.

"(4) *Choice of provider*—The consumer should also have the ability to select the provider of his choice.

"(5) *Choice of delivery system*—The consumer should also have the ability to select the method of delivery which he prefers.

"(6) *Financial security*—The consumer must know that he is protected against the threat of financially burdensome medical bills.

"(7) *Simple claim & payment procedures*—Procedures for filing and processing claims should be simple, convenient and expedient.

"(8) *Improved delivery*—Continuing improvement in the health care system through experimentation, research and development of new methods of delivery.

"(9) *Universal coverage*—All Americans should be covered by the program.

"(10) *Due process*—The rights of the consumer should be protected through adequate administrative appeal procedures and judicial review available to both patient and provider."

The National Consumers League proposed this "model patients bill of rights" in a statement to the committee Aug. 6:

"(1) The maintenance of the health of its citizens is essential to the well being of the nation. Every person has the right to receive high-quality personal health services without regard to ability to pay, age, race, sex, religion, and national origin.

"(2) The right of privacy and protection against self-incrimination shall prevail during examination, diagnosis, and treatment. It shall govern the maintenance of all health records, verbal or recorded.

"(3) Except in emergencies, patients must be informed of treatment to be received, of who provides the treatment to be received, of risks and benefits to the extent known, and of whether or not the treatment is experimental. Patients have the right to withhold consent to treatment. If the patient is unable to give informed consent, it must be sought from next of kin or others responsible for the patient's rights, including the physician or institution, as a last resort.

"(4) The patient-provider relationship shall be free of any representatives of enforcement, investigative, financial, religious or social agencies, unless the patient, without duress, approves.

"(5) No person needing care shall be turned away or otherwise abandoned by providers of care.

"(6) No person shall be denied access to care because he or she has advocated or worked for change in the provision of health care.

"(7) Every person has a right to all information of a public nature on the quality of care, the administration of health services and their governance and economics.

"(8) Health care shall be organized to benefit the general public; therefore, elected consumer representatives under national health insurance shall have an ongoing role in decisionmaking with respect to local expenditures for health-care services, including services educational, preventive, curative, restorative and mental health.

"(9) Every citizen has the right to select and change physicians at will or to select a preferred system of medical care.

"(10) The right of health-care consumers to pursue complaints to a satisfactory conclusion shall not be denied."

The National Association of Manufacturers, in a statement to the Senate committee, held that "the problems of the present health care system seem to lie mainly at the margin. The major goals of any new program, therefore, should be to fill the gaps left in coverage and delivery and to bring the costs under more stable control. Industry believes that any national health plan should seek to achieve the following objectives: (1) Target benefits primarily to those people for whom present health care is unavailable; (2) provide effective controls on the rapidly expanding costs of health care; (3) acknowledge the economic impact of massive new health care costs on employment and on the private sector's ability to provide goods and services; (4) improve health care availability and delivery; (5) Build upon the strengths of the existing system rather than move toward a federal takeover of a viable portion of the private sector."

Nursing home cost rule barred. A federal district court in Washington Feb. 7, 1974 barred the Cost of Living Council from enforcing its price control guidelines for nursing homes. The ruling jeopardized the Administration's plans to continue wage-price restrictions for the health industry after the Economic Stabilization Act expired April 30.

According to the court, a 6.5% ceiling on price increases conflicted with Medicare and Medicaid statutes requiring that institutions be reimbursed for all "reasonable care" cost increases. The court also declared that the guidelines were "arbitrary and capricous" because they singled out nursing homes without demonstrating they had an inflationary influence on the economy. An estimated 20,000 nursing homes were affected by the ruling.

HEW drops pre-admission review plan. Caspar W. Weinberger, secretary of health, education and welfare, announced abandonment Feb. 8 of an HEW proposal that would have required physicians treating Medicare and Medicaid patients to obtain prior approval from a hospital committee of "health professionals" before admitting them to a hospital in a non-emergency situation.

The pre-admission review plan, published in the Federal Register Jan. 9, was withdrawn because of opposition from doctors who warned they might refuse to serve on the admission panels, Weinberger said.

HMO benefits called too expensive. Administrators of prepaid group health insurance programs warned federal health officials that regulations for implementation of the new Health Maintenence Organization (HMO) Assistance Act would make their plans too expensive to market, it was reported Feb. 14, 1974.

If required to provide such benefits as diagnostic mental health services and dental care for children, the administrators said, their plans could not compete with less comprehensive but cheaper ones now being devised and put into practice by private health insurance companies and the Blue Cross-Blue Shield systems across the U.S. Moreover, the large companies would not bother with government certification, since they already had 90% of the market, the administrators warned.

Dr. Frank Newman, president of the Group Health Association of America, suggested that a "grandfather clause"

—creating exemptions based on previously existing circumstances—was needed to certify existing prepaid programs. However, Dr. Harold P. Buzzel, director of the Health Services Administration of the Department of Health, Education and Welfare, said, "If the existing plans, which are also a vested interest group, want to qualify for certification, they will have to comply with the law."

In a prepared answer to questions of the Senate Finance Committee, Casper W. Weinberger reported May 21 on the use of HMOs under Medicaid: "The Medicaid statute provides an opportunity for states to contract with . . . [HMOs] to provide for the delivery of health maintenance and treatment services to Medicaid eligible populations. Since July 1969, states have contracted with HMOs to provide or arrange for medical services to be provided on a prepayment basis to Medicaid eligibles. During fiscal year 1973, twelve states (California, District of Columbia, Hawaii, Maryland, Massachusetts, Michigan, Minnesota, New York, Pennsylvania, Rhode Island, Utah and Washington) had negotiated Medicaid-HMO contracts. There are 67 prepaid health plans, providing care and services to an enrolled population of over 370,000 Medicaid eligibles and a potential population of almost one million. The ceiling on reimbursement to these HMOs is the actuarial value of the cost of services provided under the contract, had these services been provided outside of the HMO. In fact, in view of the emphasis of HMOs on ambulatory care and health education, and, as a result of the financial incentives of a prepayment system, costs in HMOs tend to be lower than alternatives and services tend to be delivered in a more effective manner. A draft study of the experience of 1,000 Medicaid eligibles enrolled in a Washington, D.C. HMO demonstrated that the average cost of care was approximately 20% less than comparable services provided on a fee-for-services basis."

Care denial invalid. In an action announced Feb. 26, 1974, the Supreme Court, over the dissent of Justice William H. Rehnquist, struck down an Arizona law denying indigent health and hospital care to individuals who had not met the state's residency requirement of one year.

Kennedy criticizes drug promotion. Sen. Edward M. Kennedy (D, Mass.) accused the pharmaceutical industry of using techniques to promote sales of their drugs that smacked of "payola." Kennedy's charge was made amid Senate subcommittee testimony by former drug salesmen that the drug industry offered doctors color television sets, freezers and expense-paid Bermuda "seminars" in hopes of inducing them to prescribe certain drugs.

The former salesmen appeared before the Health Subcommittee March 8, 1974. They told of promotional schemes offering "gifts" to pharmacists, officials of hospitals or clinics and doctors who ordered or prescribed large amounts of a company's products. While they expressed high regard for their former employers, the witnesses also testified that they were under great pressure to sell but under relatively less pressure to educate physicians and pharmacists on the hazards and limitations of their drugs.

The subcommittee March 12 took testimony from executives of four leading drug manufacturing firms, who defended industry marketing practices, contending they were intended to provide doctors with a careful balance on the good and bad points of their products.

Jan Dlouhy of the Lederle Labs division of American Cyanamid Co. said: "I do not accept the proposition that a physician, after all his years of training, with all his interest in his patient's well-being, and with his professional reputation at stake, will have his judgment swayed and will use inappropriately a product simply because of a salesman presentation—even if overzealous on occasion."

Openly skeptical, Kennedy responded that doctors were inadequately educated about drugs in medical school and, forced to choose among 20,000 brand names for 700 drug entities, tended to rely excessively on information from the drug manufacturers.

Kennedy also charged that huge outlays to promote medicines had led to irrational prescribing. Kennedy said adverse drug reactions killed 30,000 persons annually and that 50,000-100,000 deaths a year could be attributed to treatment-resistant bacteria, which had emerged, in part, because of misuse and overuse of antibiotics.

Previously, the subcommittee heard testimony Feb. 25 that more than half the antibiotics given hospital patients were not needed or had been incorrectly prescribed.

Dr. Sidney Wolfe, director of Ralph Nader's Health Research Group, blamed the drug industry for the unnecessary use of medicines. "A well trained actor could probably prescribe drugs as well as the thousands of American doctors whose prescribing practices reflect drug company indoctrination in lieu of scientific evaluation." Wolfe cited unpublished drug industry statistics that two of every three Americans who saw doctors about common colds were given antibiotics that were ineffective.

Dr. James A. Visconti of Ohio State University's College of Pharmacy told the subcommittee of a study he participated in, which showed that only 13% of the prescriptions for antibiotics given 340 hospital patients were judged "rational" by an evaluating team of doctors and pharmacists. Of the remaining prescriptions, 65% were called "irrational" and 22% "questionable," he said.

Va. law against drug price ads voided. A three-judge federal panel struck down as an unconstitutional infringement on the 1st Amendment, a Virginia law barring drugstores from advertising prices of prescription drugs, it was reported March 25, 1974. The panel said the elderly, the infirm and others who spent large parts of their incomes on medicine, had the right to know prescription prices so they could shop for bargains.

Easing of VD outbreak reported. For the first time in a decade, the reported number of cases of venereal disease did not show a marked increase, the Center for Disease Control reported March 13,

NUMBER OF PERSONS
WITH HEALTH INSURANCE PROTECTION
BY TYPE OF COVERAGE

In the United States

(000 omitted)

End of year	Hospital expense	Surgical expense	Regular medical expense	Major medical expense	Disability income Short-term	Disability income Long-term	Dental expense
1940	12,312	5,350	3,000	—	N.A.	N.A.	—
1945	32,068	12,890	4,713	—	N.A.	N.A.	—
1950	76,639	54,156	21,589	—	37,793	*	—
1955	101,400	85,681	53,038	5,241	39,513	*	—
1960	122,500	111,525	83,172	25,371	42,436	*	N.A.
1961	125,825	116,376	90,393	32,334	43,055	*	N.A.
1962	129,407	119,766	94,717	37,130	45,002	*	N.A.
1963	133,472	124,105	100,095	42,003	44,146	3,029	N.A.
1964	136,304	127,092	106,007	47,338	44,992	3,363	N.A.
1965	138,671	130,530	109,560	53,020	46,727	4,514	N.A.
1966	142,369	133,995	113,986	57,881	49,731	5,068	N.A.
1967	146,409	138,898	119,913	63,428	51,675	6,778	2,399
1968	151,947	143,625	126,233	68,171	55,236	7,836	3,242
1969	155,025	147,774	131,792	73,752	57,270	9,282	5,230
1970	158,847	151,440	138,658	77,061	57,589	10,966	7,454
1971	161,849	153,093	139,399	80,252	58,580	12,284	8,912
1972	164,098	154,687	140,873	83,668	60,848	14,538	10,272
1973:							
Under 65	156,595	149,409	137,896	86,223	63,468	17,011	N.A.
65 and over	10,552	9,215	8,446	1,616	—	—	N.A.
Total	167,147	158,624	146,342	87,839	63,468	17,011	12,178
1974:							
Under 65	160,483	153,346	143,493	89,555	64,582	17,799	N.A.
65 and over	11,277	9,225	8,287	1,766	—	—	N.A.
Total	171,760	162,571	151,780	91,321	64,582	17,799	16,842

*Included in "Short-term," with the possibility of some duplication of disability income coverage for these years.

Note: Data have been revised due to a change in methodology to improve the accuracy of reporting health insurance coverages. The data refer to the net total of people protected, i.e., duplication among persons protected by more than one kind of insuring organization or more than one insurance company policy providing the same type of coverage has been eliminated. The "Hospital expense," "Surgical expense," and "Regular medical expense" categories represent coverage provided by insurance companies, Blue Cross, Blue Shield and medical society-approved plans, and other plans. The "Major medical expense" and "Dental expense" categories represent insurance companies only. The "Disability income" category represents insurance companies, formal paid sick leave plans, and coverage through employee organizations.

N.A. — Not available.

Source: Health Insurance Association of America.

1974. The last six months of 1973 had a 2% decrease in the number of reported cases of infectious syphilis, compared to the same period in 1972. Gonorrhea, a considerably more widespread disease, showed a July–December 1973 increase of less than 1%, which was a "striking change" from the past, one physician at the center commented.

Final figures for fiscal 1973 (July 1, 1972–June 30, 1973) were 25,080 newly reported cases of syphilis, up 4.5% from fiscal 1972, and 809,681 newly reported cases of gonorrhea, an increase of 12.7% from fiscal 1972.

Funds for cancer & diabetes research. Nixon July 23, 1974 signed into law a bill extending the National Cancer Act through 1977. The bill, which authorized $2.8 billion for cancer research for fiscal 1975–77, was approved by voice vote in the House July 9 and the Senate July 10. One section of the act required Senate confirmation of all future directors of the National Institutes of Health.

The President also signed into law July 23 legislation authorizing for fiscal 1975–77 $41 million for new diabetes research centers and for establishment of a national commission to formulate long-range plans to combat diabetes.

Governors discuss health care. At the National Governors Conference, held in Seattle June 2–5, 1974, a health-care discussion was held June 3, featuring Sen. Edward M. Kennedy (D, Mass.), Health, Education and Welfare Secretary Caspar W. Weinberger and Dr. Russell B. Roth, president of the American Medical Association (AMA). The first two pushed for support of their competing national health-insurance plans. Kennedy insisted that the "profit motive" should be taken out of health insurance. Weinberger said the strength of the private medical profession and private insurance industry must be maintained. Roth called both plans "inflationary" and said the "health crisis" had been "trumped up" by politicians frustrated by the economic and public safety problems of government.

Report analyzes health insurance effect. According to a Rand Corp. study published in the New England Journal of Medicine June 13, a national health insurance plan covering most medical expenses would cause physicians and outpatient clinics to be swamped with patients but have little effect on hospitalizations. On the whole, the report said, national health insurance would lead to higher physicians' fees without improvement in the health of most Americans or increase in average life expectancy.

Among the conclusions of the report:

A comprehensive, full coverage national health insurance plan would add $8 billion–$16 billion to the $62 billion currently spent each year for health care. Such a plan would increase the demand for ambulatory medical services by at least 75%.

A health insurance plan requiring participants to pay 25% of their medical costs would cost $3 billion–$7 billion more than current levels and bring about at least a 30% rise in the demand for ambulatory medical care.

Patients would experience longer delays in obtaining appointments and doctors would have less time to spend with each patient. The net effect of such a change would be to "reduce the demand for ambulatory services among the relatively affluent, who are primarily time-poor (reluctant to spend time waiting in line), and thus to enhance the tendency of a national insurance program to reallocate services toward the dollar-poor."

Catastrophic health insurance designed to prevent financial disaster brought on by unusually large medical bills would have little effect on demand for either ambulatory services or hospitalization.

Hospitalizations would be little affected by national health insurance because 90% of them were covered by third parties like Blue Cross-Blue Shield and Medicare.

AMA eases peer review opposition. Delegates to the American Medical Association's (AMA) semiannual convention in Chicago, voted to cooperate with the federal government in establishment of Professional Standards Review Organizations (PSRO) to monitor the quality of service under Medicaid and Medicare. By a vote of 185–57 June 26, 1974, the delegates agreed to not to wage, as some had demanded, a campaign of outright opposition to PSROs, but to work for the programs' success while seeking to amend portions of the law creating the organizations.

The AMA board of trustees and its Council on Medical Services had spent much of the meeting warning the delegates that fighting PSROs would be futile. A continuance of efforts to seek repeal of the PSRO law could seriously weaken AMA impact on pending health legislation and destroy its public credibility, they said. One trustee said, "I believe the federal government, which purchases care for 38% of our population, is entitled to assurances that that care is efficient, effective and economical."

Utah PSRO begins operation—The peer review system became operative June 18 with the signing of a $951,000 contract by the Utah PSRO. In existence for two years, the Utah organization had served as a model for peer review legislation.

Doctors had warned that the PSRO would be costly to administer, would add hours of paperwork to a doctor's day, allow the federal government to interfere in medicine and lead to "cookbook medicine" by discouraging innovative practices. But the Utah doctors involved in the pilot project asserted that none of these fears was valid.

Only 5.5% of all cases required additional review by the PSRO, and in only 24 of 20,000 cases was payment denied. Dr. Alan R. Nelson, chairman of the Utah PSRO, said there was "zero paperwork" and most physicians in Utah had agreed to participate in the program. The cost of review, Nelson said, was about $2 a year for each Medicare and Medicaid patient.

Court supports review of doctors' Medicare billing—The 1972 law that gave the government the right to review billing for Medicare and Medicaid was ruled constitutional by a three-judge federal court May 8, 1975. The law had been contested in a June 1973 suit brought by the Association of American Physicians and Surgeons against the Department of Health Education and Welfare.

The suit challenged the legality of legislation known as the Professional Standards Review Act, which was an amendment to the 1972 Social Security Act. Under the act, PSROs had already been established in several areas of the U.S.

In the ruling, which was unanimous, the judges said that the law didn't "bar physicians from practicing their profession," but only provided "standards for the dispensation of federal funds." The panel ruled that Congress had a constitutional right to see to it that physicians were kept from abusing Medicare and Medicaid funds.

The ruling was upheld by the Supreme Court Nov. 17, 1975.

(The Supreme Court Jan. 13, 1975 upheld a lower court decision denying reimbursement under Medicare to persons treated by chiropractors.)

More foreign-trained MDs. According to a report in the June 29, 1974 issue of the New England Journal of Medicine, a growing "medical underground" of thousands of foreign trained doctors were practicing medicine without licenses and often without supervision. Although many of these uncertified doctors were officially hired as laboratory technicians or assistants in other low-level jobs, the report said, they often assumed responsibility for patient care without consulting licensed physicians.

The study, conducted by five U.S. doctors, was undertaken at the request of the Educational Council for Foreign Medical Graduates (Philadelphia), the body which examined foreign graduates to determine their fitness to seek licensure in the U.S. (Foreign trained doctors had to pass this examination to qualify to take examinations for state certification.)

In a related development, a report prepared for the Association of American Medical Colleges urged a program to drastically cut the number of foreign medical school graduates entering U.S. medicine, it was reported July 20. The study asserted that such graduates were becoming "a category of second-class physicians," and said these "products of unaccredited educational systems" threatened the quality of U.S. care.

The study group recommended a standard and "adequate" qualifying examination to be given graduates of both domestic and foreign institutions before they were admitted to internship or residency. (It would replace the test administered by the Educational Council for Foreign Medical Graduates.) The number of foreign graduates given internships and residencies should be limited. A pilot program, giving preference to U.S. citizens, should be started to help raise foreign graduates to levels of competence generally reached by U.S. graduates.

Graduates of foreign medical schools currently made up nearly a fifth of the 356,000 doctors in the U.S.

In a study commissioned by the U.S. HEW Department, Rosemary Stevens and Joan Vermeulen of the Yale University Medical School had reported in early 1973 that 63,391 of the 334,028 physicians in the U.S. in 1970 had received their primary medical education abroad. The number of foreign-trained doctors who came to the U.S. in 1971 was 10,540, or more than 1,500 more than the 8,974 doctors who graduated from medical schools that year.

Drs. E. Fuller Torrey and Robert L. Taylor had noted in the April 1973 issue of the American Journal of Psychiatry that "taking this medical manpower from other lands saves the United States a large amount of money. If the 3,016 foreign doctors who were permanently licensed in the United States in 1970 had to be trained in the United States, they would require the addition of 30 new medical schools. To build a medical school costs at least $50 million and to operate one for a year averages $3.8 million. Thus the total amount needed to replace the foreign-trained doctors who were permanently licensed last year would be $1.6 billion. This is the equivalent of over half of the total U.S. foreign aid program. When this amount is added to other aspects of the brain drain, it may well be that our foreign aid program is in effect canceled altogether."

There seemed to be some evidence, however, that the bargain, in respect to medical care, was not as good for the U.S. at it at first had seemed. According to the Stevens-Vermeulen study, "indications are that foreign medical graduates continue to perform less well than their American counterparts even after several years of American training." As an example, 37% of foreign medical graduates but only 9% of graduates of American medical schools failed to pass their tests for American licenses.

Needless X-ray use charged. Dr. Karl Z. Morgan, professor of health physics at the Georgia Institute of Technology in Atlanta, told the American Cancer Society's seminar for science writers in St. Augustine, Fla. March 27, 1974 that Americans were getting harmful radiation overdoses from diagnostic X-rays. Asserting that most U.S. doctors and dentists "didn't have the remotest concept of the risks associated with exposure to diagnostic X-rays," Morgan charged that 3,000 Americans died each year from cancer resulting from unnecessary exposure to diagnostic X-rays.

Morgan, director of health physics at the Atomic Energy Commission's Oak Ridge (Tenn.) National Laboratory 1943–72, urged that outmoded, high-dose X-ray equipment be replaced with new low-dose apparatus; that radiation technologists be appropriately educated, trained and certified; and that dentists reserve use of X-rays for special needs only.

The Food & Drug Administration July 29 published new standards that were designed to reduce public exposure to unnecessary radiation. Under the new rules, which were effective for medical and dental diagnostic equipment manufactured after July 31, X-ray beams were limited to the smallest size necessary to produce an acceptable picture. The rules also contained provisions to minimize film retakes by requiring improvement in equipment reliability.

National Research Act. President Nixon July 12, 1974 signed into law the National Research Act, which created a commission to monitor the use of human subjects in biomedical research and established a biomedical research training awards program. The bill had been passed by the Senate 72–14 June 27 and by the House 311–10 June 28.

The first U.S. legislation ever to consider the ethical questions of medical research, the act aimed at developing guidelines for research involving humans. A temporary, two-year commission appointed by the secretary of health, education and welfare (HEW)—to be succeeded July 1, 1976 by a permanent National Advisory Council for the Protection of Subjects of Biomedical and Behavioral Research—would study and make recommendations on controversial research and procedures. The temporary commission would pay close attention to research on children, prisoners, the mentally ill and live human fetuses, as well as psychosurgery, a brain operation designed to control behavior.

The commission would be without any power to enforce its recommendations and could be overruled by the HEW secretary, who would be only required to publish his reasons for rejecting the proposed guidelines. However, the permanent commission would not be obligated to publish its recommendations nor could it be overridden by the HEW secretary.

The act also required appointment of the 11-member temporary commission within 60 days of the bill's signing. Within four months of the members' appointment, the commission would recommend policies for research involving live human fetuses. Until these recommendations were presented, all fetal research using HEW funds would be prohibited, except to save the lives of infants.

The other major section of the act created a national program of research training grants to young scientists and doctors. Individuals receiving the awards would have the options of repaying them along with accrued interest or repaying each year of support by teaching or doing research in the health field for one year. Recipients trained in the health care professions might also repay the grants by working in geographical areas not adequately staffed with professionals in their specialties.

Mass. law curbs fetal research—Gov. Francis Sargent (R) signed into law June 26 legislation prohibiting Massachusetts doctors from testing vaccines on developing fetuses.

Rep. William Delahunt, principal sponsor of the bill, said June 27 that the law would not interfere with most fetal research. He added that researchers should be grateful that the law was not as restrictive as a recently enacted Illinois statute barring research on living or dead human fetal tissue.

Dr. Michael N. Oxman, a Boston microbiologist, was critical of the new legislation. Vaccine studies, he contended June 28, "can only be done by administering the vaccine to women already planning abortions and then testing the fetal tissues to see if the vaccine reached the fetus."

Equivalent-drug differences cited. A report to Congress by the Office of Technology Assessment (OTA) July 12, 1974 indicated that prescription drugs containing the same active ingredients did not necessarily produce identical therapeutic results. The OTA found "roughly a score" of chemically equivalent drugs produced by the same or different manufacturers that could be absorbed into the blood at different levels and speeds. This was potentially dangerous, the panel said, for drugs that were toxic at high levels.

Robert W. Berliner of Yale Medical School, chairman of the OTA panel, said that 85%–90% of ethical drugs would not require screening for equivalency, but he urged greater FDA control over the manufacturing of medicines that did. He also proposed creation of FDA advisory groups to make lists of interchangeable drugs.

C. Joseph Stetler of the Pharmaceutical Manufacturers Association (PMA) called the OTA's report "superb," and claimed that it undercut the new Health, Education and Welfare (HEW) Department policy of limiting Medicare and Medicaid drug reimbursement to the lowest-cost drug generally available. Generic drugs, chemically the same as brand-name drugs, were usually less expensive than brand-name counterparts.

However, Berliner disputed Stetler's assessment, arguing that HEW could act promptly to insure equivalency among the 10%–15% of drugs requiring screening.

Sen. Edward M. Kennedy (D, Mass.), chairman of the Technology Assessment Board overseeing the OTA and the Health Subcommittee of the Senate Labor and Public Welfare Committee, had requested the study. Kennedy said he would incorpo-rate the OTA's conclusions into his proposed bill to reform the pharmaceutical industry's advertising and marketing practices.

Kennedy had released statistics May 2 showing that in 1973, 20 leading drug concerns had given doctors, nurses and other health professionals promotional gifts valued at $14 million. These firms had also distributed more than two billion free drug samples. Kennedy said such marketing practices were indefensible.

Ford & Health Care

Ford Succeeds Nixon

Richard M. Nixon resigned as President of the United States Aug. 9, 1974 after admitting wrongdoing in the Watergate scandal. Vice President Gerald R. Ford, who succeeded Nixon as President, indicated soon after assuming office that his viewpoints and policies on the issue of health care were similar to Nixon's.

Appeal to Congress. In his first major address as President, Ford appeared before a joint session of Congress to make a nationally televised appeal for the legislative body's cooperation in confronting the problems of the nation. In regard to health-care problems, Ford said:

As vice president, I have studied various proposals for better health-care financing. I saw them coming closer together, and urged my friends in Congress and in the Administration to sit down and sweat out a sound compromise. The comprehensive health insurance plan goes a long way toward providing early relief to people who are sick. Why don't we write—and I ask this with the greatest spirit of cooperation—why don't we write a good health bill on the statute books in 1964 before this Congress adjourns?—74, excuse me.

Cost-cutting. Ford sought to cut the budget as closely as possible. He indicated in a message to Congress Nov. 26, 1974 that health programs would have to bear a large share of the spending reduction.

Among the changes proposed were an increase in Medicare costs to the patient, a decrease in the federal share of Medicaid funding, less funds for dental care for the poor and in the amount of money that working welfare mothers could earn without losing benefits.

In a message to Congress Jan. 30, 1975, Ford requested that $2.6 billion in federal spending be rescinded or deferred. The requests for recissions included $285 million scheduled for health care planning.

Inflation & health-care costs. The rising costs of health care were explored in Washington Sept. 19–20, 1974 by representatives of the poor, the aged, the handicapped, the young, minority groups and consumers, who held discussions with Administration officials and Congressional leaders on ways to curb inflation in the areas of social welfare, health and education.

Citing the impact of inflation on social services, Sen. Edward Kennedy (D, Mass.) quoted from an HEW position paper prepared for the conference showing that $2 billion–$3 billion in the total $43 billion increase in Medicaid and

Medicare appropriations was caused by rising prices.

(According to the HEW paper, "direct out-of-pocket payments by consumers for medical care fell from 68% to 35% of personal health care expenditures" between 1950–1973. "However, due to inflation, population growth and expanded use of services, out-of-pocket expenditures actually increased by almost $21 billion during the same period" to total $28 billion.)

The problem of rising health costs was also discussed Sept. 20, when the Consumer Price Index for August was released showing that the 1.5% monthly increase in the cost of health care outpaced the average inflation rate, which was 1.3%.

In the four months since wage and price controls had been lifted, the medical component of the index had increased at an annual rate of 17.6%, compared with a 13.5% increase for the index as a whole.

A statement endorsed by 16 major national groups and signed by 69 participants to the conference was issued Sept. 20 as a counter-position paper to protest possible budget cuts by the Administration.

"No evidence was presented at the conference that federal spending levels have been one of the major causes of high inflation of the past 18 months," the paper declared. "Rather, the inadequacy of federal health, education and welfare expenditures have resulted in a deterioration of services to the poor and low income groups, which is unjustified at any time and particularly undesirable during a period of rapid inflation. Any increases in the already too-high unemployment rate is a completely unacceptable approach to meeting the current inflationary period."

"Major tax reform" and "tax increases based on the ability to pay" would prove more effective anti-inflation weapons than budget cuts penalizing the poor, the statement said.

Signers of the statement included nearly all of the meeting's participants who represented the poor, the aged, the handicapped, minority groups and consumers. (The balance of the delegates—about 150—represented professional groups in the health and education fields.) Among the wide-ranging groups which endorsed the statement were the AFL-CIO, the League of Women Voters, the National Council of Churches, the National Urban League, and the National Conference of Catholic Charities. Wilbur J. Cohen, a former HEW secretary and developer of Medicaid and Medicare, was a chief backer of the consensus statement.

At a news conference following the tumultuous two-day meeting, HEW Secretary Caspar Weinberger justified cutbacks in the federal budget, saying that many persons regarded federal spending as a major cause of inflation and therefore, attempts to reduce expenditures would be perceived as progressive steps in the inflation fight.

"The Administration will not base its anti-inflationary effort on increasing the burdens of our less advantaged citizens," Weinberger said. "Our efforts will be to deliver more benefits at less cost to those who are most in need. Such sacrifices as are required will be borne by all our citizens."

Health budget increased. Ford submitted his fiscal 1976 budget to Congress Feb. 3, 1975. It included a request for a $1.6 billion increase in Medicare and Medicaid funds.

In the budget message, Ford requested $27.3 billion for fiscal 1976 spending on health programs. The total was $1.5 billion above previous-year funding although the department's (Health, Education & Welfare) fiscal plans were being shaped by an intensive cost-control effort.

A 20% spending cut was imposed on direct service programs such as neighborhood health centers, maternal and child health and community mental health centers. The department expected state and local governments to provide the deleted funds. The spending reductions would hit migrant health care, family planning, drug abuse, alcohol control, immunization and venereal disease programs.

For Medicare, Congress was asked to endorse a cost-control plan to limit the rate of increase in average daily costs reimbursable to hospitals from the government. The Administration also was seeking legislation for authority to raise the monthly premium for Medicare paid by the aged as well as legislation to increase the non-premium, or out-of-pocket, payments by the aged for Medicare benefits, up to an annual ceiling of $1,500.

The Administration further requested legislation to reduce to 40% the current 50% federal share of Medicaid programs funded in cooperation with the states.

Federal spending on health research would be augmented, with about half the total going to the drive against cancer.

Ford requested $620 million for the training of health professionals during fiscal 1976. He said that "measures undertaken since 1969 have assured major increases in the number of graduates of U.S. health professions schools. From 1965 to 1974, medical school enrollments and the number of graduates each grew

by 56%. Medical school enrollments have grown from 32,428 to 50,477 and the annual number of graduates has increased from 7,409 to 11,580. As in other fields of higher education, Federal assistance in 1976 will emphasize aid to students rather than to institutions. Unnecessary federal institutional subsidies will be gradually phased out. Since students in the health professions can anticipate high earnings, they can be expected to finance a greater share of their own educational costs. Federally guaranteed private loans are available, and recently increased ceilings on such loans will heighten their usefulness to students in the health professions. Proposed legislation will reflect this appropriate federal role in the support of health professions training. An expanded National Health Service Corps program of scholarships in return for service will both assist students financially and help meet federal needs for health professionals."

CONSUMER PRICE INDICES FOR MEDICAL CARE ITEMS

In the United States   (1967 = 100.0)

Year	All medical care items	Physicians' fees	Dentists' fees	Optometric examination and eyeglasses	Semi-private hospital room rates	Prescriptions and drugs
1947	48.1	51.4	56.9	67.7	23.1	81.8
1950	53.7	55.2	63.9	73.5	30.3	88.5
1955	64.8	65.4	73.0	77.0	42.3	94.7
1960	79.1	77.0	82.1	85.1	57.3	104.5
1961	81.4	79.0	82.5	87.8	61.1	103.3
1962	83.5	81.3	84.7	89.2	65.3	101.7
1963	85.6	83.1	87.1	89.7	68.6	100.8
1964	87.3	85.2	89.4	90.9	71.9	100.5
1965	89.5	88.3	92.2	92.8	75.9	100.2
1966	93.4	93.4	95.2	95.3	83.5	100.5
1967	100.0	100.0	100.0	100.0	100.0	100.0
1968	106.1	105.6	105.5	103.2	113.6	100.2
1969	113.4	112.9	112.9	107.6	128.8	101.3
1970	120.6	121.4	119.4	113.5	145.4	103.6
1971	128.4	129.8	127.0	120.3	163.1	105.4
1972	132.5	133.8	132.3	124.9	173.9	105.6
1973	137.7	138.2	136.4	129.5	182.1	105.9
1974	150.5	150.9	146.8	138.6	201.5	109.6

Note: In 1972, a composite index of Hospital Service Charges was developed. This index rose from 102.0 in 1972 to 115.1 in 1974.

Source: U.S. Department of Labor.

Table from Health Insurance Institute

But Ford Jan. 2 had vetoed (announced Jan. 3) a bill increasing federal support for the training of nurses because of its "excessive" appropriations levels—more than $650 million over three years. "Federal spending for nursing education would be intolerable at a time when even high priority activities are being pressed to justify their existence," he said.

Drop in heart-attack death rate reported. The death rate from coronary heart disease among white males, aged 35 to 64, dropped 8.7% between 1968 and 1972, Dr. Jeremiah Stamler, chairman of the department of community health and preventive medicine at Northwestern University, said Jan. 23, 1975. The death rate from the disease dropped to 427.7 deaths per 100,000 white middle-aged males in 1972, down from 463.1 in 1968. Dr. Stamler said similar results were reported for black men and for women. He attributed the decline largely to the drop in the percentage of men who smoked cigarettes—from a high of 60 per cent in 1955 to 40 per cent in 1970, with a smaller decline among women. (The FTC said March 9, however, that cigarette consumption in 1974 was up 3 per cent from the previous year. The report asked Congress to disclose some of the diseases associated with smoking on package labels.)

Incidence of VD reported leveling off. For the first time in nearly a decade, the reported number of cases of venereal disease dropped, the federal Communicable Disease Center said Feb. 15. During the fiscal year ending June 30, 1974, the incidence of infectious syphilis fell .4 per cent and remained stable the following six months, the center reported. Gonorrhea, a far more widespread disease, increased 4.8 per cent in 1974 and 3 per cent in the current fiscal year spokesman said, noting that that was a far slower pace than in previous years.

The spokesman said that since 1972, when an intensified gonorrhea detection program began nationwide, the number of cases had dropped in 15 cities and the rate of increase had declined in another 28.

Controversy Batters Health Agencies & Programs

FDA staff charges agency harassment. Eleven staff scientists of the Food and Drug Administration (FDA) charged in Senate testimony Aug. 15, 1974 that their superiors in the FDA had harassed, transferred and overruled them when they had produced adverse findings on drugs needing final FDA approval before being marketed.

Caspar W. Weinberger, secretary of health, education and welfare, Aug. 24 announced a "full review" of the procedures and practices by which the FDA evaluated the safety and effectiveness of new drugs for use in general medical practice. The review was being called, Weinberger said,

VENEREAL DISEASE TRENDS

	Primary and secondary syphilis		Gonorrhea	
	Cases reported	Rates per 100,000	Cases reported	Rates per 100,000
1941	68,231	51.7	193,468	146.7
1950	32,148	21.6	303,992	204.0
1957	6,251	3.8	216,476	129.8
1965	23,250	12.3	310,155	163.8
1969	18,679	9.3	494,227	245.9
1970	20,186	10.0	573,200	285.2
1971	23,336	11.5	624,371	307.5
1972	24,000	11.7	718,401	349.7
1973	25,080	12.1	809,681	392.2
1974	24,728	11.9	874,161	420.1

at the request of FDA Commissioner Dr. Alexander M. Schmidt.

The testimony before the combined Health Subcommittee of the Labor and Public Welfare Committee and the Administrative Practice and Procedure Subcommittee of the Judiciary Committee was backed by three outside consultants, who had been named to FDA panels created to review staff work. One consultant, Dr. Gerald Solomons of the University of Iowa, characterized his dealings with the agency as "one of the most frustrating, embarrassing and degrading experiences I've had in my medical career."

Solomons had been called in to review an FDA staff member's finding against Cylert, a drug made by Abbott Laboratories for use on hyperkinetic children. Noting that his review panel had also recommended against Cylert, Solomons testified that he had sensed "a lack of cooperation if not obstructionism" against the review committee's position. "It appeared that our deliberations were being relayed to the drug company after confrontation with administrative officers," he said, adding, "Professional personnel who had been involved and enthusiastically supported our findings were assigned to other projects."

Dr. Roger D. Freeman of the University of British Columbia, who was a member of the same reviewing team, testified that his own findings had confirmed the original staff report that Abbott Laboratories had presented insufficient data to back its application for approval of Cylert. Moreover, Freeman said, he had not been permitted to comment on a rebuttal from Abbott and when a second medical review team was set up, "we were to have no contact with this new committee." He called it a "personal and professional insult."

Dr. Carol Kennedy, the FDA staff member and psychiatrist who first recommended against Cylert, said she had been subsequently transferred to the dental-surgical section to study soft contact lenses.

Schmidt appeared before the joint subcommittees Aug. 16. He rejected Sen. Edward Kennedy's (D, Mass.) assertion that FDA decisions often reflected the "power and influence of the drug companies," but conceded that the previous day's testimony had been "highly disturbing." He had always emphasized "scientific integrity" and a need to explain the FDA's work "openly, honestly and well," Schmidt said.

Kennedy challenged Schmidt on another assertion that his policy had been to keep records. Kennedy produced a Dec. 1, 1972 internal FDA memorandum ordering destruction of verbatim transcripts of advisory committee meetings as soon as summary transcripts had been approved by the committees. Under oath, Schmidt said the memorandum was in error and said the policy had never been implemented. However, Schmidt conceded that a second memorandum correcting the error had never been sent.

Dr. Richard Crout of the FDA's Bureau of Drugs testified Aug. 16 there were "real misconceptions" among the 11 staff members and three consultants testifying Aug. 15. Disapproval of a drug "commonly [was] not a permanent turndown," as adverse reports were often re-reviewed in the light of new information, he said.

Senate study assails nursing homes. A report by the Long-Term Care Subcommittee of the Senate Special Committee on Aging, made public Nov. 19, 1974, criticized the Department of Health, Education and Welfare (HEW) for laxity in the enforcement of laws and administrative standards intended to end abuses in the nation's nursing homes.

In many cases, the report asserted, the aged "haven't even received human treatment. And, in an alarming number of cases, they have actually encountered abuse and physical danger, including unsanitary conditions, fire hazards, poor or unwholesome food, infections, adverse drug reactions, overtranquilization and frequent medication errors."

Federal policy on nursing homes was confusing and incoherent, the report charged. It was especially critical of HEW, which, the report said, was "reluctant to issue forthright standards to provide patients with minimum protection." Moreover, HEW left en-

COMMUNITY HOSPITAL STATISTICS – 1974

State	Average Cost to Hospital Per Patient Day	Average Length of Hospital Stay (days)	Average Cost to Hospital Per Patient Stay
Alabama	$ 98.90	7.4	$ 732.00
Alaska	190.00	4.7	892.90
Arizona	148.70	7.3	1,085.30
Arkansas	89.30	6.6	589.20
California	180.90	6.7	1,211.70
Colorado	126.00	6.6	831.70
Connecticut	161.80	7.5	1,213.60
Delaware	131.60	8.4	1,105.70
D. C.	172.60	8.0	1,380.60
Florida	124.60	7.4	922.30
Georgia	116.10	6.6	766.30
Hawaii	140.40	6.9	968.70
Idaho	100.60	6.5	653.60
Illinois	134.60	8.2	1,103.90
Indiana	107.10	7.8	835.00
Iowa	94.00	7.8	733.50
Kansas	95.70	7.9	756.10
Kentucky	95.30	7.1	676.80
Louisiana	111.30	6.5	723.70
Maine	112.40	7.4	831.50
Maryland	153.20	8.4	1,286.70
Massachusetts	175.30	8.5	1,490.10
Michigan	140.70	8.2	1,154.10
Minnesota	105.80	8.8	931.00
Mississippi	87.10	6.9	600.90
Missouri	107.70	8.4	904.70
Montana	93.10	6.6	614.20
Nebraska	97.70	8.3	810.60
Nevada	159.10	6.4	1,018.30
New Hampshire	110.00	7.1	780.90
New Jersey	123.60	8.8	1,087.30
New Mexico	117.30	6.0	704.00
New York	160.50	9.8	1,573.30
North Carolina	99.70	7.6	757.70
North Dakota	82.80	8.4	695.60
Ohio	119.10	8.2	976.30
Oklahoma	106.60	6.7	714.10
Oregon	133.60	6.4	854.80
Pennsylvania	119.90	8.7	1,043.40
Rhode Island	156.10	8.4	1,311.00
South Carolina	95.40	7.2	686.70
South Dakota	83.00	7.3	605.80
Tennessee	96.80	7.5	725.90
Texas	107.80	6.8	732.70
Utah	127.60	5.6	714.30
Vermont	112.80	8.2	925.00
Virginia	102.30	8.1	829.00
Washington	141.70	5.6	793.50
West Virginia	92.30	7.7	710.60
Wisconsin	108.20	8.3	898.20
Wyoming	94.00	5.9	554.40
United States	$127.70	7.8	$ 996.20

Source: American Hospital Association and Health Insurance Institute.

forcement of inadequate standards to the states, whose efforts, the study complained, were, with few exceptions, "scandalous, ineffective, and, in some cases, almost non-existent."

Sen. Frank Moss (D, Utah), chairman of the subcommittee, said the report was intended, "more than anything else," to spur consideration of "expanded nursing home coverage within the context of national health insurance legislation." He said the report was the first in a series of 12 studies to be issued by the subcommittee.

Frank C. Carlucci, undersecretary of health, education and welfare, took exception to the report. He said through a spokesman that the report ignored significant progress made since 1971, when former President Nixon announced steps to improve the country's nursing homes. (The subcommittee report took note of the Nixon reform plan, but said its effect had been "minimal" and that HEW's current efforts fell "short of any serious effort" to carry out promises by Nixon.)

NIH head's ouster deplored. Six prominent scientists Dec. 17, 1974 issued a statement deploring the forced resignation of Dr. Robert S. Stone, director of the National Institutes of Health (NIH). In their statement the scientists also criticized the abrupt dismissal in December 1972 of Stone's predecessor, Dr. Robert Q. Marston.

"We deplore the firing of the NIH director, the second such forced change of leadership in a two-year period, as one more indication of the degree to which NIH can be vulnerable to unwarranted and counterproductive political control," the statement said. The scientists called for Congressional repeal of the section of the National Cancer Act providing for Presidential appointment of the NIH director, and they urged President Ford "to show his commitment to a politically independent and more effective NIH by involving the scientific community in the selection of a new director as promptly as possible."

The Washington Post Dec. 12 reported conflicting reasons for Stone's dismissal. The Post cited unnamed NIH scientists, who said Stone had been asked to leave because he had pushed for more research funding while officials of the Department of Health, Education and Welfare (HEW) were seeking cutbacks. However, unnamed HEW officials cited by the Post claimed that Stone had been unable to solve NIH problems, which included determining how medical research fit into the national health program; how the NIH's resources should be divided between basic and clinical research and whether NIH should concern itself with delivery of health services.

The scientists signing the statement of protest were Drs. Christian Anfinsen, Julius Axelrod and Marshall Nirenberg, Nobel laureates in 1972, 1970 and 1968 respectively; Dr. Robert Goldberger of the National Cancer Institute; Dr. Franklin Neva of the National Institute of Allergy and Infectious Diseases and Dr. Earl Stadtman of the National Heart and Lung Institute.

Regional agencies. Congress Dec. 20, 1974 gave final approval to legislation to establish regional agencies for planning and improving health services. President Ford signed the bill Jan. 4, 1975.

Dispute re tax financing of Medicare. The Social Security Advisory Council's final report to Congress and the President March 7, 1975 proposed that impending deficits in the retirement system be avoided by paying for most of the costs of Medicare from general tax revenues. Otherwise, the 13-member panel's 239-page report urged that the "basic principles" of the system remain unchanged.

In a statement March 7, President Ford applauded the council's confidence in the system. He also endorsed a recommendation for a technical change in the benefit formula that would make future costs predictable and avoid large deficits. However, Ford flatly rejected the recommendation to transfer the financing of Medicare (health insurance for the aged) from the Social Security trust fund to the general tax revenue fund of the Treasury Department. Such a change would be a departure from the principle of compulsory payroll contributions by workers, he said.

Medicare-Medicaid 'fraud.' Dan Thomasson and Carl West reported in the Scripps-Howard newspapers Feb. 15, 1975 that, according to estimates by Congressional investigators, "fraud and abuses in ... Medicare and Medicaid programs total at least $3 billion a year," or more than 10% of the total cost of the combined programs. The two reporters cited "Congressional and GAO [Government Accounting Office] critics" as contending that "only one out of 100 cheaters ... is being caught, and the Justice Department often is reluctant to prosecute...."

In a report Feb. 25 on the situation in Illinois, the two reporters listed among possible "frauds" or "abuses": (a) "Seventy Illinois physicians were paid $10 million in 1973 for treating welfare patients; one got $447,995." (b) "Twenty drug stores received $7.4 million in Medicaid payments." (c) "A physician in a poor area writes $1,000 worth of Medicaid prescriptions a day, and every recipient is prescribed tranquilizers, sleeping pills and panty hose [possibly for varicose veins]." (d) A woman "posed as a surgeon and fraudulently billed the state for performing open heart surgery, then double-billed because she posed as the patient and then triple-billed by posing as the patient's housekeeper." (e) "From May 1973 to March 1974, 23 optometrists prescribed three or more pairs of glasses to each of 1,804 Medicaid recipients." (f) "A physician billed Medicaid for 32 visits to six nursing homes to treat patients who denied he had seen them." (g) "The owner of a medical laboratory admitted kickbacks of up to 40% to physicians."

Health bill enacted over veto. A $2 billion health bill was enacted into law by Congress July 29, 1975 over a presidential veto.

The bill authorized $2 billion in fiscal 1976–78 for the programs—$1.42 billion in fiscal 1976–77 for formula grants to the states for public health services programs, family planning programs, community mental health centers, migrant health centers, community health centers in rural and inner-city areas. Another $553 million was authorized in fiscal 1976–78 for training programs for nurses; $30 million was authorized in fiscal 1976 for the National Health Service Corps.

The bill also authorized funds for establishment of a center for rape prevention and control, centers for treatment of hemophilia, a study group on nervous disorders and programs for health care at home.

The bill was passed by voice votes of the Senate July 14 and House July 16.

President Ford vetoed it July 26 because he considered the appropriations levels "excessive" and its program conception "unsound." The levels were "far in excess of the amounts we can afford," he said. As for the programs, the community mental health center projects, having undergone adequate demonstration, should be absorbed into the regular health services delivery system, he said. Similarly, the nursing schools had enough enrollments, especially in light of a tightening job market. The hypertension, rape prevention, hemophilia treatment and home health service programs he criticized as "narrow, categorical and potentially costly programs which duplicate existing authorities."

The Senate met later July 26 to consider a motion to override the veto, Ford's 36th in office and ninth of the session. It carried, 67–15, 12 more than the two-thirds majority required.

The vote in the House, taken July 29, was 384–43, 99 votes over the requirement.

Doctors strike N.Y. hospitals. Interns and resident doctors at 21 New York hospitals went on strike March 17–20, 1975 to shorten work schedules. It was the first major doctors' strike in U.S. history. It ended March 20 with an agreement to limit work hours and to set up scheduling committees at individual hospitals.

More than 2,000 doctors went on strike at the hospitals, which had 14,000 beds, a third of the city's total, and normally handled 10,000 outpatients daily. Medical service was maintained by private attending doctors and staff and faculty members. The striking union, the Committee of Interns and Residents, pledged to cover emergencies where doctor shortages existed. The state health department also sent doctor-nurse teams to monitor patient care during the action.

Formed in 1958, the committee had labor contracts with municipal, voluntary and independent hospitals. It struck 15 voluntary ones and six affiliated municipal hospitals to get relief from schedules it said ran up to 110 duty hours a week with uninterrupted stretches of up to 56 hours. Federal mediators assisted the negotiations.

The union received an unexpected assist March 18 from the American Medical Association, whose two top officers said "in important respects, it is a strike for better patient care." Dr. Richard E. Palmer, board chairman, and Dr. Malcolm C. Todd, president, said 50 hours straight or 100 hours a week were "tough" on the doctor and a threat to quality patient care. They noted that patients were covered during the strike, which was not a right the AMA believed a doctor had, the right to strike against a patient.

The work hours would be limited, under the agreement, to not more than one night's duty in a three-day period unless approved by a committee, to be established, of union and hospital representatives. The committee would devise guidelines for schedules focusing on "optimum patient care" and "the health and well-being of house staff officers, including their reasonable social needs and providing for adequate rest." The guidelines were to be implemented by the hospitals "subject to budgetary limitations."

Senate tables anti-abortion amendment. The Senate April 10 rejected by a 54–36 margin an amendment to a health services and nurse training bill that would have prohibited federal funding of abortions under the Medicaid program for the poor. The vote to table the amendment reversed a 1974 Senate vote on an amendment to a labor-health, education and welfare (HEW) appropriations bill that barred

abortions paid for with Medicaid. House-Senate conferees on the appropriations bill later dropped the amendment.

Sen. Dewey F. Bartlett (R, Okla.), a Catholic, who said HEW spent more than $40 million for 270,000 abortions in 1973, contended that the federal government had adopted a policy of encouraging abortions despite the national controversy surrounding the issue. "If this amendment is passed into law," Bartlett said, "we can eliminate those programs whose purpose is the taking of human life."

Opponents of the amendment, on the other hand, avoided the emotional side of the issue and maintained that the amendment was illegal, vaguely written and unfair to women too poor to afford abortions without Medicaid.

Report links decrease in abortion deaths to legalization. A report made by a panel of the National Academy of Sciences showed a sharp decline in maternal deaths and injuries related to abortion since the liberalization of abortion laws. The report, released May 27, 1975, said that women who had abortions since its legalization had displayed no measurable increase in mental problems.

The project was lead by 11 specialists in the health and behavioral sciences who were named by the science academy's Institute of Medicine in early 1974. They were commissioned to make what members called "as objective an analysis as possible" of available abortion facts.

The impetus for the report was a 1973 Supreme Court decision that greatly liberalized states' abortion laws and the subsequent number of protests.

The report, titled "Legalized Abortion and the Public Health," noted that in 1961, when illegal abortions were common, there were 320 known abortion-related deaths. This contrasted with 47 deaths in 1973, with 16 attributed to illegal abortions.

The report noted that a healthy woman undergoing a competently performed abortion during the initial three months of pregnancy had only about six chances in a thousand of a major medical complication. During the second six months, however, the risk increased to 21 chances in a thousand.

Figures as to the number of medical complications when abortions were illegal were difficult to calculate, the committee said. But it cited a sharp drop in admissions to New York City municipal hospitals for two serious complications of abortion between 1969 and 1973. Incoming patients from septic and incomplete abortions, the report said, went from 6,524 to 3,253 in those years. Most restrictions on legal abortion in New York City were dropped in 1970.

At a news conference the day the report was released, a member of the committee said that a return to restrictive laws would probably lead to a rise in illegal abortions and the dangerous health consequences they entailed.

The committee also found that estimates of post-abortion psychoses (serious mental breakdowns) ranged from .2 to .4 per 1,000 legal abortions. This compared with the one or two associated with normal deliveries. Depression or guilt feelings reported by some women after abortions were usually described as mild and temporary.

The study panel cited figures indicating that 745,400 legal abortions were performed in the United States in 1973 and 900,000 in 1974. Of these, a third of the women were under 20, a third were between 20 and 25 and the remainder over 25. One in four was married and two-thirds were white.

The Associated Press reported May 26 that a Harris Poll survey had found that 54% of the American people supported legalized abortion, 38% opposed it and 8% were unsure.

HEW lifts fetal research ban. Acting on a recommendation from a national review board that conducted hearings on the subject, Caspar W. Weinberger, secretary of health, education and welfare, June 29, 1975 ended a ban on federally funded medical research with human fetuses.

The new regulations, which ended a 13-month moratorium, allowed experimentation with fetuses both inside the mother's womb and, in many cases, on aborted fetuses temporarily alive. Research was still prohibited on live fetuses if it would kill them, or keep them alive artificially.

If the fetus was still in the womb, the research had to be either necessary for keeping it alive, or to seek important facts which could not be learned otherwise. The regulations added that the experimentation must pose only "minimal" risk beyond any the fetus already faced.

The recommendations, which were first made by the National Commission on Protection of Human Subjects of Biomedical and Behavioral Research, were approved by Weinberger without major changes. The review board was commissioned by Congress after it banned fetal research in June 1974.

The rules required the mother's consent in all cases. They required the father's consent except where his identity could not be learned or if pregnancy resulted from rape.

Because risks to the fetus could be assessed differently in different cases HEW was charged by the commission to establish a set of national ethical review boards to review questionable research. The new rules applied officially only to HEW projects, but almost all fetal research was federally funded. Also, hospitals' ethical review committees generally applied the same rules to all research as was applied to federal projects.

Opposition to the renewal of such research came, in large part, from anti-abortion groups, including the U.S. Catholic Conference, which maintained that no fetal research was ethical. The anti-abortion groups argued that a fetus was unable to give consent and that a woman planning an abortion had given up her right to decide what was done to the fetus.

However, an introduction to the new rules said a woman "may not be presumed to lack interest in her fetus" even if she had decided to opt for an abortion. Therefore, she could be "validly asked to consent for research."

The study commission heard a number of research reports on the usefulness of fetal research. One such report, made by the Battelle Institute of Columbus, Ohio, said that certain fetal research had saved the lives of hundreds of thousands of babies.

The report focused on four medical advances that resulted from such research. Included was a treatment of Rh hemolytic disease of the newborn. The disease resulted from an incompatibility of blood types between the mother and the fetus. Advances through fetal research eventually led to a vaccine that saved 450,000 fetuses between 1930 and 1975, the Battelle report said.

Also touched on in the report were the development, through fetal research, of a vaccine to fight rubella, a viral infection, and its resultant birth defects; research on a respiratory distress syndrome of newborns; and the development of amniocentesis, a technique for sampling fetus cells from the fluid surrounding the fetus of the womb. The director of the Battelle project said that none of the research could have been done on animals.

One member of the commission hearing the report said the study, submitted March 14, was the "most striking evidence we've heard yet on the potential future importance of fetal research."

Dr. Maurice J. Mahoney, a Yale scientist who was heading another research project for the commission said there had been a "quantum jump" in fetal research in recent years. In the report, first submitted to the Commission for the Protection of Human Subjects Feb. 15, Mahoney cited over 1,000 studies worldwide. He attributed the rapid growth to advancing medical science and the legalizing of abortions that made fetuses more available.

"By far the smallest" number of studies Mahoney said, was in one of the most controversial areas of research involving the early fetus outside of the womb. Mahoney said he could only cite three studies in which fetuses were purposely kept artificially alive for a time. They were all part of attempts to develop a new type of fetal incubator for "test-tube births," where the mother could not herself carry the baby.

Another report made by a team of scientists headed by Dr. Richard Behrman, head of pediatrics at Columbia University, and presented to the commission March 15, said more prematurely born fetuses survived than was expected. The survey indicated that annually, several hundred babies might be surviving birth before the end of the first two-thirds of pregnancy in the U.S.

The report also said that research done on fetuses younger than 24 weeks still in the womb, and studies after birth on a fetus younger than 25 weeks, were biologically safe. No fetuses that young had been known to live more than minutes without artificial assistance, and none survived to leave the hospital, the report said.

HEW approves health network. A new national network of health-planning agencies was approved June 18 by Secretary of Health Education and Welfare Caspar W. Weinberger. The agencies would administer federal hospital building funds and help distribute over $2 billion annually in locally spent federal health funds.

The network was initially begun with 159 federally aided local and regional agencies in 45 states. They would plan building of hospitals, nursing homes and other major health facilities. The new local and regional "health systems agencies" would replace and strengthen a spotty system that covered some regions well and others poorly.

Weinberger at the same time rejected 33 local proposals and two state plans for such agencies. He made the rejections on the ground that the areas were unsound geographically or economically, or by virtue of too much or too sparse population.

AMA fights decline. The financially troubled American Medical Association voted June 18, 1975 to raise its national dues from $110 to $250. Its new president, Dr. Max Parott, said the move could cost the organization up to 15,000 members. The vote came at the annual House of Delegates meeting in Chicago.

The move to higher dues was an attempt to rebuild the AMA's vastly depleted reserves, which had fallen from $5 million to $200,000 since 1970. During that time its membership decreased to 158,000 of the nation's 380,000 doctors.

Parott said the money from the dues increase would be used as a "war chest" for court battles against federal laws and regulations that many doctors felt interfered with their duties. The AMA was also in the midst of a dispute with the Internal Revenue Service and the Postal Service which, if lost, could cost the organization several million dollars.

The federal actions that the AMA was fighting in the courts included the health-planning bill passed by Congress, and Department of Health Education and Welfare regulations that restricted payments under Medicare and Medicaid to the lowest priced drugs.

The new dues of $250 were in addition to those a doctor paid his local and state medical groups or his surgical specialty society. Total dues could run as high as $1,000 a year, the New York Times reported June 18.

In a related development, it was reported June 28, that the AMA had developed a referral system designed to channel doctors who agreed with AMA policy into 315 Federal health advisory panels. The existence of the referral system became known only after confidential memos of the AMA were made available.

The documents indicated, according to a New York Times article, that the association went out of its way to keep the referral system secret, even from its own members. An AMA consultant group spokesman, which helped set up the referral system, defended the need for secrecy explaining that it was unlikely "that should such information become publicly known, it would be properly understood by the federal government, AMA members and the general population."

The advisory panels offered policy and technical guidance to the Department of Health Education and Welfare. But, more important, according to the AMA consulting firm, they influenced the distribution of health grants, funds that affected the investment in health programs, etc.

To insure that physicians recommended by the AMA for appointment followed the association's philosophy, the consultant report said state medical societies would be used as a prime source of recruitment.

Secret AMA memos reveal political activities. Secret, official memos of the American Medical Association were leaked to the press, the Internal Revenue Service, and members of Congress, it was reported in a series of Washington Post stories July 1-30, 1975. The papers had led to questions concerning the legality of the AMA's lobbying activities, political contributions and its ties with the drug industry. In addition, the organization's low-cost mailing rates were being reviewed and charges of fraud were being considered by the U.S. Postal Service.

One of the memos, it was reported in the Post July 1, revealed that 27 of the largest drug companies in the United States had given the political arm of the AMA $851,000. The association had long maintained, despite testimony to the contrary in the past, that it was independent of the pharmaceutical industry.

The corporate contributions were said to have been given to the AMA's American medical political action committee (Ampac) between 1962 and 1965. According to Joseph C. Stetler, a former official for Ampac and now president of the Pharmaceutical Manufacturers Association (PMA), the money was used for "political education campaigns" during the 1960s.

During those years the AMA and the PMA worked, purportedly independent of one another, to fight new federal requirements that drug companies must prove the effectiveness of their drugs. The organizations argued that the requirements would cost drug companies millions of dollars if their products were thrown off the market. The laws in question were passed in 1962 but the fight over the way they should be enforced was still going on.

The Post said that the contributions were revealed in a memo that was attached to a 1965 letter from Ampac's executive director, Joseph D. Miller, to Stetler, who was then PMA president. Miller admitted that those early contributions provided the financial foundations for Ampac, it was reported July 1. But in a statement issued by the AMA, also July 1, the group said it had "scrupulously complied with the laws governing legislative and political activities.

Another memo, it was reported July 19, described how in 1970 the AMA teamed up with the PMA in a secret, successful drive to kill a bill aimed at reducing the costs of drugs. Although opposition to the measure, an amendment to the Social Security Act, was made known by both groups, the existence of the joint lobbying effort was kept secret.

The amendment, offered by Sen. Russell B. Long (D, La.), would have required the use of generic drugs instead of the more expensive brand name products for Medicare and Medicaid patients. The backers of the proposal believed the requirement would have eventually been adopted by group health insurance groups nationwide and would have led to a substantial decline in the cost of drugs for all Americans. The bill did not pass at the time, but most of its provisions had been incorporated in new Federal regulations regarding Medicare and Medicaid patients.

The documents about the effort to kill the amendment showed careful coordination between the AMA and drug companies and a desire to keep the relationship secret. Lobbyists were given PMA material criticizing the Long ammendment and were told to see to it that contacts were made by a physician constituent of each senator to express concern over the proposal. The AMA lobbyists were reportedly told to make sure that the doctors stressed the AMA's interests and that it was "to be an AMA project with no reference to PMA's interest."

Many AMA critics have charged that the association's support for the manufacturer's positions was related to the AMA's dependence upon drug advertising in its journals. According to a July 19 report in the New York Times, the AMA admitted it received $9.5 million of its $34.7 million 1974 budget from advertising, much of which was from drug companies.

Earlier in July it was revealed that the AMA allowed salesmen of a drug company to use a letter by one of its executives minimizing the danger of certain oral diabetic drugs.

In a letter to IRS Commissioner Donald C. Alexander, Sen. Abraham Ribicoff (D, Conn.) urged "a full and immediate investigation" of AMA's tax-exempt status, it was reported July 19. Ribicoff referred to the recently released secret memos regarding its lobbying and political activities.

The senator, a member of the Finance Committee, which had jurisdiction over tax laws and the IRS, said the documents "raise serious questions about possible abuses of the tax system."

The documents in question reportedly showed that the medical association lobbied on matters unrelated to health. This included the support of F. Clement Haynsworth's nomination to the Supreme Court in 1969, which failed. In addition, the AMA reportedly handled campaign contributions from Ampac. Tax-exempt organizations were barred from general lobbying or making political contributions to candidates.

In reaction to the secret memos revelations, consumer advocate Ralph Nader July 30 charged that the AMA had juggled its income to create paper losses, allowing it to avoid paying income taxes.

In a letter to Chairman Charles A. Vanik (D, Ohio) of the House Ways and Means Committee's Oversight Subcommittee, Nader called for a congressional investigation to find out why the AMA had not paid taxes on advertising in its journals.

As a further result of the memos' release, a U.S. Postal Service spokesman said July 15 that the AMA was being investigated for possible criminal fraud for allegedly concealing information, which could affect its mailing rates. According to one memo, reported in the Washington Post July 16, the AMA had a "friend" in the Chicago Post Office who allowed it to refrain from revealing what fraction of its members' dues went for its journals—a postal requirement.

"The memo, and the way it was written, seemed to indicate some kind of fraud," James H. Byrne, assistant postmaster general for communications, said July 16.

The man who divulged the secret memos was reported July 7 by the Washington Post to have described himself as a doctor and former employee of the AMA. The medical organization had recently fired 77 staff members, the Post pointed out in its report, but the informer did not say if he had been amongst the most recent cuts.

In a note accompanying the first packet of photocopied AMA documents, the man said he was making them public in the hope that they would spur an investigation. He said he hoped such action would restore the AMA to its original constitutional objectives: "To promote the science and art of medicine and the betterment of public health."

HEW acts on drug costs. In a move designed to save state and federal governments up to $75 million on drug costs, the Department of Health Education and Welfare (HEW) gave final approval to a plan known as Maximum Allowable Costs. The plan provided that the government would not pay for high-priced medicines for Medicare and Medicaid patients if less expensive ones, readily available, would do as well.

Under the plan, which took effect July 25, 1975, the Food & Drug Administration had the power to declare that there was no difference in the biological effects of different brands of the same drug. HEW would then set the price it would reimburse pharmacists for each drug based on the lowest cost at which it was available to the druggists.

Doctors would then be given a list, published and continually updated by HEW, which would catalogue the most frequently prescribed drugs and the price the area druggists paid for them. This list would help doctors become aware of which drugs were covered by the federal program. The list would also be made available to the general public to allow them to know of the least expensive drugs.

HEW officials said that less than a fourth of commonly prescribed drugs were sold under more than one brand name. Sources estimated that only about a dozen of the best-selling drugs would ultimately be included in the program in its first year.

The new regulations still gave doctors the right to prescribe any drug they wanted to Medicare and Medicaid patients regardless of cost. But they had to certify in writing on the prescription that they believed there was a "medical necessity" for that brand.

The provision was included in the regulations in an attempt to appease American Medical Association (AMA) objections, according to an HEW official. Nevertheless, the AMA sued to halt implementation of the plan.

According to the suit, filed in Chicago federal court July 29, the AMA contended that doctors would be forced to prescribe only the cheapest drugs, when they otherwise would prescribe a drug "which they believe to be safer, more reliable, or more effective." Caspar W. Weinberger, Secretary of HEW was named as the defendant in the case.

Drug price advertising proposed. The Federal Trade Commission June 2, 1975 proposed new regulations that would permit druggists to advertise the retail prices of prescription drugs. The proposed regulations would supersede any state and local laws to the contrary and bar any private attempts, such as by pharmacists' associations, to restrict a druggist from disclosing or advertising prescription drug prices.

Pharmacists would not be required to advertise drug prices, but if they did the commission was considering formulating guidelines for such ads. It was also considering rules on whether a druggist must provide price data, if requested, over the telephone and whether a printed price list should be made available.

Currently, such advertising was prohibited by laws and regulations in 33 states and codes of ethics of at least three dozen state pharmaceutical associations.

The commission's staff report said consumers were "woefully uninformed" about prescription drug prices, that they could vary widely. FTC Chairman Lewis A. Engman, in a speech before the American Advertising Federation June 2, said the consumer was "ignorant" about such pricing and "I have reason to believe that he is ignorant because advertising bans keep him that way." Engman cited a survey in the San Francisco area showing that 100 tablets of a high-blood-pressure drug were for sale at 38 different prices ranging from $2.50 to $11.75.

Consumer spending on prescription drugs totaled nearly $7 billion a year and potential savings through awareness of the availability of lower-priced drugs were estimated at $130 to $200 million a year.

Pharmacist trust case. The Department of Justice filed a civil antitrust suit in federal court in Grand Rapids Nov. 24, 1975 on charges that the 50,000–member American Pharmaceutical Association and the Michigan State Pharmaceutical Association had conspired to prohibit advertising by their members of retail prices for prescription drugs.

Assistant Attorney General Thomas A. Kauper said this was the first antitrust suit in which the government had ever challenged advertising restrictions practiced by a national association. The suit charged the two groups with "adopting, publishing and distributing a code of ethics containing a provision which prohibited pharmacist members of associations from advertising the retail prices of prescription drugs." The court was asked to order the defendants to cancel such prohibitions from their codes of ethics.

Anesthesiologists accused. An antitrust suit had been filed Sept. 22, 1975 in federal court in New York against the American Society of Anesthesiologists, charging the organization with having violated the Sherman Antitrust Act "for many years" by fixing the fees its members asked of patients for anesthesia services. The court was asked to order the society not to send any more fee guidelines to members or to make other recommendations on calculating charges.

Overhaul of FDA recommended. Sen. Edward M. Kennedy (D, Mass.) proposed revising the Food & Drug Administration Nov. 2, 1975 because of "fundamental defects in our nation's current regulatory procedures for prescription drugs."

He suggested division of the agency into two separate and independent units—a drug and devices administration, itself split into a scientific division and an enforcement division, and a food and cosmetics administration.

Kennedy also suggested establishment of a national drug review board composed of scientists to help the new adminis-

tration regulate drugs after clearance for marketing.

Kennedy said the FDA as set up was "overextended and unable to do its work responsibly" because of "its inadequate budget, its incredible range of unrelated responsibilities and its insufficient scientific expertise."

Kennedy, chairman of the health subcommittee of the Senate Labor and Public Welfare Committee, presented the recommendations at a medical symposium at Tulane University in New Orleans.

Food and Drug Commissioner Alexander M. Schmidt, in remarks at the Tulane symposium Nov. 5, proposed revision of the agency's drug role to speed entry of drugs onto the market and to provide more time for his agency's investigation of the drugs. This would be accomplished by permitting sales of the new drugs to the public under limited conditions, and under strict reporting requirements for adverse reactions.

Schmidt opposed Kennedy's suggestion for splitting the FDA into two new agencies.

Schmidt Nov. 4 denied charges made at a Kennedy subcommittee hearing in August 1974 that the agency favored the drug industry. Schmidt said he found from a year-long investigation of his own that the most common problem of the agency was "one of faulty communication, not one of malicious behavior."

FTC seeks end to ban on doctors' advertising. The Federal Trade Commission charged Dec. 22, 1975 that the American Medical Association's ban against advertising by physicians illegally restrained trade and thus violated U.S. antitrust laws.

The FTC's complaint attacked a section of the AMA's principles of medical ethics that barred physicians from soliciting business through advertising. The FTC argued that the prohibitions stifled competition, caused prices to be "stabilized, fixed, or otherwise interfered with," and deprived patients of "information pertinent to the selection of a physician and of the benefits of competition."

The AMA, with 170,000 members, represented about half the nation's physicians. Also named in the complaint were the Connecticut State Medical Society and the New Haven (Conn.) County Medical Association, which an FTC spokesman said, were typical of state and local medical groups that adhered to and enforced the AMA's ban against advertising.

The AMA denounced the FTC action, saying, "We think there is enough hucksterism in this country without hucksterizing medicine." In its statement, the AMA said "advertising by a professional is the very antithesis of professionalism. Physicians shouldn't solicit patients. A patient should go to a doctor on the basis of need, not the basis of advertising."

An FTC spokesman said that an end to the AMA ban on advertising would have a "substantial" impact on fees charged by physicians, but he declined to give a dollar figure. If the agency were successful in overturning the AMA ruling, "at the very least," he said, "the public would be made aware of the prices doctors are charging for specific services, the qualifications of doctors, which medical schools they attended, their specialties, the honors they have received." This information, he said, would "provide the public with a decisional basis" for selecting a physician.

Ads for eyeglasses sought. The Federal Trade Commission proposed a rule Dec. 23 to allow eye doctors, optometrists and eyeglass-makers to advertise the price of their services. Such advertising was barred, under law or professional codes of ethics, in all states for doctors and optometrists. Opticians were barred from advertising in 24 states.

The commission said lack of data on prices and availability led to higher consumer costs.

Behavior modification reviewed. The National Institute of Mental Health (NIMH) July 9, 1975 released the first federal policy statement on the controversial topic of behavior modification. According to the NIMH, 60,000 Americans were undergoing behavior modification treatment by doctors.

According to the new study, behavior modification had been a "marked success" for the treatment of such problems as phobias, compulsive behavior and sexual dysfunction. However, it was noted that the use of the treatment for depression and schizophrenia had been far less successful "and may not be as good as existing forms of treatment."

Scientifically, behavior modification was the process of trying to change a person's way of reacting by applying "positive" or "negative" reinforcement. In practice, this generally amounted to giving rewards like food treats or punishments like electric shocks or loss of privileges.

The institute's conclusions were published in a report, intended as a guide to therapists, titled "Behavior Modification: Perspective on a Current Issue." The report noted that persons considering such treatment should carefully review its overall benefits and drawbacks.

"One of the main problems" of the treatment, according to an NIMH spokesman, was the lack of "quality control." He said that at least a third of the sex therapists using the method were "outright quacks." Aside from private patients, the technique was being used at hospitals, prisons and schools.

The Institute was financing $2 million in research into the method in 1975, and another $1 million in research was being done by federal alcohol and drug abuse agencies. The Law Enforcement Assistance Administration and the Bureau of Prisons, after a rash of public criticism of the uses of the method, had ended most such programs in federal prisons in 1974.

However, in a report released by the General Accounting Office Aug. 6, 1975, it was revealed that the Bureau of Prisons still applied such techniques to some prisoners in solitary confinement. Rep. Ralph Metcalfe (D, Ill.), who had asked for the report, said the programs were "inhuman" and should be discontinued.

According to press reports Aug. 6, Metcalfe said the treatment as administered was "nothing short of long-term punishment under the guise of what is in fact pseudo-scientific experimentation."

The GAO report on the programs, which were begun in 1972, was somewhat less critical of the program than Metcalfe. It said "the effort has not been well managed," but added that it had stressed rewards and minimized punishments and included "counseling, work, education, recreation and other activities."

Other Developments

Report on U.S. health. The Department of Health, Education & Welfare Jan. 12, 1976 made public its first report assessing the state of health of the U.S. population. The report found that Americans were generally healthy.

The three-volume report to Congress and the President, titled "Health, U.S., 1975," was an attempt to merge health statistics with figures on population trends and health costs so planners and policymakers could make decisions with some knowledge of potential impact.

The report found that excessive use of alcohol and tobacco and lack of proper exercise and diet contributed greatly to cancer, heart, kidney and liver disease, respiratory ailments and accidents among Americans.

According to data compiled by HEW, the U.S. infant mortality rate fell from 29.2% per 1000 live births in 1950 to 16.5% per 1000 in 1974. The rate among non-white babies was twice that for white babies. Even with the decline, the U.S. ranked below 14 other countries with lower infant death rates.

The heart disease rate among persons between the ages of 55 and 64 dropped nearly 15% in the last six years, but the rate of death from cancer for the same age group increased almost 4% in the same period, according to Dr. Theodore Cooper, HEW assistant secretary for health, whose staff prepared the report.

Among younger persons, the report said, accidents and homicide were major causes of death.

Life expectancy among white women was 75.9 years and among non-white women, 72 years. White men were expected to live an average of 67.4 years while the life expectancy of non-white males was about 62 years. The increase in life expectancy (up by four years since 1950) produced a rise in the number of elderly persons suffering from chronic diseases such as arthritis and diabetes, which should receive better medical management, the report said.

Statistics in the report showed that Americans received more medical care now than 10 years ago and that "considerable progress" had been made in "lowering the income barrier to [medical] care."

Among families earning less than $2,000 a year, an estimated 13% of their income went to health care. But for most families, insurance companies paid two-thirds of health costs—a reversal since 1950, when individuals paid two-thirds. Statistics showed a steady rise in the proportion of the gross national product spent on health from 1929 through 1971 and then a leveling off at about 7.7%. In 1975, 8.3% of the GNP was consumed by health costs, according to the New York Times Jan. 15.

Although there was one doctor for every 562 persons in 1973 (an increase of 64% over 1950), medical specialists were still unevenly distributed, the report said.

U.S. health-care data. Among data reported by the Office of Management & Budget in its special analyses of the fiscal 1976 federal budget:

● The most prominent postwar health-care trend has been the increase in total spending for health, which has grown from $12 billion in 1950 to $104 billion in 1974—from $78 to $485 per capita. During 1950–74, such annual spending by federal, state, and local governments increased from $3 billion to $41 billion—from 26% to 40% of all spending—mainly due to the enactment of the Medicare and Medicaid programs.

● Another significant trend has been the aggregate growth in health resources. The number of active physicians has risen from 272,000 in 1963 to an estimated 363,000 in 1975, and the number of active registered nurses has grown from 582,000 to about 940,000. More than 4.4 million persons are employed in health-related careers—about 4% of the civilian labor force. Health workers comprise the third largest occupational grouping in the United States.

• Simultaneously, there have been downward trends in the overall death rates and infant mortality rates, which have been underway since early in the 20th century. Significant advances through research have taken place in medicine. Knowledge of how to prevent and treat disease has made possible the virtual elimination of certain diseases, particularly infectious diseases that previously were major health problems. These advances have lengthened life for many persons. On the other hand, the degenerative processes that come with age result in increased incidence of chronic diseases—which generally are more costly to treat or cure than the acute and infectious diseases.

• The federal government supports the majority of biomedical research in the U.S., with 65% of total biomedical research funding. The largest federal biomedical research agency is the National Institutes of Health (NIH). NIH administers 65% of federal health research funds. Other federal agencies also support and conduct health research in support of their program missions. The three largest such agencies are the Energy Research & Development Administration, the Department of Defense and the Veterans Administration; together, these agencies account for 15% of all federal biomedical research expenditures.

• Between 45% and 50% of the revenues of the nation's medical schools are derived from federal grants or contracts. These outlays do not include payments for medical services from Medicare and Medicaid.

• Despite growing numbers, the geographic distribution of physicians and other health professionals is generally far from optimal. Among the states, the number of physicians per 100,000 population range from 196 in New York and 178 in Massachusetts, to 76 in Mississippi and 71 in South Dakota. Approximately 25% of the nation's 25,000 psychiatrists practice in the New York, Boston and Washington, D.C. metropolitan areas. General practitioners are found in somewhat larger proportions in nonmetropolitan counties, but their numbers are steadily declining as older physicians retire from practice and fewer new physicians choose general

practice. The uneven distribution of health resources, especially health professionals, is frequently cited as a reason for this country's poor health status in relation to that of other comparable countries. The relationship between the availability of physicians, however, and one common indicator of health status, mortality rates, is ambiguous. Clearly, there are factors that bear heavily upon health other than the availability of health care services: genetic and hereditary factors; the quality of the natural environment; social and economic well-being; safe working conditions; proper housing, sanitation, and nutrition; as well as personal patterns of exercise, smoking, and drinking. All of these influence individual health status.

• In contrast to the distribution of health professionals, the less populous states are relatively well-endowed with hospital beds. This geographic distribution probably reflects the impact of over 25 years of federal hospital construction assistance through the Hill-Burton program. Under its statutory formula, which favored the less populous and poorer areas, the Hill-Burton program allocated more than $4 billion in grants to the states. The basic task for which the Hill-Burton program was created—improving the supply of health facilities in shortage areas—is largely completed. The Hill-Burton program's expenditures have declined over the past decade, from about 13% of total national medical facility construction expenditures in 1963, to 5% in 1972. The vast majority of medical facility construction is now financed through long-term debt service of loans from the private capital markets. Depreciation costs and debt servicing are legitimate expenses included in reimbursements from health insurance. In just the four years from 1969 to 1973, for instance, the percentage of private nonprofit hospital construction being financed by debt service increased from 40% to 60%. This trend offset reductions in the share of construction costs borne by government, philanthropy, and internally generated funds. Federal programs for the construction of health care facilities include the support of both community health care facilities to serve the general public, and facilities operated by federal agencies for special beneficiary groups.

• The principal efforts to improve the organization and delivery of health services include health services research, support of health planning at the state and local level, and limited demonstration activities. Health services research includes studies of ways to improve the organization, delivery, quality, and financing of health care services. In 1976, health planning was scheduled to be assisted through recently authorized federal funding of health systems agencies throughout the country and federal matching grants to state health planning agencies. This program replaces the expired comprehensive health planning, regional medical program and Hill-Burton programs. The primary federal health care delivery demonstration activities include: grants and contracts to assist states and localities in developing comprehensive emergency medical services systems; grants, loans, and contracts to plan, develop, and provide initial operating support for health maintenance organizations that deliver comprehensive medical care on a prepaid basis; and the National Health Service Corps, which had been directed to locate approximately 405 health professionals in underserved areas in 1976, to demonstrate the ability of such communities to support health personnel.

• In 1969, $56 billion of total health expenditures—6.2% of the gross national product (GNP)—went for health services and supplies. By 1974, national spending on such health services reached $97 billion and 7.2% of GNP. Per capita health services expenditures in the U.S. rose from $271 to $457 during this same period. These huge sums purchase annually over one billion physician visits by the U.S. civilian population, approximately 30 million incidents of hospitalization, 2.5 billion drug prescriptions, and other health services by the public, payment mechanisms that reduce out-of-pocket expenditures by individual consumers and encourage inflation of charges and unnecessary utilization, expansion of health resources, and advances in medical therapies. The impact of the increased public spending for health care for the low-income population is reflected in changing utilization patterns for health services. While the numbers of physician visits and

hospitalizations per capita have not changed markedly in the past decade, surveys disclose that the low-income population uses these health resources at higher rates than the nonpoor population. Another result of the changing trends in health spending is the more than 100% growth from 1964 to 1974 in the number of residents of U.S. nursing homes. These developments stem, in large part, from increased government financing of medical services through Medicare and Medicaid together with the different health status of the poor and nonpoor.

Hospital admissions decline. The American Hospital Association Jan. 14, 1976 reported a 0.4% decline in the number of persons admitted to U.S. hospitals in the first nine months of 1975. The decline was the first on record since the association began keeping survey statistics 15 years ago.

At the same time, according to the periodic survey taken by the association of its 7,000 member hospitals, data indicated an increase of 9% in the use of clinics.

Cancer institute reports show increasing survival rates. Two separate studies released by the National Cancer Institute (NCI) concerned survival rates for persons afflicted with cancer in the U.S. The first study, released July 17, 1975, compared the survival rates of white cancer patients diagnosed between 1960-71. The second, reported Aug. 28, compared treatment results of white and black and male and female patients.

The July 17 report, "Recent Trends in Survival of Cancer Patients 1960-71," measured one-year and five-year mortality rates of white patients suffering from 48 types of cancer. The report made use of 230,500 patients in the 1960s and 45,400 patients in 1970-71. NCI used an earlier report for its 1950s statistics.

Among the most encouraging results were the survival rates for sufferers of Hodgkins disease. Five-year survival rates for males went from 31% (1950s) to 38% (1960-64) and 52% (1965-69). For women, rates for the corresponding time intervals went from 38% to 46% and 56%.

One-year survival rates for acute leukemia in males under 15 years of age increased from 26% (1950s) to 40% (1960–64) and 60% (1965–69) and finally, 76% (1970–71). The rate in females went from 21% to 41% to 62% to 71%. However, the five-year survival rate progressed at a much slower rate, going from 1% (1950s) to 4% (1965–69) in males and from 1% to 7% for the corresponding time period in females.

Female breast cancer patients' five-year survival rates increased from 60% in the 1950s to 64% in the late 1960s. According to NCI, the upward trend reflected an increased proportion of early diagnosis of the cancer. (The World Health Organization disclosed that statistics covering the past half-century showed breast cancer as the third leading cause of death, after accidents and suicides, among women 35–54, it was reported Aug. 10.)

Upward survival rates were also recorded for prostate, testis, kidney, bladder, brain, thyroid, larynx and skin cancers. Little change, however, was shown in the survival rates of lymphosarcoma or reticulum cell sarcoma.

The second study, which used data from the same hospitals, found that between 1955–64 white cancer victims lived, on the average, 40% longer than blacks who got cancer. It was further discovered that white women had the best chance of survival, followed by black women, white men and black men.

NCI officials, who edited the report, said the study indicated that cancer in blacks was more likely to be fatal because it was usually discovered later than it was in whites. In the Aug. 28 Washington Post report of the findings, Dr. Paul Cornely, a Howard University professor emeritus and former public health official, blamed the high cancer mortality rates in blacks on the inaccesibility of medical care as well as the environmental hazards of the ghetto and low-paying jobs. He said he felt that the mortality rate was probably approximately the same among blacks and whites of the same economic status. However, NCI officials said that physiological reasons for blacks' poor survival "should be explored."

The longer survival rate among women has been attributed in large part to the defenses provided by their hormonal makeup. In addition, women generally went to doctors more often and had cancers more susceptible to cure. Of the 240,580 cases of cancer studied, if other causes of death were not taken into account, 42% of white women escaped cancer death after 10 years, 33% of black women, 25% of white men and 15% of black men.

Cancer death rate at record high. The cancer death rate for the first seven months of 1975 was at a record high, the National Center for Health Statistics reported. As of July 31, the death rate was at 176.3 persons per 100,000, the highest rate since the government began compiling the statistics 42 years before. It was in contrast to the rate of 105.9 in 1933 and 169.5 at the end of 1974. The rate of increase for the first seven months, 5.2% was far above the increase of 1% averaged since 1933.

The National Cancer Institute said Nov. 6 it had no explanation for the high rate. However, at the same time Dr. David Baltimore and Rep. L. H. Fountain (D, N.C.) suggested environmental causes as the reason. Baltimore said the rise might be the start of a long-term trend which reflected "an increasing exposure to the cancer causing agents in the environment."

Fountain, a member of the House Intergovernmental Relations and Human Resources Subcommittee, pointed specifically to the problems of adding DES, a carcinogen, to cattle and sheep feed, and nitrates and nitrites to processed meat products.

The Center for Health Statistics said that of 665,000 people expected to fall victim to cancer in 1975, about one out of three would survive at least five years. This compared with one in five in the 1930s.

Developmental disability aid. Congress completed action Sept. 24, 1975 on legislation authorizing the expenditure of $287 million in fiscal 1976–78 for programs to aid the developmentally disabled. (Developmental disabilities, which usually began in childhood and continued indefinitely, included mental retardation, cerebral paisy, epilepsy and other afflictions.)

One section of the measure authorized $150 million in formula grants to states for aiding the developmentally disabled and also authorized funding for the training of persons to care for them.

A second section required the states to guarantee the legal rights of the developmentally disabled and the use of individual treatment plans for the developmentally disabled in federally funded institutions.

HMO development. The Health, Education & Welfare Administration Oct. 28, 1975 issued its final regulations on the mandatory dual choice provisions of the 1973 Health Maintenance Organization Act. Under the new rules, each employer of 25 or more workers, if covered under the Fair Labor Standards Act, must include the option of choosing membership in a qualified HMO whenever the employer offers any health benefit plan to eligible employes and their dependants.

By the end of 1975 the number of operational HMOs increased to 181 in 25 states, and the number of persons enrolled rose to 5.7 million.

Foundation seeks rural physicians. The Robert Wood Johnson Foundation Sept. 29, 1975 announced the start of a $14 million national project aimed at alleviating the severe shortage of doctors in rural areas.

The project would be coordinated by the University of North Carolina School of Medicine and would create medical groups in 25 rural communities. Each group would be made up of an adminis-

HEALTH INSURANCE BENEFIT PAYMENTS OF INSURANCE COMPANIES

In the United States

(000,000 omitted)

Year	Grand total	Group Total	Medical expense	Dental expense	Loss of income	Individual and family policies Total	Medical expense	Dental expense	Loss of income
1945	$ 278	$ 139	N.A.	N.A.	N.A.	$ 139	N.A.	N.A.	N.A.
1950	755	438	N.A.	N.A.	N.A.	317	N.A.	N.A.	N.A.
1955	1,785	1,252	N.A.	N.A.	N.A.	533	N.A.	N.A.	N.A.
1960	3,069	2,350	$1,809	N.A.	$ 541	719	$ 421	N.A.	$ 298
1965	5,160	4,000	3,322	N.A.	679	1,160	792	N.A.	368
1966	5,559	4,357	3,608	N.A.	749	1,203	814	N.A.	389
1967	6,030	4,790	3,953	$ 42	796	1,239	824	*	415
1968	6,717	5,362	4,360	54	948	1,355	894	*	461
1969	7,575	6,202	5,027	79	1,096	1,374	897	*	476
1970	9,089	7,476	6,043	140	1,293	1,613	1,090	*	523
1971	9,497	8,018	6,541	175	1,301	1,480	1,006	*	474
1972	10,622	8,943	7,315	201	1,427	1,679	1,148	*	531
1973	11,863	9,764	7,924	262	1,578	2,099	1,462	*	637
1974	13,636	11,439	9,260	332	1,847	2,197	1,517	*	680

*Less than $500,000.

Note: Figures do not add to totals in some cases due to rounding. The data include loss of income benefits and exclude accidental death and dismemberment benefits. Data for 1973 are revised.

N.A. — Not available.

Sources: *Health Insurance Review, Spectator Health Insurance Index,* Health Insurance Council and Health Insurance Association of America.

trator, one to three primary-care physicians (family doctors, interns and pediatricians) and nurse practitioners or physicians' assistants.

The $14 million would be used primarily to underwrite the salaries of the medical groups during the first three or four years it would take for them to become self-supporting.

Communities eligible for a foundation grant would have a population of from 6,000 to 20,000 and be at least 15 miles from the nearest commercial center with a population of more than 25,000 and at least 30 miles from the nearest metropolitan area. The community would also have to be without a local doctor or about to lose its doctors.

The medical groups would be established in affiliation with a community-based non-profit organization created for that purpose. In addition, the community would be expected to raise the necessary funds to build or renovate a medical clinic where one did not already exist.

Insurance benefits & health-care costs up.
The Health Insurance Institute reported in early 1976 that benefits paid to (or for) holders of private health insurance "have been rising even faster than spiraling medical-care costs." Using 1967 as the base year (in which costs and benefits would be set at 100), benefits per insured person rose from an index of 61 in 1960 to 91 in 1965, 143 in 1970 and 218 in 1974. By comparison, the medical-care component of the Consumer Price Index (1967 also set at 100) rose from 79 in 1960 to 89 in 1965, 121 in 1970 and 150 in 1974.

Quinlan life-support halt barred. A New Jersey Superior Court judge refused Nov. 10, 1975 to authorize the disconnection of the breathing device that was keeping Karen Anne Quinlan, 21, alive. In refusing her parents' request, Judge Robert Muir Jr. cited the fact that, although Miss Quinlan had lost all ability to think or function as a normal person, she was still legally and medically alive and as such retained the right to live.

The legal dispute began in September when Joseph and Julia Quinlan, convinced their daughter had no chance of recovery, petitioned the court to have her returned to "her natural state" and "leave her to the Lord" by having the respirator

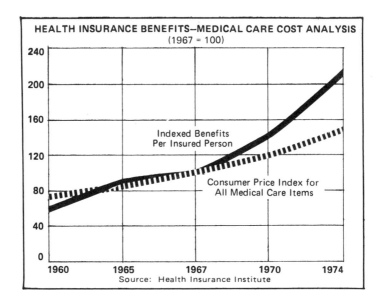

HEALTH INSURANCE BENEFITS—MEDICAL CARE COST ANALYSIS
(1967 = 100)

Indexed Benefits Per Insured Person

Consumer Price Index for All Medical Care Items

Source: Health Insurance Institute

removed. The Quinlans, Roman Catholics, were upheld in their views by their parish priest. The parents had made their decision after Miss Quinlan had been in a coma for seven months and had fallen into an irreversible "persistent vegetative state," according to doctors.

The Quinlans went to court after a request to attending physicians to disconnect the respirator was turned down. Muir left the final decision on use of the respirator with the doctors. He authorized Daniel R. Coburn, a Morristown lawyer who acted as Miss Quinlan's guardian for the court hearings, to continue as the guardian of "her person." Coburn would not be authorized to initiate any new medical procedures but would be available for consultation with the attending physician.

In a related development, a woman in a St. Louis, Mo. hospital who had been the subject of court battles to have her life-supporting machines disconnected, died Nov. 9. Judith Ann Debro, in a coma since Oct. 16, died of unknown causes with the machines that had kept her lungs breathing and heart beating still connected. A circuit court had ruled that it did not have jurisdiction in the case.

Malpractice Dilemma

Doctors in Revolt as Malpractice Insurance Costs Rise

One of the hazards physicians face is the suit for malpractice—in which a patient goes to court to try to collect monetary damages from his doctor for allegedly improper medical or surgical treatment. To avoid possibly catastrophic financial losses in such suits, virtually all doctors, dentists, hospitals and others involved in health-care delivery buy malpractice insurance from commercial insurance companies.

In recent years, judges and juries have been granting increasingly large malpractice damage awards. The insurance companies called on to pay the growing claims have raised their premium rates for such coverage. And even with doubled or tripled rates, most insurance companies claim that medical malpractice insurance is a losing business. Some companies, therefore, have stopped writing malpractice insurance.

The medical profession has thus been placed in a difficult predicament. Where malpractice insurance is available, it has become so expensive that doctors and hospitals often say they are unable to afford it. Where insurance companies have withdrawn malpractice coverage, many medical practitioners fear to undertake high-hazard or even routine medicine and surgery for fear

that an unfortunate incident might result in a bankrupting law suit.

All those involved have their own nominees for villain in the situation. Medical and insurance spokesmen have denounced judges and juries as awarding damages for unjustified reasons and as setting damages unreasonably high because of the presumably widespread notion that nobody is harmed when a big insurance company pays a large award. Lawyers have been attacked for allegedly inflating claims in order to profit by the high contingent fees usually collected in malpractice cases. The lawyers reply that patients who suffer injury through negligence usually deserve high awards and that frequently even the large sums awarded are insufficient to pay for the suffering and years of treatment that may follow medical errors. The insurance companies are frequently assailed for alleged overcharging, and they reply that their high premiums are both necessary and often insufficient.

The malpractice dilemma has driven many doctors to the verge of revolt. Many threaten to go on strike, to retire at an early age, to move to areas in which malpractice awards (and therefore malpractice insurance premiums) are low or to practice "defensive" medicine, which would increase the costs of medical care tremendously as physicians seek to avoid malpractice charges by ordering numerous and possibly unnecessary laboratory procedures, by insisting on *expensive and possibly unneeded consultations or by refusing difficult cases.*

The malpractice problem had become obvious as early as at least the 1960s, and it reached the crisis stage during 1973-75.

Malpractice panel asks changes. The Commission on Medical Malpractice, appointed by President Nixon in 1971, issued a final report April 17, 1973.

"The malpractice problem is like a proliferation of cancerous cells which have spread throughout the health care system," the report said.

Among the recommendations offered by the panel to reduce the $100 million paid annually in malpractice claims: to make certain that skills were kept up to date, doctors, dentists and other health professionals should be relicensed periodically; state laws should be changed to make medical license revocation easier; and simpler methods for settling malpractice claims should be adopted, such as arbitration or a "no fault" approach to compensate patients even in cases where negligence was not established.

The commission reported that medical practitioners paid $300 million for malpractice insurance in 1970.

Companies end coverage. Insurance firms across the U.S. were reported Jan. 12, 1975 to be dropping malpractice insurance coverage, citing losses in suits that surpassed premiums. A crisis was temporarily averted in New York when the Argonaut Insurance Co., which insured 80 per cent of the state's doctors, agreed Jan. 6 to drop a planned 200 per cent rate increase and retained current rates, which had been increased nearly 100 per cent in July 1974. However, the company said it would end its coverage in the state completely by July 1. There had been charges that Argonaut's financial problems were due to bad investment rather than poor profits but the company refused to comment on the issue.

The St. Paul Fire and Marine Insurance Co. of St. Paul (Minn.), which provided malpractice coverage for some 48,000 doctors in 47 states (excepting Alaska,

Hawaii and Nevada), said Jan. 23 it would offer a new and different type of insurance after June 30, but was discontinuing insurance in Maryland at that time because of the state insurance commission's rejection of a 48 per cent increase there. The new coverage would be based on the claims records of doctors in previous years. St. Paul blamed its problems on an increased number of suits and the tendency of juries to side with the patient. The company also noted that lawyers who often received one-third to 40 per cent of the settlement encouraged larger suits. Nearly 5,000 physicians in Maryland would be affected by the cancellation.

In Los Angeles, 2,000 doctors had to seek new carriers when Pacific Indemnity and Star Insurance Co. Jan. 1 quit issuing malpractice insurance after incurring heavy claims losses. Some 50 physicians were reported unable to get new coverage by the main carriers because they had bad claims records.

The American Hospital Association (AHA) House of Delegates Feb. 5 endorsed the establishment of a captive insurance company, funded by a special assessment of up to $4 a bed, to provide malpractice insurance for the nation's hospitals. The money would be forwarded to a national casualty insurance company, which would retain a portion for service and forward the rest to a captive insurance company established by the AHA for the payment of claims. The program was established in response to reported cancellation of hospital coverage in 14 states by Argonaut and rate increases of up to 700 per cent in others. A preliminary injunction was issued April 1 which barred Argonaut from raising its premiums on hospital malpractice policies in New York and from canceling the policies for 35 hospitals across that state.

Hastings on problem. Rep. James F. Hastings (R, N.Y.) reviewed the malpractice problem in the House of Representatives April 17, 1975. Hastings said:

"Between 1960 and 1970, malpractice insurance premiums for dentists rose 115%; for hospitals, 262%; for physicians other than surgeons, 540.8%; and for surgeons, 949.2%. Available evidence since

1970 shows malpractice insurance rates continuing to climb. In early 1974, physicians in New York State had to pay 93.5% more for their malpractice insurance than for the previous rating period. The insurer in that state recently proposed an additional increase of almost 200%, raising the rates for some specialists as high as $45,000. As a result of objections by the state insurance commissioner to the proposed increase, the insurer announced it would not renew policies or write new business after July 1 of this year. Hospitals too are experiencing extraordinary increases with rates doubling, tripling, and sometimes increasing as much as 700%. Argonaut Insurance Co., the major hospital malpractice insurer, has recently announced it will no longer cover hospitals in at least 14 states.

"The availability and cost of medical malpractice insurance has reached emergency proportions in many states because of dramatically increased claims and skyrocketing award levels. Factors contributing to the availability and cost situation include: Increased technology and complexity of medicine, rising patient expectations, strained patient-provider relationships, expanded use of the judicial system as an alternative for provider accountability, and the lengthy time span between the adverse medical occurrence and the settlement of a malpractice claim. . . .

"A serious question has arisen as to whether or not medical malpractice is becoming an uninsurable risk. Inability to predict the ratio of expected claims against premiums to anticipate loss experience is being likened to the risk of natural disasters. Providers, viewing every patient contract as a possible medical injury claim are practicing 'defensive' medicine—ordering extra and often unnecessary tests, procedures and consultations as protection against a malpractice claim—at a cost of billions of dollars a year to the nation's consumers who in the end must pay for it all: the medical care, including defensive medicine, the cost of the providers' malpractice insurance as reflected in fees, and the cost of any necessary legal action.

"Despite skyrocketing medical malpractice insurance costs, only a small portion of medical malpractice premiums actually goes to the injured patient or his legal representative. The amount of each premium dollar actually awarded to the patient or his legal representative may range from 16 to 38 cents, depending upon which estimate is accepted. The remainder goes to lawyers for the plaintiff and the defendant, and for costs and profits of insurers. Settlements are seldom prompt; the average time for cases heard by a jury is five years. It takes over 10 years to settle all alleged medical malpractice incidents occurring in any one year.

"An unanswered question is the extent of medical injuries caused by the negligence of health care providers which do not result in malpractice claims. One study, . . . commissioned by the Secretary's Commission on Medical Malpractice, found that of 23,750 discharges from two hospitals studied, 517 patients had received medical injuries during treatment which were caused by negligence. The investigators found that only 31 malpractice claims would be filed during the year in which the study was made. Since there were only 12,600 claims asserted in 1970 throughout the nation, and over 30 million hospital admissions a year—according to the National Center for Health Statistics—it appears that malpractice claims are instituted in only a small fraction of cases where medical injuries through negligence have occurred.

"Both the Congress and the administration have responded to the medical malpractice crisis. Legislation has been introduced in both the Senate and the House proposing various alternatives to the medical malpractice problem. . . .

". . . On Feb. 26, the American Insurance Association approved the establishment of joint underwriting associations in states where there were problems, and has prepared draft state legislation for this purpose. State legislatures have also been extremely active. According to the American Medical Association, over 200 bills dealing with the medical malpractice problem have been introduced this year in our state legislatures, proposing a wide variety of solutions. . . ."

Legislation proposed. Various malpractice bills were introduced in Congress but met serious opposition.

Casper Weinberger, Secretary of Health, Education and Welfare, at a subcommittee hearing April 10 argued against federal action, saying that the situation varied so widely from state to state as to make a federal law impractical. He added, however, that HEW would monitor the situation in the states and would aid in finding long-range malpractice solutions. At the same hearings, an American Hospital Association spokesman concurred with Weinberger's opinion saying state actions were the most "effective" way of dealing with the problem. The American Medical Association (AMA) said April 10 it was also against the federal bills, in part because of physician licensing or other medical standards that the bills incorporated. It said that such action should be considered separately from malpractice bills. The AFL-CIO Executive Council, however, agreed May 6 to support the bills, pointing out that the high cost of such insurance was eventually passed on to consumers.

The AMA May 2 said malpractice cases had risen 1,000% since 1969 and an insurance company spokesman said that the average claim had doubled to $12,500 between 1969 and 1974. It was reported March 21 that applications for medical commissions in the military (which paid doctors' insurance fees) had risen dramatically since insurance companies began to increase rates. According to officials, Navy commissions had risen from 10 in January to 90 in February. One Navy recruiter said there hadn't been as many applications for medical commissions "since the early days of the Vietnam War." Five hundred civilian doctors were reported March 21 to have been on waiting lists for the armed services, according to Department of Defense officials.

AMA action on problem. The American Medical Association (AMA) June 19, 1975 reaffirmed its support of a doctor's right to withhold services to protest what he considered "unwarranted burdens on his patients."

The vote, taken at the association's closing session of its annual meeting, was apparently directed at recent work slowdowns and threats of more such slowdowns by doctors protesting increased malpractice costs.

However, the final resolution deleted earlier wording that gave the AMA, as an association, the right to run organized protests. An AMA spokesman said the association feared that such a statement might violate antitrust regulations should further work slowdowns occur. Labor unions were exempted from antitrust laws but the AMA had long contended that doctors were individual businessmen.

At the same time, the AMA agreed to form a reinsurance company to cover insurance companies run by state medical societies for malpractice judgments that ran higher than the society's basic coverage.

The new insurance company, however, would only cover those companies which were in states which had changed their malpractice laws to an extent satisfactory to the association. An official said four states were considering action that would make them eligible for the reinsurance—New York, Indiana, Michigan and Maryland.

The AMA was spending $20,000 to file an insurance charter and was authorized by its delegates to deposit $1.5 million to form the company once five states became eligible for the coverage. Officials estimated it would take one year for the reinsurance company to come into formal existence.

State-by-State Action

State developments. Among malpractice developments in the states during 1975:

Alabama—The state legislature enacted the Alabama Liability Act, which became effective Sept. 23, to deal with the malpractice insurance issue. The act authorized the state insurance commissioner to establish a joint underwriting association composed of all insurers who wrote property and casualty insurance. The insurance pool would supply malpractice coverage to those who otherwise could not get any. The act also provided for arbitration of claims and set a time limit on the filing of suits. It stipulated that doctors, surgeons, dentists and hospitals were not liable for the success of their treatment or services and that advance payments could not be considered admissions of liability.

Alaska—Doctors in Alaska had begun a work slowdown, the New York Times reported Aug. 12. Earlier, doctors had been working uninsured or suspended practice.

Patients in most cases found themselves unable to obtain elective surgery, cancer treatment or nonessential checkups. The state's only heart surgeon advertised his decision to quit in several Alaskan newspapers, explaining that adequate insurance protection would cost him $40,000 a year, the Times reported July 26. In Juneau, rates had tripled for malpractice coverage and doctors were being charged $12,000 for coverage they considered inadequate.

Alaska had been known for its low number of malpractice suits. However, with 15 suits already filed in 1975, compared with 74 in the previous 16 years, any coverage at all was hard to find. The only policies available were the "claims made" type, which covered only those malpractice claims made the year the policy was in effect.

The state legislature passed a bill in the spring that would have established a joint underwriting association, the Times said in its July 26 report. But the resolution was criticized by physicians and insurance men because of technical flaws and Gov. Jay S. Hammond vetoed it. The governor, instead, created a committee to study the problem and according to Sept. 2 reports, the group had a proposal which was backed by many doctors, lawyers and insurance companies. The key element in the commission's proposal was the establishment of an adjustment board to review claims, which in many cases would obviate the need for a jury trial.

California—In the northern part of the state some 2,000 physicians, including virtually all anesthesiologists and surgeons, refused to pay for new, more expensive, insurance and went on strike May 1. The Argonaut Insurance Co. had ended its old coverage that day and had instituted a new type of policy that cost between 200% and 400% more, depending on the doctor's "risk" category. (Surgeons and anesthesiologists were generally in the most expensive category.) Only operations considered emergencies were being performed, with other operations being postponed or transferred to public hospitals.

A one-day sympathy strike was reported in Southern California May 7 after the strike in the north reached its sixth day. In Los Angeles, non-emergency surgery was cancelled at 10 hospitals and reduced at two others, while in San Diego a sampling showed less than 25% of the operating rooms in 10 major hospitals in use.

The doctors' strike was finally ended May 28 after Gov. Edmund Brown signed what was considered stopgap legislation. The strike, which lasted 28 days, and caused layoffs of 13,000 hospital workers, had ended nearly all elective surgery in the San Francisco Bay Area and affected 200 hospitals statewide.

The emergency legislation provided for the establishment of a joint underwriting insurance pooling system for areas where malpractice insurance was unavailable or where it was only available at high rates. Dr. Seymour Wallace, president of the California Society of Anesthesiologists, ending the strike, said the state legislature's action showed "that a permanent acceptable solution is in the works."

California's insurance commissioner said June 6 he would not set up an insurance pool in any of the eight counties in northern California where the protest was most severe. He explained that he did not see the need for it after hearing testimony at a series of public hearings on the subject. In reaction, Wallace said that he expected doctors would stay on the job anyway, noting that most of them had already bought short-term insurance despite high premiums. He said that the doctors were willing to "bite the bullet for three months" but most would not renew their insurance without lasting relief.

Delegates representing the 26,000 members of the California Medical Association gave their state legislators a mid-September date for enactment of a permanent solution to the malpractice problem, it was reported June 3.

The bill that finally emerged, and which Gov. Brown signed, extended the life of the Joint Underwriting Association (JUA) from Jan. 1, 1976 to March 1, 1978. As enacted, the legislation required the JUA, which was composed of all the liability insurers in the state, to issue malpractice policies, where otherwise unavailable, in amounts of $100,000; $250,000; $500,000 and $1,000,000. The bill also created a three-member actuary panel which would conduct public medical malpractice rate hearings. The panel would pass its findings on the JUA's rates to the state insurance commissioner for a final decision on appropriate premiums.

The legislative action, however, did nothing to dampen a volatile situation in Southern California where physicians, facing a 486% rate increase Jan. 1, 1976, had threatened work stoppages.

In northern California, doctors wishing to circumvent similar rate conflicts with their insurers had begun forming physician-owned insurance companies, it was reported Sept. 19. One such firm, the Medical Insurance Exchange of California, headquartered in San Francisco, had already received a charter from the state and had received its initial funding from doctors.

Connecticut—A comprehensive insurance program known as the "Connecticut Plan," scheduled to expire in 1975, was renewed for five more years, the Journal of Commerce reported Aug. 20. The plan, developed jointly by the Connecticut State Medical Society and its major insurer, Aetna Life and Casualty, covered 91% of the medical group's members. Premiums were raised an average of 40.7% Oct. 1 but remained among the lowest in the nation. New rates ranged from $913 annually (up from $678) for general practitioners, to $7,511 yearly (up from $5,258) for neurosurgeons.

Delaware—The Aetna Casualty & Surety Co. was granted a major rate hike in its malpractice premiums by the Delaware Insurance Department, the Journal of Commerce reported Sept. 18. Aetna, which threatened to halt its malpractice

coverage in the state if the increase was rejected, was allowed increases ranging from 67% to 150% for insuring the state's hospitals and over 600 doctors.

Florida—A Florida malpractice bill, signed into law May 20, was aimed at reducing malpractice suits. The bill imposed a four-year statute of limitations on the filing of law suits. It also required patients to take their claims to a mediation panel as a prerequisite to going to court. Particularly significant was the bill's inclusion of a clause aimed at negligent doctors. For the first time, Florida's Board of Medical Examiners and hospitals were given the authority to revoke the licenses of doctors found guilty of malpractice.

One measure considered by the Florida legislature, but not part of the final bill, would have outlawed contingency fees for lawyers. The system provided that a set fraction of the final settlement, if won, would go to the lawyer as a fee for arguing the case. Although it was argued that such fees might encourage suits for excessive amounts, lawyers contended that it was the only way many poorer plaintiffs could afford to go to court.

Anesthesiologists in northern Florida ended a seven-day strike April 28 over rising malpractice costs. Meanwhile, the New York Times reported May 21 that a U.S. District Judge in Jacksonville had ordered the Argonaut Insurance Co. not to raise its malpractice rates above the Jan. 1 level. The court also directed Argonaut not to cancel policies of Florida physicians who refused to pay higher rates.

Idaho—The Journal of Commerce reported May 12 that Idaho had enacted a malpractice law limiting liability to $150,-000 in cases involving one person, $300,-000 in cases involving more than one, and establishing a limit on fees for lawyers. Doctors and hospitals would be subject only to malpractice claims for compensatory damages not paid by other sources. Further, the law clarified the idea of "informed consent" (how much a physician must explain of his procedures and options before he treats a patient).

The law provided for a joint underwriting association for medical malpractice insurance for doctors who could not get coverage when their company pulled out of the field. Implementation of this section of the law almost became necessary when the Argonaut Insurance Co. indicated it was pulling out of Idaho by the end of May. But St. Paul Fire and Marine Insurance Co. said it would provide coverage to those doctors facing loss of coverage, the Journal of Commerce reported. The company said it was doing so because of the "unusually favorable operating conditions in the state" following passage of the malpractice law.

Illinois—Gov. Daniel Walker (D) signed a bill that set a $500,000 limit on the amount recoverable through malpractice suits, it was reported Sept. 13. The bill, whose approval had been unsure, set a time limit on filing a suit—five years from the occurrence of the alleged malpractice.

The legislation set up pretrial review panels in each judicial circuit to screen claims and make nonbinding recommendations on the amount of the awards. Most of the bill's provisions had been lobbied for by state hospital and physician groups as a solution to the malpractice problem. The bill was passed by the state legislature, the Wall Street Journal reported July 1.

Indiana—Gov. Otis Bowen (himself a physician) April 17 signed into law a medical malpractice bill which he hailed as "a bill for the people." An attorney for the Indiana State Medical Association said the measure "may set some valuable precedents for the nation and for the industry."

The bill preserved the right of trial by jury, but limited the total award in any suit to $500,000. It confined the insurance carrier's liability to $100,000 while setting up a patients' compensation fund, financed from a surcharge on insurance premiums, that would be responsible for further liability. At the same time, the bill limited the plaintiff's attorney fees to no more than 15% of the total claim payment from the fund, with similar limitations on the first $100,000 claimed. A statute of limitations of two years from the date of the alleged malpractice was instituted with the exception of children under six.

Minors would have until their eighth birthday to file a claim.

The bill established a risk management authority within the Indiana Department of Insurance to grant malpractice insurance to qualified physicians or others who were deemed unjustly denied coverage. It also allowed for a panel of physicians to be set up to issue an opinion to the courts on any malpractice suit. An important clause in the bill set up a study commission that was expected to recommend a long-term solution to the problem of malpractice. The commission would be composed of four state legislators, the state insurance commissioner, a representative of the insurance industry, three medical representatives, two attorneys and two laymen.

Louisiana—The Louisiana state legislature enacted a law setting a $500,000 limit (plus costs and interest) on the amount recoverable by a patient as a result of malpractice. The law, which took effect Sept. 12, also provided that physicians could not be sued for alleged breach of contract for assuring the results of medical treatment unless such a guarantee had been put in writing.

Two separate malpractice bills, which also took effect Sept. 12, dealt with the issue of coverage for hospital and federal employes. Hospitals were granted the authority to provide malpractice coverage for any medical doctor, dentist or professional nurse employed by, or related to, that institution. In a separate bill, state agencies were allowed to provide, at no charge, liability coverage for medical personnel under contract with the state.

Maryland—Gov. Marvin Mandel April 29 signed a bill creating the nation's first nonprofit, doctor-run, insurance company. The firm was scheduled to begin offering malpractice insurance coverage June 1, the day a major insurer was scheduled to drop coverage in the state. St. Paul Fire & Marine Insurance Co., however, agreed to extend its coverage to July 31 to allow time for the new insurance company to get started.

A second bill signed April 29 permitted the insurance commissioner to establish a pool arrangement requiring all insurance companies in the state to share losses from malpractice insurance. A third measure, signed at the same time, shortened the time-limit for filing malpractice suits to five years from the date a patient was treated.

The new laws were criticized by doctors and insurance companies as being only stop-gap measures that failed to deal with the basic issues. Several doctors said they would halt all but emergency surgical cases when the commercial insurance expired. The doctors wanted assurances that Gov. Mandel would support new legislation to limit the role of juries and the size of awards in malpractice cases.

St. Paul Fire & Marine was granted a rate increase of up to four times its old premiums May 20 but only for June and July, after which it no longer handled malpractice insurance in Maryland.

A $300 tax was levied on every licensed physician in Maryland in order to provide capital for the new doctor-run company, to be known as the Mutual Medical Liability Insurance Society of Maryland. All doctors had to pay the tax whether or not they were members of the state medical society and whether or not they were covered by the new insurance plan.

In a related development, the Maryland insurance commissioner approved a basic rate structure for the new insurance company, which could as much as triple doctors' malpractice insurance premiums, it was reported July 7. The rates, though higher than normally would have been approved, were allowed because it was the company's initial year. Insurance firms were permitted to charge higher rates for their first year of coverage to provide a rapid buildup of reserves to meet claims.

Physicians in Baltimore who chose the doctor-run company as their insurer would be paying annual rates ranging from $1,154 for those who do not perform surgery to $9,602 for certain high-risk surgeons. This compared with St. Paul's rates which had ranged from $583 to $3,887.

A decision by the Maryland Court of Appeals in Annapolis was reported Oct. 16 to have rejected the so-called "strict locality" rule, which required that a physician's performance be judged by what other local doctors regarded as reasonably careful practice. In its place, the court adopted a guideline known as the "similar circumstances" standard which allowed testimony from physicians from different geographical locations who practiced under similar circumstances.

In its decision, the court noted that the original rule was instituted in the 1870s to protect small town doctors who were often less trained and equipped than their urban counterparts. This justification was no longer valid, the court decided. The ruling resulted from an appeal by plaintiffs who charged negligence during the birth and early treatment of their son, which they alleged led to permanent brain damage. Testimony from expert witnesses was disallowed at the original trial because of the locality rule but a new trial was scheduled. The appeals court decision was expected to end the practice in which local doctors refused to testify against their accused colleagues.

Massachusetts—Gov. Michael Dukakis (D) June 19 signed into law an amended malpractice bill which created a Joint Underwriting Association (JUA) in the Bay State. The bill had been amended to make the association responsible for maintaining itself. The original bill had made it mandatory that all property and casualty insurers join in the pool and share in any losses it might occur. But in the bill's enacted form, doctors would have to make up any deficit the JUA might incur by paying further assessments.

A major provision, which was enacted over the criticism of a major malpractice insurer in the state, mandated that insurance be provided on either an "occurrence" or "claims made" basis, at the discretion of the doctor. (Under an "occurrence" policy insurance companies were liable for all claims made the year the policy was in effect regardless of when an alleged malpractice took place. "Claims made" coverage, however, provided coverage only for suits brought for alleged malpractice the year the policy was in effect.)

A spokesman for the St. Paul Fire and Marine Insurance Co., which covered

40% of the state's doctors, said June 26 the company would have "no choice but to discontinue" coverage of malpractice in the state once the new law took effect. St. Paul initiated "claims made" coverage in the state May 1 and contended that they had found it impossible to price "occurrence" policies.

The situation in Massachusetts was further aggravated by the fact that the Argonaut Insurance company, which insured 1,600 doctors in Massachusetts, had announced plans to pull out of malpractice insuring there by the end of 1975, United Press International reported June 3.

Michigan—Gov. William G. Milliken signed into law May 12 a malpractice bill which made Michigan the first state in the nation to establish a malpractice insurance fund. The governor said the bill should eliminate the threat of a mass exodus of physicians from the state. The fund was set to be self-supporting, paid for by premiums charged to those who used it. If those premiums were insufficient to cover costs, additional assessments would be made depending on the risk category of each physician involved.

The Michigan state legislature later passed 15 bills concerning the malpractice issue, the New York Times reported July 27. Among the actions taken was the establishment of an arbitration system which could avoid jury trials in many cases. Under the new law, patients could sign a voluntary arbitration form which need not be signed as a prerequisite for care. However, should the patient decide to sign the form, any alleged malpractice would be submitted to an arbitration board which would make a final decision on the matter.

The board would be composed of a physician, a lawyer and a qualified lay person. By agreeing to this system, the patient could expect a speedier decision at less cost to all parties concerned.

Missouri—Physicians in Missouri formed their own insurance company, the Journal of Commerce reported May 15, with the objective of halting rapid rate increases and providing more extensive coverage. The doctors contended that their premiums, which had recently risen

300%, had been based on an unfavorable national climate which was far worse than that in their own state. They laid this difference, in part, to a legal system in Missouri more favorable to doctors.

The newly formed insurance company, Missouri State Medical Insurance Inc., would be a wholly-owned subsidiary of the Missouri Medical Association. Under the new premium schedule, Missouri's urban physicians, who encountered more expensive suits, would pay 20% more for coverage than those in rural areas. The plans had a limit of $300,000 on individual policies but "umbrella" policies of up to $5 million would be available at a higher premium.

Nevada—A joint medical legal screening panel, to which all malpractice claims had to be submitted prior to court action, was established in Nevada. In a separate action, all malpractice court proceedings would be required to include expert medical testimony. Such testimony would be required in order to prove that there had been deviations from established standards of care. The laws took effect April 30.

New Hampshire—A bill, taking effect in August, authorized the commissioner of insurance to establish a Joint Underwriting Association to assure the continued availability of malpractice insurance, the Journal of Commerce reported June 20. A long-term study was also established.

New Jersey—The Argonaut Insurance Co. decided to halt writing medical malpractice insurance in New Jersey as soon as possible, it was reported April 18. The announcement followed severe official criticism April 16 of a proposed 410% rate hike by the company. Argonaut was the principal writer for policies in the state, covering almost all of its hospitals. A crisis was averted, however, when Chubb & Sons volunteered to cover any hospital which Argonaut dropped, it was reported May 1.

The state legislature April 30 created a special six-member commission—three Assemblymen and three Senate members—to study the state's malpractice insurance problem.

The state's hospital malpractice insurance rates became subject to rapid insurance rises when the Insurance Services Office, which regulated the hospital's premiums, filed for a 250% increase. According to the Journal of Commerce May 28, the raise could affect malpractice policies for hospitals as well as doctors and interns who were full-time staff members. Gov. Brendan Byrne said the state would consider going into the malpractice insurance business if private rates became unreasonable, the Journal of Commerce reported June 3.

Later, New Jersey's doctors, in a meeting of the Medical Society of New Jersey June 4, said they would wait six months for new, "remedial" legislation before withholding all but emergency services. The threatened action came after a decision by the Federal Insurance Co., reported June 3, asking the state to approve a rate increase of 53.8% for medical malpractice insurance. Federal, a division of the Chubb group, covered 6,700 New Jersey doctors. The state insurance commissioner announced Oct. 1 that Federal had been granted a 49.5% rate increase.

A threatened "job action" (slowdown) by New Jersey anesthesiologists was averted when an agreement with a new reinsurer was reached June 30. The threatened work slowdown was scheduled for July 1, the day the Commercial Union Insurance Co. was dropping "umbrella" coverage in that state. ("Umbrella" coverage, which provided insurance beyond the basic coverage of other malpractice policies, was considered necessary for those surgeons in high risk positions.) However, in an agreement worked out with the state insurance commissioner, the Crum and Forster Insurance Co. agreed to step in and provide the extra coverage, though at substantially higher rates. Thus, highest risk rates, for $1 million in "umbrella" coverage, which had been $253 with Commercial, would rise to $1899 annually with the new insurer.

Another firm, the St. Paul Fire & Marine Insurance Co., said that it would no longer offer hospital malpractice coverage in New Jersey and would stop renewing policies as of Jan. 1, 1976, the Journal of Commerce reported Oct. 24.

St. Paul provided coverage for 39 hospitals in the state, 35% of the total. According to the report, St. Paul made its decision after the state insurance commissioner refused to allow the company to provide coverage on a claims-made, rather than a claims-incurred basis. (The claims-made policy provided coverage only during the year it was in effect, while the claims-incurred policy made the company liable to suits at any time as long as they related to an alleged malpractice while the policy was in effect.) A spokesman for the New Jersey Hospital Association said the withdrawal created a "potential emergency." Nine hospitals had policies with St. Paul which expired in January and February 1976.

New York—Gov. Hugh Carey and legislative leaders of both parties in the state announced May 15 that they had reached an agreement on a compromise bill to resolve an impending malpractice crisis stemming from a decision April 16 by the Argonaut Insurance Company, the major insurer in the state, to end its coverage there by June 30.

The proposal called for the creation of a Medical Malpractice Underwriting Association, consisting of the state's 300 private insurance companies that offered personal liability insurance. The association, along with other insurance companies—including the Medical Liability Mutual Insurance Co., then being formed by the State Medical Society—would offer malpractice insurance. It was hoped that the increased competition would help curb rate hikes. Doctors' premiums were expected to rise, however, by at least 75%. In the event the assets of the underwriting company were exhausted, and insurance was not available from the private sector, the state insurance fund would provide coverage.

The measure reduced the time in which a case could be brought to trial from three to $2\frac{1}{2}$ years, except for infants, where the statute of limitations was set at 10 years. Limits were also put on the amount a patient could sue for. In addition, all malpractice charges would first be heard by a panel of doctors and a consumer advocate. Recommendations for action would be sent to the commissioner of health for a final determination on appropriate judicial action.

The Medical Society of the State of New York had decided April 27 that it could not "realistically provide patients with anything but emergency care" if its physicians were left without an insurer. In response to a poll by the society, a third of the member doctors said they would leave the state if they could not obtain coverage, it was reported May 1.

When enacted, however, the new bill was rejected by delegates of the New York State Medical Society May 25, and protesting doctors observed a 10-day slowdown of all but emergency services in New York. The slowdown ended June 11 after Gov. Carey appointed a panel to study the malpractice problem.

A new Medical Malpractice Insurance Association was formed under the May law, and the state Insurance Department announced June 23 that the new unit had been granted an increase in malpractice insurance premiums 20% above the current rates. Under the same law, the Medical Society of the State of New York had established a doctor-run insurance company.

The Medical Malpractice Insurance Association had applied for an increase of 100% over current rates. It began accepting applications under its new rates, as approved, June 27. Premiums for hospitals by both companies would remain at current rates.

North Carolina—A superior court judge ruled that North Carolina's malpractice reinsurance exchange law was unconstitutional, the Journal of Commerce reported Nov. 12. Some 350 companies providing liability insurance in North Carolina had charged in a week-long hearing that the new law would require them to enter the malpractice business as well as share in its losses.

In its decision, the Wake County Superior Court said the law gave the state insurance commissioner too much authority over rates, and denied the insurance companies' right to due process and equal protection under the law. The court upheld the insurance companies' contention that the commissioner had sought to establish rates so low that the firms would

incur substantial losses. This amounted to confiscation of property, the court ruled.

The malpractice situation in North Carolina had reached a crisis Sept. 30 after the major insurer, the St. Paul Fire and Marine Insurance Co., announced it would no longer provide malpractice coverage in the state. However, St. Paul later reappraised the situation and decided to reenter the malpractice field, it was reported Nov. 12. At the same time the State Medical Society established a mutual insurance company and began accepting applicants. Meanwhile, the North Carolina Hospital Association announced it had set up a trust fund covering hospitals.

Ohio—Some 200 physicians signed up for malpractice insurance with Ohio's new Medical Professional Liability Insurance Association, the Journal of Commerce reported Aug. 27. However, insurance under the new joint underwriters association pooling plan required about as much cash outlay from doctors as was required in the open market. Although applicants paid a premium of only 45% to 70% of the going rate, they were required to deposit an amount equal to their premium in a physicians' stabilization fund. Doctors would eventually get back a portion of their deposit.

Pennsylvania—Gov. Milton J. Shapp (D) signed the Health Care Services Malpractice Act, which established a statewide system of compulsory arbitration panels to hear malpractice claims, it was reported Oct. 22. The seven-member panels would include, "wherever possible," one health-care provider of the class involved in the claim. Decisions of the panels could be appealed to the courts. Attorneys' fees were limited to 30% of the first $100,000 of an award, 25% of the second $100,000 and 20% of the balance.

Insurance companies were made liable for $100,000 per occurrence with the balance to be paid by a catastrophe loss fund capitalized by an annual surcharge on all health care providers. This fund would also be responsible for all claims filed four years or more after the alleged malpractice.

A joint underwriting association was also established by the act to provide high-risk doctors (such as neurosurgeons) with coverage. License fees would be made available to finance improved policing of the medical profession by their licensing and disciplinary boards. A commission was also established to study the malpractice problem on a continuing basis. The act would become effective Jan. 12, 1976. The president of the Pennsylvania Medical Society said that under the new system rates would probably come down 20%–30% within a few years, but this would still leave premiums "too high."

The new law was signed after the Medical Protective Co., Pennsylvania's largest writer of malpractice insurance, had approved a 68% rate hike effective Sept. 1. The boost affected 6,000 doctors and 4,000 dentists covered by the company. At the same time, the company agreed to renew all malpractice policies on an annual rather than monthly basis. In addition, it promised to end its moratorium on new policies.

Rhode Island—The State Director of Business Regulations announced June 8 the formation of a Joint Underwriting Association for malpractice coverage.

South Carolina—Acting under a joint resolution adopted by the state general assembly, the state's Insurance Commission ordered the establishment of a Joint Underwriting Association, the Journal of Commerce reported June 9. The commission said it would require all companies writing bodily injury liability insurance, other than auto liability, to participate in the pool. The action was limited to surgeons and physicians.

Texas—The Texas legislature passed two malpractice insurance laws, it was reported June 13, following a series of work slowdowns around the state protesting increased malpractice costs.

The new legislation guaranteed that medical liability insurance would be made available at reasonable rates. The first measure created a medical liability underwriting pool for doctors and hospitals that had difficulty getting insurance on the open market. The second bill put previously unregulated malpractice rates under the authority of the State Board of Insurance. Following the passage of the bill, the state insurance commissioner ordered all insurance companies selling malpractice to file rate schedules by June 15, the Journal of Commerce reported June 17.

The second bill also cut the time a patient could file a malpractice claim to two years from the time of treatment and established a commission to report in two years on the results of changes in the malpractice laws. The Texas House of Representatives narrowly defeated a bill, passed in the Senate, which would have placed a $100,000 limit on malpractice suits. Another provision in that bill would have established a panel of physicians to rule on whether a case should go to court.

Wisconsin—The State Insurance Department, under state legislation signed into law March 14, established an emergency malpractice insurance pool.

In mid-1975, Gov. Patrick Lucey signed a compromise malpractice bill into law after vetoing portions of a previous law, the Wall Street Journal reported July 22. The bill, which had been passed by the state legislature July 10, set up a risk-sharing pool of insurers that would provide malpractice insurance. This pool would pay claims up to $200,000 per case and $600,000 annually for each physician, hospital or other health care provider.

In addition, doctors would be assessed $200 each year and 10% of their coverage to set up an "umbrella" fund for claims in excess of the original coverage. If the capital in the fund fell below a certain level, claims would be limited to $500,000 plus lifetime medical expenses. The bill also created screening panels to consider malpractice claims before they went to court.

A number of physicians in the state had limited or ended their services because of inadequate insurance coverage, the Wall Street Journal reported in its July 22 article. In the beginning of July it was reported a survey had shown that surgery had dropped 45% in 18 Milwaukee hospitals.

Index

181